Lady Insurrectionists

Lady Insurrectionists

Women, Reform and Revolution in Victorian Britain

Judy Cox

VERSO
London • New York

First published by Verso 2026

The manufacturer's authorized representative in the EU for product safety (GPSR) is LOGOS EUROPE, 9 rue Nicolas Poussin, 17000, La Rochelle, France
Contact@logoseurope.eu

1 3 5 7 9 10 8 6 4 2

Verso
UK: 6 Meard Street, London W1F 0EG
US: 207 East 32nd Street, New York, NY 10016
versobooks.com

Verso is the imprint of New Left Books

ISBN-13: 978-1-83674-190-9
ISBN-13: 978-1-83674-193-0 (US EBK)
ISBN-13: 978-1-83674-192-3 (UK EBK)

British Library Cataloguing in Publication Data
A catalogue record for this book is available from the British Library

Library of Congress Cataloging-in-Publication Data
A catalog record for this book is available from the Library of Congress

Typeset in Sabon by MJ & N Gavan, Truro, Cornwall
Printed and bound by CPI Group (UK) Ltd, Croydon, CR0 4YY

This book is dedicated to the memory of
Malcolm Chase (1957–2020)
Peter Cox (1927–2022)

Contents

Preface

Chartism was the largest working-class political movement of the nineteenth century. This book will recover the lives and contributions of iconoclastic Chartist women. It corrects a misapprehension that women were confined to the margins of Chartism, valued only for their novel and decorative presence at events – 'glorious auxiliaries' in a movement geared to the interests of their husbands, fathers, brothers and sons.[1] In fact, Chartism offered unprecedented opportunities for working-class women not just to engage with politics, but to shape, influence and lead an unprecedented national campaign. As we shall see, women Chartists were an important relay in the struggle for women's rights that led from Mary Wollstonecraft's *A Vindication of the Rights of Woman* to the Suffragettes.

Chartism took its name from the People's Charter drafted by the London Working Men's Association and published early in 1838. The Charter did not call for votes for women. Its authors felt that to do so would delay the concession of their six points: the vote for every man over twenty-one years of age, a secret ballot, abolition of property qualifications for parliamentary candidates, a wage for members of Parliament, redistribution of seats and annual elections. But the National Charter Association established in Manchester two years later – the first working-class, mass-membership party in the world – admitted women on the same basis as men. And calls for female suffrage rang out in influential Chartist periodicals from the first months of the movement to its last.

Chartist women did more than make the tea and sandwiches, embroider banners and mind the children. They went on strike and joined marches, boycotted hostile shopkeepers, collected signatures and advocated for the Charter in their communities. They did not give up their precious time and energy out of altruism for their male relatives. The movement offered them opportunities to socialise, organise and theorise. It provided them with access to a public platform in mass meetings and the widely read Chartist press. In 1839, Chartism's foremost paper, *The Northern Star*, outsold *The Times*, making it the biggest selling newspaper in history at that point.[2] Women raised demands for their own political rights as democrats, as women and as workers. And they shaped Chartist organisations into a means of amplifying these demands. Women assumed positions of authority by chairing meetings and proposing motions, publishing addresses and delivering lectures. They may have been more welcome in some local associations than others, but everywhere they found ways to insert themselves into the movement.

It would be anachronistic to use the term feminism to describe the political aspirations of women in the mid-nineteenth century. They had no shared name for their political hopes. Anne Knight, a radical Quaker and Chartist sympathiser, called her approach 'womanism'. Most Chartist women combined their womanism with class consciousness. They rarely, if ever, sought alliances with middle-class women. They raised their demands for greater equality in a movement that aimed to increase the rights of the whole working class. Histories of Chartism have tended to treat women as an undifferentiated part of the crowd or to judge female Chartism according to standards provided by the feminist movement of the 1970s. According to these accounts, in Chartism's later years, women were pressured by Victorian standards of respectability to abdicate their independence and withdraw from radical politics into domestic life. At a moment when the organised working-class could have embraced gender solidarity, it instead fell back on male supremacy. This is a partial and misleading picture based on a failure to give sufficient weight to the voices of Chartist women themselves.

Repositioning working-class women at the centre of historical accounts matters. This century, neoliberal feminism has dwelt on the 'mindset' and 'positivity' that women supposedly need to succeed in adverse social conditions. A plethora of books celebrate the achievements of 'inspirational' women who changed history or shattered glass ceilings. These women can seem like isolated individuals, without context or comrades.[3] Even much more serious accounts of women's history have long abandoned Marxism and the centrality of class, which tends to leave them ill-equipped to understand movements that involved high levels of unity between working-class men and women. My hope is that recovering women's role in the mass campaigns of the past can encourage the revival of emancipatory strategies and solidarities today. The Chartist women were not 'gutsy', they are not 'role models' or 'pioneers'. What they did was to participate in establishing the first mass working-class movement in the world and they ensured women's voices were influential within it.

Approaching Chartism through the lens of gender reveals an enduring legacy of female activism in working-class politics. A distinct current of support for women's rights was incubated at the intersection of radical political currents and Chartist organisation in the late 1830s and 1840s. It was here that socialist and Chartist women developed their capacity for what Sheila Rowbotham called 'optimistic imaginings' and envisaged the possibility of broad and radical social transformation and egalitarian relationships between the sexes.[4] This component of Chartism was sufficiently entrenched and cohesive to survive the decline of the movement, and to energise the late Victorian women's suffrage movement. When that campaign emerged in the later nineteenth century, erstwhile Chartists contributed their experience, and their strategies gave the campaign for votes for women some of its dynamism and breadth of support among working-class women.

No history of nineteenth-century British radicalism can be complete without an exploration of the Chartist movement from the perspective of its female participants. Capturing that perspective means retrieving women such as Eliza Cook, the youngest of eleven children born into a working-class family in Southwark, South London. Cook was encouraged to write by her mother and her first volume of poetry, *Lays of a Wild Harp*, was published in 1835 when she was just seventeen. One poem alone, 'The Old Armchair', made her a household name in Britain and the United States. Cook had a long-term and public relationship with the American actress Charlotte Cushman. Her enormously popular poems were printed in Chartist publications and she frequently explored Chartist themes in her work. She hasn't attracted much interest from literary historians nor been considered in the context of female Chartism. She did not occupy a formal position within the Chartist movement as some male poets did, but she identified with the campaign, wrote poems celebrating Chartism and publicly attempted to influence its direction.

Given the time and energy that women expended on work and providing care, their energetic commitment to fighting for political and social change was nothing short of heroic. They created a tradition of support for women's right to interfere in politics, which endured to become a constituent element of suffragism and the Suffragettes. This book tells the women's stories and places them in the heart of the movement they did so much to create.

Our story opens one October evening in 1842 when a young working-class woman stepped up to address a Chartist meeting in London, across the street from the Old Bailey. Her impromptu speech would become a sensation.

1

The 'Hen Chartists' Take Flight

In an upstairs room at number 55, Old Bailey, men and women jostled together on crowded benches, pressing their bodies forward for a better view. The front row was so close to the stage that people in the audience could reach out to shake the hand of a speaker or pat them on the shoulder. The large female contingent was not in the mood for reticence and decorum. They waved their handkerchiefs, clapped and cheered.[1]

The purpose of the meeting was to form a Female Chartist Association to cooperate with the Male Association and for other objectives connected with the People's Charter. The main speaker was a man, Mr Ridley, who was probably the London Chartist leader Daniel Ruffy Ridley. Ridley was delivering his planned defence of women's right to engage in politics when he was interrupted by a Mr Cohen, who questioned women's constitutional suitability for the rough and tumble of politics. Cohen declared 'it would be more in her proper character and station to rest at home, where she was the pride and ornament of the domestic hearth, than in the political arena'. According to press reports, his intervention prompted some cries of 'hear, hear' but caused a 'sensation among the ladies'.[2] The young woman chairing the meeting, Susanna Inge, demanded that Cohen tell her how much physical force was required to cast a vote.

Undaunted, Cohen rose again to assert that women could not vote according to their conscience because they would be incapable of resisting the influence of 'attractive young Tory sprigs'. This time, it was a pale young woman dressed in black who responded. She delighted the audience by observing that women must always be able to withstand the influence of men, because a man who would lead a woman astray in political matters could also lead her astray in other ways. At the end of her short speech,

> she declared herself a Chartist in name and feeling; and having appealed to her fellow-country women to 'come out' in favour of the Charter, and, however ungrammatical their language, not to be dismayed by any shaft of ridicule that might be pointed against them, concluded by giving them the encouraging hope that if it were only from the curiosity to hear 'a woman' speak, the young men would come out and speak to them.[3]

The speaker, Mary Ann Walker, had succinctly expressed the obstacles faced by working-class women who advocated for Chartism in public. She acknowledged women's awareness of their lack of education and fear of becoming objects of curiosity and ridicule, while also encouraging them to exploit the novelty of women speaking in public to generate support for the Charter.

Widely circulated press reports of Susanna Inge's role in the meeting and of Mary Ann's speech propelled them into the pages of the mainstream newspapers. *The Times*, popularly known as *The Thunderer*, published articles attacking them as 'hen-Chartists'.[4] The jibe drew on misogynistic tropes of hen-pecked, emasculated husbands and scolding wives recognisable from popular culture. Hen-pecking wives might topple the authority of their husbands; hen-Chartists might topple the authority of the British political establishment. Another London paper sneered that for the female Chartists, 'no good can come of legislation until the women have the paramount authority in Parliament and Polly Walker sits in the Speaker's chair'.[5]

'Why is Miss Mary Ann Walker like a lightening conductor?', asked the *Newcastle Journal*. 'Because she attracts bolts from the *Thunderer*!'[6] At the opposite end of the country, the *Bristol Times* remarked on the great novelty of women entering into the public arena: 'Tired of the slow progress which their male friends and relatives are making in the march of reform and revolution, a society of female Chartists have sprung forth from among the fair portion of our *ultra-politicians*, their more "tardy sons to chide" and shame into renewed energy by ardent example.'[7] Walker proudly told one meeting that the 'scoffs and gibes' of *The Times* had made her famous in 'all parts of the world'.[8] The Chartist women had gone viral, or as viral as the print media of the mid-nineteenth century allowed.

Such a display of female audacity could not go unanswered. Chartist women were portrayed as 'vulgar viragos', 'unsexed' deviant females with 'masculine proclivities'.[9] Women who were so abandoned that they could invade the public arena might be capable of other shocking transgressions. The *Hereford Journal* accused Walker and Inge of helping to dissect the body of a socialist to prepare themselves for public speaking.[10] The press constantly reminded Chartist women that they were members of the lower orders, that their 'accomplishments smacked rather spicily of Billingsgate', invoking the misanthropic trope of the sharp-tongued fishwife.[11] A correspondent for the *West Kent Guardian* wrote of his 'disgust' at the sight of 'English women, the daughters, sisters or wives of somebody, exhibiting themselves in this fashion, before a set of ragged, reeking fellows in a corner of the Old Baily [sic]'.[12] A *John Bull* reporter declared he was 'panting' to know more about Mary Ann Walker's eyes, hair, complexion, mouth and voice, while another openly speculated on whether she was a virgin.[13] Any woman who has engaged with left-wing or feminist movements in the past 200 years will be all too familiar with such sexualised jibes.

Even the Chartist *Northern Star* newspaper noted Walker's low-cut dress, 'very graceful bust' and 'interestingly proportioned body'.[14] Some historians see these descriptions as symptomatic of Chartist preferences for women as 'decorative symbols of working-class virtue', whose busts were more important than their political views.[15] The context for the *Star*'s description was a *Punch* cartoon that caricatured Walker as a hideous *sans-culotte* with thin hair pulled back into the shape of the cap of liberty.[16] The *Star* may have been defending Walker from attacks on her appearance. The historian Helen Rogers

Sarah Parker Remond

suggested that Walker adopted a black mourning dress for her lectures to present herself as a dutiful and Christian daughter. When combined with Walker's good looks, it turned her into a 'Chartist sex symbol'.[17] There is evidence, however, that Walker adopted her black dress as a political rather than a personal statement. At one event, Walker declared herself in mourning, not for a relative but for her 'deject and wretched' country.[18]

Newspapers had always lampooned women in reform movements, but the reporting on Chartist women was unique in its scope and intensity. Mary Ann Walker never admitted to being intimidated by this media onslaught. She said *The Times* had done her a huge favour by making her popular, so that 'numbers of people had been crowding in on her asking her "Did you see the *Times*?", "Did you see the *Times*?", "Why, it calls you hen Chartists!", to laughter and cheers from the audience'.[19] Copies of the *Times* reports had poured in on her from her friends and supporters, she told them, mocking the newspaper's efforts to pillory both her reputation and her person.

Female Chartists were not actually a novelty in 1842: they had been in the public eye since the Chartist agitations of 1838. What was new was that Chartist women were taking to the public platform not to sweetly and demurely encourage their male comrades, but to 'chivvy' them. The 'hen-Chartists' held themselves up as an example men should follow, not a docile flock to be led.

Walker also seems to have become a link between Chartism and radicals in France, which must have given her some influence over how Chartism was seen abroad. Several papers reported that Walker read out a letter received by the 'lady Chartists of Great Britain' from a Parisian man, Messier de Clarge, who had also sent them a copy of his unpublished pamphlet, *The Rights and Deserts of Woman*.[20] Walker was commissioned by the Female Charter Association to give an official response to his letter, and both the letter and her response were included in some of her speeches.[21] This correspondence was mocked in the British press, which found foreigners taking female Chartists seriously both absurd and infuriating. The existence of this radical fan mail suggests that the Chartist women were providing an example of female activism to democrats in Paris and creating networks of mutual support.

A few weeks before Christmas, Mary Ann Walker appeared at another rally in High Holborn.[22] The meeting was convened by public advertisement and attracted a big crowd, including 'a large proportion of very elegantly dressed ladies, many of whom were of the superior classes of society'. It was due to start at 8:00 p.m. and by 8:10 p.m. members of the audience, superior or not, were loudly stamping on the floor to signal their eagerness to begin. When Mary Ann appeared, surrounded by a group of female friends, there was a simultaneous burst of applause. As she walked through the body of the hall towards the platform, she was greeted with cheering, clapping hands, the waving of handkerchiefs, mingled with the loud 'Huzzas' and other demonstrations of welcome so enthusiastic as to be 'almost beyond description'. A few hostile hisses were drowned out by the 'reverberating din of acclamation'.[23]

Walker began her speech by acknowledging that it was bold for a woman to speak out in public, but her feelings about her country's wrongs, and men's and women's sufferings, were so strong that she would not apologise for making a public stand. She then described a cruelty perpetrated by the present economic system. A young female shirtmaker had been driven to suicide, she said, after working sixteen hours for sixpence making shirts for the 'lords of creation', a phrase commonly used by radical women to ridicule male authority. What were the causes of such miseries and who were the beneficiaries? The 'penny a shirt' pay was caused in part by taxation levied on the finished product. Those taxes supported a host of royal parasites who lived in luxury on the money wrung from the starving needlewomen. Walker was a young woman who probably had little education or experience. Yet, her speeches combined pathos with social analysis in an extraordinarily effective way.

As proceedings ended, members of the audience attempted to shield Walker from a heckler but she willingly faced his question. In her speech, Mary Ann had criticised Lord Abinger, a cousin of the Queen, as a 'modern-day Judge Jeffreys' for his harsh treatment of Chartist prisoners. The heckler asked her whether one overbearing judge meant the whole judiciary was rotten. Mary Ann replied by saying one diseased limb could contaminate a body unless it was amputated, which Abinger should immediately be. Her riposte was greeted with loud and prolonged cheering.[24] This spontaneity is very striking in all the reports of Mary Ann's speeches, coming as it did at a time when interactions between lecturers and their audiences were otherwise highly regulated and controlled. Sympathetic audiences sought to protect Mary Ann from potential insults, but also vastly appreciated her capacity to deal with hecklers and critics with unscripted wit and verve.

Walker broke all the conventions governing female public speech. She did not apologise for her presence, she did not emphasise her virtue or reticence, she did not clothe herself in the respectable garb of a wife or mother. On the contrary, she was bold and audacious, witty and satirical. She called the Church 'holy robbers', who had stolen Westminster Abbey. She declared the Whig party to be dead and 'woe on the first body-snatcher to drag them from the grave'.[25] She redeployed *The Times'* jibe of 'hen Chartism' to express her womanly equality with Queen Victoria, asking one appreciative audience why no one called the Queen a 'hen-sovereign'?[26]

Walker's public identity was shaped by satire and wit more attuned to libertine Jacobinism than Victorian prudery. When another heckler suggested that support for women's rights could cause disunity in the movement, Walker retorted that she had always favoured union with her fellow man, prompting laughter and cheers.[27] She also defended so-called physical force Chartists, pointing to the physical force regularly deployed against them by the state. 'What were the soldiers, the guns and the bayonets if not physical force?' she demanded.[28] In January, she told a meeting in Bristol that she would 'strongly advise "Bobby Peel" and his friend Wellington to grant the poor their rights ... and take care least if the French came over, she and the people would not assist them, as she would just as soon be enslaved by one nation as another'.[29] This was a daring statement for a woman to make, given the recent history of laws which criminalised potentially treasonous sentiments.

Walker was particularly adept at reversing assumptions of gender and class disadvantage. She encouraged the members of one audience to bring their wives and daughters to hear the female Chartists speak, because, 'as she would tell *The Times*, they might hear reason and sound political wisdom from the lips of a woman, and from the daughter of a working man'.[30] A working-class identity was not a source of shame but a cause for pride. The experience of work gave women like her insight and experience which was not available to those who mocked and satirised them.

Susanna Inge is an acknowledged supporter of women's

rights, one who expressed her frustration with the confinements imposed on women whose province was 'only to make a pudding, prepare a dinner, clean the house, tend to her children'.[31] In contrast, Walker's commitment to her sex has been contested by historians.[32] She seemed less concerned about the frustrating restrictions on women's public activities than with the terrible conditions endured by women workers. Her speeches, however, articulated a deep concern with the impact of low pay, job insecurity and welfare reform on women. These were important elements within her broader radical political commitments.

We know nothing of Mary Ann Walker's early life or what brought her to the Chartist movement. She described herself as coming from 'humble origins' but nothing else is known of her background. By the summer of 1843, she had returned to obscurity. In August, newspapers reported on a commotion which occurred at the Blackfriars Rotunda, a site of radical meetings and theatricals. A performance of *Hamlet* was disrupted by audience uproar when Walker, whose presence had been wrongly advertised, failed to appear as Hamlet's mother.[33] By then, Walker's celebrity may have descended into caricature and become divorced from both her politics and her control.

The right to interfere in politics

The Chartist movement which engaged women such as Susanna Inge and Mary Ann Walker was born out of frustration with the Whig Reform Act of 1832. The Reform Act was driven through a reluctant Parliament by agitation from ordinary men and women, agitation which left an organisational form in pro-reform political unions including some women's unions. When the Lords rejected the bill, riots broke out in Nottingham, Derby and Bristol and speculation about a possible revolution was rife. The act itself did little to assuage a growing thirst for political reform and increased democracy. Historians estimate that the act increased the electorate from 11 percent of the adult male population to 18 percent.[34] This increase not only failed to address the expectations aroused by the popular campaign, but some working-class electors were deprived of their former voting rights.[35]

Any surviving illusions about the capacity of the reformed Parliament to legislate in the interests of the working classes were dispelled by the passing of the New Poor Law Amendment Act in 1834. Popularly known as the New Poor Law, it deprived the sick and old, disabled people, single parents and the destitute of outdoor relief, and forced them into poor houses, where appalling conditions were deliberately created to dissuade applicants. The legislation prompted a mass movement of opposition which prevented its new structures being imposed for up to two years in some areas. Many working-class women gained their first experience of campaigning in the anti–Poor Law movement, and many women and men drew the conclusion that Parliament must be thoroughly reformed for the act to be repealed and future attacks on the poor prevented.

The London Working Men's Association (LWMA) drew up the Charter in the summer of 1837, but it was much revised and delayed. A version was circulated for amendments to be submitted, and one proposal was to include women in the expanded franchise. The LWMA rejected the suggestion, arguing,

> Against this reasonable proposition we have no just argument to adduce, but only to express our fears of entertaining it, lest the false estimate man entertains for this half of the human family may cause his ignorance and prejudice to be enlisted to retard the progress of his own freedom.[36]

The inclusion of women was rejected on the basis of expediency, not principle.

The campaign for the Charter was intensified by the 'politics of hunger' amid the severe economic recession of the 1840s. Anger and despair generated an explosive campaign which opened with monster rallies and continued through the threat of insurrection, Britain's first general strike and the involvement of tens of thousands of working-class women in political activism.

Women embraced Chartism in large numbers because it offered them the possibility of redressing both class and gender inequalities. Those familiar with other histories of Chartism will recognise that this is a controversial claim. The Chartist movement has been characterised as socially conservative and hostile to the idea that women could be independent political activists. Chartist men, it is said, wanted to buttress their power over women's labour and sexuality. Historians of female Chartism have characterised the women's stance as one of 'militant domesticity'.[37] This positioning legitimised women's presence in the movement as defenders of their family, but it also circumscribed their role to one of supporting their menfolk.

In contrast, *Lady Insurrectionists* will show that throughout the Chartist years, women consistently and loudly demanded their share of any newly acquired rights. Some of their public justifications for acquiring the franchise demonstrate women's confidence that their intellectual abilities were equal to those of men. An address issued by the Ashton Female Political Association in February 1839 argued that intelligence should replace property as the qualification for voting because 'then, Sisters, we shall be placed in our proper position in society and enjoy the elective franchise as well as our kinsmen'.[38]

An uneasy consensus developed within the early years of Chartism that the movement should focus on winning the vote for working-class men and then a reformed Parliament could undertake the more controversial work of extending the franchise to women.[39] There were encouraging signs that the official organisations of the Chartist movement recognised women as valued comrades in the cause and would, therefore, promptly deliver the vote to them. As we have seen, membership of the National Charter Association (NCA) was open to both women and men.[40] Another Chartist organisation, William Lovett's National Association for the Political and Social Improvement of the People committed its members to supporting women's right to vote.[41] The London Democratic Association, the most important Chartist organisation in the capital, also expressed support for women's political rights. Its cognate women's organisation campaigned for the female franchise and insisted that female members would rule themselves and not allow men into their meetings except by a majority vote.[42]

There was no opportunity to test the women's optimism because the Charter was never accepted by Parliament. But the campaign to pressure Westminster into conceding the Charter generated multiple associations and societies which provided women with opportunities to articulate and popularise support for their political rights. Women such as Elizabeth Neesom in London, Elizabeth Hanson in Elland, Mary Savage in Nottingham, Jane Stow in Keighley and Mrs Lapworth in Birmingham established themselves as leaders in female Chartist organisations. Many female Chartists joined societies in which they could assume positions of authority by chairing meetings and proposing motions, publishing addresses and delivering lectures. There is also growing evidence that women played a role in the official business of mixed-sex Chartist meetings. Mrs Lapworth seconded a resolution which pledged support to the National Charter Association at a mixed meeting in Birmingham in May 1841.[43] Further examples will be presented throughout this book.

It is possible that women could be energetic and valued supporters of Chartism but still be confined to the margins of the movement in which they could contribute only in ways that were an extension of their domestic roles, such as presenting homemade caps and sashes to male leaders. Indeed, some female Chartists appeared to accept their marginalisation, and they invoked their role as mothers and wives to justify their involvement with politics. In their addresses, some female Chartists argued that they had not sought out politics, but that politics had found them, had forced them to work outside their homes and ruptured their hopes of effective care-giving and domestic fulfilment. Women, however, did not always frame their addresses in apologetic tones or limit their concerns to the restoration of their lost domesticity.

Women justified their support for Chartism in multiple ways, citing their authority as wives and mothers, claiming a radical heritage of natural rights and positioning themselves as contributors to the wealth of the nation.[44] The ascension of Victoria to the throne in 1837 provided another argument in favour of women's right to assume a public role. In May 1839 Elizabeth Neesom, the secretary of the recently established London Female

Democratic Association (LFDA), issued an address in which she rebuked 'those who may be, or rather appear to be, surprised that females should be daring enough to interfere with politics; to them we simply say, that as it is a female that assumes to rule this nation in defiance of the universal rights of man and woman, we assert in accordance with the rights of all, and acknowledging the sovereignty of the people, our right, as free women (or women determined to be free) to rule ourselves'.[45] Neesom used the rhetoric of universal rights to position women within the 'sovereign people' whose rights were being denied. Six months later, the Birmingham Female Political Union responded with an address to Neesom and the women of East London.[46] While Neesom had referred to universal rights, the Birmingham women invoked their position as labourers who deserved a fair share of the wealth they produced:

> Be not deterred by the hypocritical cant, that women have no right to interfere with politics. We are told we want to destroy the ancient institutions of the country, and to appropriate the property of others for our own use; but we only ask for a fair renumeration for our labour – nothing less will satisfy, nothing more is required.[47]

Another feature of Chartist women's rhetoric was their regular appeal to emotions to create a community of shared feeling, to disarm critics and to encourage support.[48] Their deployment of emotions was closely connected to their working-class identities. Many of the female Chartists' earliest addresses invoked the pathos of starving children. Others adopted a broader and more sophisticated approach to understanding how feeling could intensify the misery arising from poverty and physical hardship. On 9 February 1839, the Chartist women of Newcastle issued an address in which they described how the deleterious effects of poverty were exacerbated by the 'scorn' directed towards them:

> The fear of want hangs over our heads; the scorn of the rich is pointed towards us; the brand of slavery is on our kindred, and we feel the degradation. We are a despised caste; our oppressors

are not content with despising our feelings but demand the control of our thoughts and wants.[49]

This class antagonism influenced how women experienced supposedly private life events such as motherhood. Mrs Lapworth, the secretary of the Birmingham Women's Political Union (BWPU), frequently described how the contrasting expectations of rich and poor women fractured any potential for a shared female experience.[50] Motherhood had intensified her sense of indignation at inequality and encouraged her to 'sally forth and force a combination of the working classes'.[51] Rich ladies, Lapworth claimed, were not unaware of the sufferings of poor women, but were 'insensible' to them because they were more interested in procuring 'more labour for the least money'.[52] Poor women should not fear the displeasure of the rich or feel ashamed of their poverty, she argued. Poverty was not an individual failing and women should not hide it – they should 'make it known, and talk about it, and ask the cause of it'.[53]

'Workwomen': Where gender meets class

Both popular literature and court records from the early nineteenth century provide evidence of gender-based conflict within plebian marriages over who controlled men's weekly wages, how much money and time men spent in the pub, and domestic violence.[54] Wife beating was not recognised as a crime until 1853 and it remained a common feature of life for many women. Misogynistic ideas about female attempts to usurp men's natural position as head of the family influenced attitudes and relationships within the working class, but they were contested by affection, mutual support, sociability and shared social and economic interests.

The entry of women into paid employment outside the home was one of the great social changes prompted by the Industrial Revolution. In the late eighteenth and early nineteenth centuries, the enclosures of land and changes in agricultural production meant the traditional family economy was undermined. Women turned instead to domestic production based on spinning and weaving in the home, and then to employment in the factories that began to spread out from the centre of the textile industries in the rapidly expanding urban centres of Manchester, Stockport and Glasgow. Some men organised to exclude women from their trades and refused to allow them to join their unions, fearing competition from women who were often paid lower wages. The entry of women into the labour force, however, created solidarity as well as competition and afforded women new possibilities for financial and social independence and new opportunities for collective organisation. Women expanded their traditional identities using inherited legacies, political influences and shared experiences, and they raised their own demands for increased autonomy.

The experience of working outside the home disrupted established patterns of home-based labour which were compatible with childcare. But it also afforded women new justifications for interfering in politics. The Chartists demanded that the right to political representation enjoyed by the propertied classes be replaced with the rights of labour, so that anyone who was productive could have the right to vote. The idea that social wealth depended on the labour of workers could strengthen and energise female Chartist demands for political representation. John Reginald Richardson was one of many prominent Chartists who argued that as women contributed to society's wealth by working in agriculture and industry, unmarried women should have the right to vote.[55]

The Chartist women's addresses introduced the language of class hostility and a non-gendered labour theory of value. In April 1838, a group in Wandsworth published an address to their 'fellow workwomen'.[56] They wanted to establish social and political equality through the People's Charter, and they demanded:

> Do we not produce a superabundance of wealth, which enables an aristocracy, a host of money-changers and profit mongers, to riot in luxurious profusion, while at the same time the labourer, the producer of all the wealth in existence, can scarce procure by incessant toil a little food?

The idea of 'superabundance' was important for establishing the possibility of a world in which every citizen could live in comfort and ease if the bounty of the natural world was only shared fairly. Working outside the home gave women a justification for claiming their political rights and allowed them to form new collective identities.

The question of class has been widely debated by historians of Chartism.[57] In this book I will adopt a broad definition which avoids reductionist ideas tying the working class exclusively to those directly employed in producing commodities in factory conditions.[58] The nineteenth-century working class included those who produced commodities whether in factories or sweatshops or in their own homes, the huge number of domestic servants and those who survived in the informal economy. It included the women who were identified, or identified themselves, as housewives, but who often took in lodgers and did cleaning, childminding, laundry and mending to contribute to the household income.

Alongside the process of production and the circulation of commodities was the equally important process of social reproduction. The working class had to be reproduced in two senses. Firstly, workers had to be fed, clothed and rested to some degree to keep working. Secondly, the working class had to be reproduced generationally by childbirth, and by the provision of care for the young, old and sick. The process of producing commodities and the process of producing labourers were part of one integrated system of profit-making and life-making, but social reproduction was vulnerable to any intensification of exploitation. Long working hours and rigid patterns of employment placed increasing pressure on women's capacity to care for their families and this provoked a unified working-class response. As we shall see, the huge working-class mobilisation in defence of social reproduction against the threat posed by the New Poor Laws of 1834 was a constituent element of Chartism. Chartist women attempted to expand the time, money and emotional resources allocated to social reproduction, which necessitated confronting a system which privileged the production of profits over caregiving and life-making.

The leading female Chartists were unusual because few had children at the peak of their activism. The burden that raising large families placed on working-class women made it difficult for them to sustain regular political activism. Mary Ann Walker and Susanna Inge were unmarried and childless when they became Chartist lecturers. We cannot know whether women without children found themselves with more time and energy for politics, or whether politically committed women found ways to avoid getting pregnant. Perhaps it was a combination of the two.

Chartist men often found their way to political activity through mutual improvement societies, reading clubs and educational institutions. Such activities were much harder for working-class women to access. Women had to cope with puberty, pregnancy, childbirth and menopause without running water, pain relief, sanitary products or medical care in overcrowded houses with outside toilets shared by many families. They had to face the enormous burden of combining paid employment, childcare and housework. The Chartists had to develop their own innovative methods of creating a mass activist base by coordinating national petitions, holding mass rallies and publishing Chartist newspapers. Women had to participate in this creative process while simultaneously developing their own distinct rhetoric and organisations. Their achievements were extraordinary.

The stories of the Chartist women do more than create a more complete narrative of the fight for democracy. They open up new connections and create new encounters with women whose concerns and aspirations seem so like our own. Their stories have been marginalised and erased. They have been presented as the victims of both unscrupulous employers and working-class men who wanted to keep them in a state of domestic submission. But the Chartist women refused to be marginalised or intimidated, and they were not acquiescent victims of either their bosses or their husbands. They developed a range of political and rhetorical skills to make sure their voices were heard from the platform and in the press. They demanded that they too should benefit if their husbands forced the government to concede more democratic rights. And they propelled issues such as childcare, domestic violence and institutional sexual abuse into mainstream Chartist thinking.

The Chartist women's years of activism coincided with the historical moment in which the British ruling class was bolstering the privatised family as a guarantor of social stability and the site of social reproduction. But the Chartist women refused to allow this family building to be imposed upon them. They decorated their homes with portraits of Chartist leaders and their kitchens became debating chambers. They politicised their shopping, their clothes and their children's names. I cannot read accounts of Chartist women's boycotts, banner-making and speechifying without thinking of all the women who have spent 2024 and 2025 boycotting Israeli goods, making banners and T-shirts and protesting against the genocide in Gaza. The tactics, politics and courage of the Chartist women created a tradition which resonated through the labour movement, the women's suffrage movement and the global struggle for women's liberation.

'The Apostle of Progress' Frances Wright

In July 1848, the women of the National Female Chartist Association in Bethnal Green issued an address in *The Northern Star* in which they positioned themselves in a tradition of female leadership: 'A few ornaments have already distinguished our sex. It was a Mary Wollstonecraft who wrote the Rights of Woman, a maid of Saragossa [sic] who redeemed Spain, and a Joan of Arc who saved France; and now we have a Miss Martineau and a Frances Wright, whose incorruptible virtues and talents might bid even the sterner sex to blush for shame.'[1] The choice of antecedents reveals how the female Chartists sought to position themselves in the public mind. The Maid of Saragossa became a symbol of Spanish national resistance to Napoleon's armies when she took up arms during the Siege of Zaragoza (1808) and was known as the Spanish Joan of Arc. Wollstonecraft's name was associated with both female rationality and sexual impropriety. Martineau was a respected abolitionist but was unpopular with many Chartists because of her popularisation of Malthusian views. Frances Wright was a highly controversial figure because of her very public advocacy of Owenite socialism, free-thinking and female emancipation. The women of Bethnal Green placed themselves within a tradition of transgressive women who defied gender conventions, displayed military leadership and won respect for their intellect.

Frances Wright is not mentioned in any accounts of female Chartism, but there is ample evidence of the respect afforded to her by male and female Chartists. This respect illuminates important aspects of the movement's gender politics. At a commemoration of Thomas Paine held in 1848, a toast to Frances Wright was enthusiastically cheered. *The Northern Star*'s correspondent observed that, 'There is a curious similitude here, as Mr Paine and Madam D'Arusment [Wright's married name] were both British-born subjects and both citizens of France; the one a member of her Assembly, the other one of nature's most distinguished nobles.'[2] This comparison of Wright and the hugely popular figure of Paine suggests that she was held in very high regard within Chartism. Wright reciprocated by taking her relationship with *The Northern Star* seriously. She collaborated with a Chartist correspondent for the *Star* who wrote her biography (on which more below) and then wrote six letters to the newspaper between 6 July and 17 August 1844 responding to the biography and further outlining her philosophy.[3]

Frances Wright was a deeply controversial public figure on both sides of the Atlantic throughout the 1820s and 1830s. She followed the same intellectual trajectory as many Chartists, moving from abolitionism to social radicalism via Owenism, a movement based on the teachings of Robert Owen, an advocate of early socialism and communal living. Wright's account of her travels through America, *Views on Society and Manners in America* (1821), established her national reputation as a democrat and reformer. She became a supporter of transatlantic Owenism and spent a portion of her inherited wealth on her attempt to establish a utopian community in Nashoba, Tennessee, a venture which was widely reported in the British press.[4] Wright's community involved enslaved people who were working to buy their own freedom. She intended this to demonstrate to Southern slaveowners that slavery could be ended with no cost to them. Wright enshrined women's equality in the principles of her community: 'No woman can forfeit her individual rights or her independent existence: and no man assert any rights or power over her whatsoever.'[5] Bold principles, however, were hard to put into practice when the climate and land made it impossible for the community to prosper.

Wright's community has frequently been portrayed as an idealistic attempt to create an interracial utopia, a characterisation which fitted neatly into a wider narrative of progress from slavery to democracy.[6] More recent scholarship, however, has explored the racism embedded in Wright's plan. She assumed that the slave owners needed only gentle persuasion to relinquish their 'property' and she believed that enslaved people should buy their freedom and then be transported to a colony in Africa. The eight enslaved people Wright bought had no say in her plan and many black activists strongly opposed this idea of 'colonisation'. Wright purchased land previously stolen from indigenous people with money her uncle made in British India. Predictably, it was not the limitations of Wright's scheme which caused controversy in the press but rather the question of interracial sexual relationships. Nashoba was engulfed by scandal when it became public that sexual relationships between black and white people were sanctioned at the commune.[7] In 1830, Wright eventually 'freed' the enslaved people she had bought by shipping them to Haiti, where the American Colonization Society had established a colony for free black people to settle. There is no evidence that Wright ever consulted the wishes of the enslaved people over whose lives she had absolute control.[8]

The scandal generated at Nashoba was a serious blow to Wright's reputation, health and wealth, but she recovered and by 1828 she was a leading figure in the American secularist movement. In January 1829, she launched and edited the *Free Inquirer* in New York and delivered her 'Course of Popular Lectures' which caused an 'immense sensation' and attracted both huge enthusiastic audiences and violent opposition.[9] The press vilified and satirised Wright and her supporters. They derided new workers' organisations in New York as the 'Fanny Wright party' or 'Fanny Wrighters'. The papers also carried more personal attacks, describing Wright, who was in her early forties, as an 'old hag' and a 'haggard spectre'.[10] To Chartist women, Wright must have been both an example of what women could achieve if they entered political life and a warning of the consequences should they do so.

Wright developed a sweeping critique of the interaction between class and gender inequality and argued that male power was 'the master error in the whole conception of things'.[11] She believed that frustrated middle-class women seeking fulfilling employment and exhausted working women were oppressed by the same system which dictated that women were either excluded from useful productive activities or were paid too little for what they produced.[12] Wright was outspoken about women's sexuality. In 1828, she criticised the customs which shrouded 'women's bodies, wants, desires, senses, affections and faculties in mystery'. She articulated Owenite beliefs that sex was natural and necessary for good health. 'Let us not teach', she wrote, 'that virtue consists in the crucifying of the affections and appetites.'[13] Wright also advocated a radical solution to female inequality in which the state would assume responsibility for caring for and educating all children. This led to her being accused of seeking to snatch children from their mothers' arms and destroy the family.[14] At least one Chartist reviewer, however, approved of her 'Plan of National Education', which, he wrote, 'should be circulated by the friends of popular progress'.[15] The fact that Wright was strongly identified with opposition to marriage and advocated for female sexual pleasure did not undermine her popularity among the readers of *The Northern Star.*

Wright's works were frequently advertised in *The Northern Star* and other Chartist-leaning publications such as Henry Hetherington's *The Odd Fellow*.[16] Her reputation among British reformers was built on the publication of a British edition of her 'Popular Lectures' by the Chartist James Watson.[17] Wright's 'Lectures' advanced a theory of knowledge which provided a theoretical basis for the faith radicals and Chartists had in education and disseminating knowledge as a means of reforming society. Wright's analysis of society's evils was rooted in the failure of the American and French revolutions to deliver universal rights for women, enslaved black people, indigenous Americans and the poor. In one of her published lectures, she asked, 'Who speaks of liberty while the human mind is in chains? Who of equality while the thousands are in squalid wretchedness, the millions harassed with health-destroying labour, the few afflicted with health-destroying idleness.'[18] This analysis would have chimed with Chartists campaigning to be granted the status of citizens in the aftermath of the failure of the 1832 Reform Bill to enfranchise working-class men.

The Northern Star provided a platform for the only biography of Wright published during her lifetime. The idea was first raised in May 1844 when a T. Myles, a Chartist from Wright's hometown of Dundee, published an account of meeting Wright and securing her approval for a biography. He finished his *Biography, Notes and Political Letters of Frances Wright D'Arusmont* by September, and it was published by James Watson. The reviewer in *The Northern Star* observed that Wright's published lectures were 'in all probability in possession of not a few of our readers; and are to them as they have been to us, a source of instruction and superlative enjoyment'.[19] The reviewer concluded that the new biography will 'command an extensive circulation. At all events, we have much pleasure in giving it our hearty recommendation.'[20] While this biography was being written, Wright wrote six letters to *The Northern Star* correcting errors in her earlier writings and outlining the ideas she would incorporate into her final book, *England the Civilizer* (1848).

In May 1847, the *Star* reported that the 'justly celebrated' Frances Wright was to give a series of lectures at William Fox's Unitarian South Place Chapel and commented, 'Our readers generally are acquainted with the "Lectures" delivered in America by this lady, and all who are resident in the metropolis will doubtless embrace the present opportunity to hear for themselves this eloquent apostle of progress. Madame d'Arusmont cannot fail to have overflowing audiences.'[21] Just four months later, however, in August 1847, the *Star*'s reporter suggested that her oratorical powers were fading and that 'Madame D'Arusmont is but a distorted ghost of Frances Wright'. The *Star*'s correspondent advised that Wright cease to obtrude herself upon the public.[22] Wright did not take the paper's advice. In February 1848, she was in Sheffield addressing a series of meetings including one which was convened to celebrate the birthday of Thomas Paine and was chaired by leading Sheffield Owenite and Chartist Isaac Ironside.[23] A local paper reported that her second meeting, which was held two weeks later, was given to a 'large and respectable audience' at the Town Hall.[24] Perhaps

The Northern Star correspondent had caught Wright on an off night because her speaking engagements seemed to meet with general approval.

Whatever the ups and downs in her public performances, Wright's reputation among Chartists endured. In May 1851 Ironside read out lengthy passages from Wright's *England, the Civilizer* at a meeting of the Sheffield Women's Rights Association.[25] The influential Sheffield Women's Rights Association will be discussed below but it is important to note that these independent-minded women identified with Wright and her theories of historical change and progress. This connection was one of the last Wright established. She died of complications following a fall in 1852 aged fifty-seven. Chartist publications promoted, engaged with and commemorated Wright's evolving political and theoretical ideas, and Chartist publications and publishers helped to embed Wright's ideas within the British working-class movement.

2

Radical Foremothers

The Chartists, particularly the female Chartists, had to justify their right to engage with political affairs, which made them particularly sensitive to the power of historical precedent. They were very conscious of the presence of women in earlier reform movements. And so were their political opponents.[1] Chartist women were unfavourably compared to the women of the French Revolution of 1789. After one of the women's meetings at the Old Bailey, the *West Kent Guardian* observed, 'The fish-hags of Paris were in fact to Robespierre what the ladies of the Old Bailey seem desirous to become to [Feargus] O'Connor and his tribe of Chartists.'[2] Comparisons made to earlier reform movements were constructed to sneer at and ridicule women's activism. When Mrs Lapworth was elected to the chair of the Birmingham Women's Political Union in September 1838, a local paper reported that she was acting in imitation of the 'Lancashire witches'. The 'Lancashire witches' were women who set up female reform societies in Blackburn twenty years earlier, who were themselves named for the eight women and two men who were hanged as witches in Pendle, Lancashire, in 1612.[3]

Women played an active role in the reform agitation when it resumed at the end of the Napoleonic Wars. Reformer Samuel Bamford kept a diary in which he recounted an open-air public meeting in March 1818, at which he insisted on the right of the females present to vote for or against the resolutions. 'This was a new idea', he wrote, 'and the women, who attended numerously on the bleak ridge, were mightily pleased with it.'[4] In the summer of 1819, reform-minded women began to look at creating their own organisations. The women of Blackburn caused a stir in the press when they set up their own society, attracting vicious cartoons and accusations of immorality, drunkenness and child neglect. This wave of female activism was visible at the Peterloo Massacre of 16 August 1819. The massacre took place at St Peter's Fields, Manchester, when a peaceful crowd of about 60,000 reformers was charged by sabre-wielding militias of the Yeomanry Cavalry. Eighteen people died on the day, and as many as 700 were injured. Women were highly visible in the crowd at St Peter's Fields, on the platform and on the list of casualties. Commemorations of Peterloo became a permanent feature of the radical and Chartist calendar. The tone of these commemorations demonstrate how central women were to the mythology which was constructed around the event. At one commemoration of Peterloo held in 1821, there was a spontaneous toast to 'The Female Reformers and the Rights of Women'.[5]

'Knowledge is power': Women and press freedom

The campaign for political reform was intrinsically linked to the sustained and popular campaign for press freedom.[6] Consistent efforts to challenge censorship and abolish high taxes levied on newspapers established the reputations of many of the leaders of London Chartism, including William Lovett, James Watson, John Cleave and Henry Hetherington. It is also possible to identify a few women who gained experience in the campaign for a free press and then joined the Chartist movement. In the early 1830s, Elizabeth Neesom was involved in the campaign for unstamped newspapers, those which had avoided having tax levied on them. Elizabeth became the leading figure in the Chartist women's association, the LFDA and her role in London Chartism will be discussed below.[7]

Alice Mann ran the family bookshop in Leeds when her husband, John, died. She was prosecuted twice for selling unstamped newspapers, first in 1834 and then in 1836 when she was imprisoned for six months in York Castle. Mann was a founding member of Leeds Chartism.[8] In 1848 she published a study of the inequalities of taxation and the burden of supporting the monarchy, *Mann's Black Book of the British Aristocracy; or, An Exposure of the More Monstrous Abuses in the State and the Church*. Few female booksellers published tracts in their own name and Mann's *Black Book* suggests that she was highly politically engaged and assertive.[9] Both Mann and Neesom were sustained by networks of radical publishers and booksellers and reformers which could provide political, emotional and material support.

A group of London-based women developed these informal networks into their own organisation to provide mutual support and to extend women's role within the campaign for a free press. This new organisation, the Friends of the Oppressed, was established in 1832 to support women who had family members or had themselves been prosecuted for selling unstamped papers. The organisation received sympathetic coverage from the *Poor Man's Guardian*, a paper published by Henry Hetherington and edited by Chartist James Bronterre O'Brien.[10] The Friends of the Oppressed gave some radical London women opportunities to organise meetings, to hold protests to greet women released from prison and to advocate their cause in the press.

From radicalism to Chartism: Women 'drop a hint'

Mary Wollstonecraft anticipated a derisive response to the idea that women should be allowed to vote. She wrote in her celebrated *Vindication of the Rights of Woman* (1792): 'I may excite laughter by dropping a hint, which I mean to pursue some future time, that I really think women ought to have representatives, instead of being arbitrarily governed.'[11]

Some twenty years later, Anna Wheeler, a significant figure in the London Owenite movement, raised the same demand. Irish-born Wheeler helped to formulate the arguments put forward by William Thompson in his *Appeal on Behalf of One Half of the Human Race, Women, Against the Pretensions of the Other, Men*, published in 1825 in Britain and later republished in France and the US. The *Appeal* argued for the vote for women as part of widespread reforms which would elevate both men and women.[12] Wheeler and Thompson argued for women to become agents of their own emancipation:

> Arouse! Awake! Rescue your sex, your species, from the frightful circumstances that surround and degrade you. Demand your rights, or man, ungenerous man, intoxicated with his power, may become still more presumptuous. Demand then with confidence and dignity your portion of the common rights of all.[13]

The first petition for women's suffrage was presented to the Lords on 11 August 1832 by the radical MP Henry Hunt, on behalf of Mrs Smith from Yorkshire. The petition argued that as Smith paid taxes and had to obey the law, she should have the right to choose who represented her in Parliament. The derision anticipated forty years earlier by Wollstonecraft was directed at Mrs Smith. *The Times* declared that the petition was 'shocking' and 'disgusting' while *The Spectator* referred to Mrs Smith's 'absurd' and 'foolish petition'.[14] Parliament and the mainstream press treated Smith's petition with contempt, but the idea of votes for women crept inexorably from the margins of debate to become a consistent theme within the Owenite socialist and Chartist movements.

Abolition abroad

Radicals in Britain had long counterposed liberty with 'slavery', referencing either Biblical oppression, medieval serfdom, subjection to political absolutism or colonial conquest. Thousands of women gained their first experience of public activism in campaigns to abolish the Atlantic slave trade and the physical enslavement of black people, known as chattel slavery, in the British Empire, the Southern states of America and elsewhere. Abolition activism involved women's societies and mass boycotts of goods produced by enslaved people and the organisation of mass petitions. When Parliament abolished the slave trade in 1807, it did not abolish colonial slavery. This left some 700,000 people in enslavement in the British Caribbean.[15] The campaign to abolish colonial slavery began in January 1823 when the Anti-Slavery Society was established. The society faced some formidable opponents: the wealthy planters and merchants, intellectuals and publishers, and government ministers who collectively formed the West India Interest.[16]

Between 1787 and 1792, historians estimate that some 1.5 million British people signed petitions against slavery, out of a population of 12 million.[17] The signatures on the abolitionist petitions of 1788, 1792, 1814 and 1823 were almost exclusively those of men, and it was commonly believed that women's signatures would discredit petitions. Before 1830, only one anti-slavery petition had been signed by women. Between 1831 and 1833, however, there was an explosion of female petitioning.[18] Historian Clare Midgley identifies this campaign as the first large-scale intervention by women in parliamentary politics.[19]

Women's activism intensified in the run-up to the reading of the Emancipation Act of 1833. Anne Knight and Mary Tothill organised a massive women's anti-slavery petition, which was signed by 500,000 women in England and Wales, 135,000 in Scotland and 77,000 in Wales. In the manufacturing town of Derby nearly every adult woman lent it their signature.[20] One of the most active ladies' associations was the Sheffield Female Anti-Slavery Society, which organised house-to-house canvassing and boycotts of West Indian sugar.[21]

The women's abolitionist societies were not just auxiliaries to the men's organisations. They played a 'distinctive and at times leading role in successive stages of the anti-slavery campaign' and were almost always 'bolder' than those of the men.[22] This boldness was theoretical as well as organisational. Supporters of gradual emancipation, who dominated the official anti-slavery movement, often deployed patronising and racist arguments to justify their stance. William Wilberforce argued that 'before the slave [sic] could be fit to receive freedom, it would be madness to attempt to give it to them.'[23] Some prominent women in the abolitionist movement explored the ways in which the same arguments around denial of education were used to justify indeterminate delay in granting the franchise to working men and to women in Britain. In the 1840s, Elizabeth Pease drew on this discourse to condemn opposition to the Charter as 'nothing but a slave-holder's argument – the slave was not prepared for liberty – and the people are not prepared for their rights'.[24] Confronting moderate anti-slavery views radicalised abolitionist women, and women radicalised abolitionism as they became prominent among those advocating immediate emancipation.[25]

Abolitionist women began to defy the leaders of their movement who sought to exclude them from any public role in campaigning. As a result, radical abolitionism became closely linked to assertions of female independence. Tensions between women's growing confidence and their marginalisation from the official structures of the abolitionist movement came to a head at the World Anti-Slavery Convention of June 1840, when attempts were made to exclude American women delegates.[26] The dispute was only resolved when American abolitionists William Garrison and Charles Lenox Remond refused to take their seats until the women were given theirs. Garrison was supported by English radicals and Chartist sympathisers William Ashurst and James Stansfeld. At the convention, women from Britain and America began to create new networks and became more willing to assert their rights. But despite grassroots activism, it was not until 1853 that a mixed-sex anti-slavery society was established in Britain, and not until 1859 that the black American Sarah Parker Remond became the first woman to deliver abolitionist lectures to mixed audiences on this side of the Atlantic.[27]

The Chartist movement incorporated conflicting attitudes towards the anti-slavery campaign, which some dismissed out of racist prejudice or because it struck them as middle-class hypocrisy.[28] Chartist publisher John Cleave was influenced by the 'racist republicanism' imported from American politics, which justified the inclusion of slaveowners in the coalition of support for President Andrew Jackson by alleging enslaved people's incapacities and degradation.[29] Cleave and Bronterre O'Brien were closely associated with *The Northern Liberator*, the Chartist publication which most consistently satirised and dehumanised enslaved people.[30] The Whig government's Emancipation Bill intensified tensions between reformers and abolitionists when it granted £20 million in compensation to slaveowners, to be paid through higher taxation. Opposition to this aspect of the Emancipation Bill sometimes slid into resentment against enslaved people and a downplaying of the horrors they endured. In June 1833, O'Brien wrote in *The Poor Man's Guardian*, 'We have said enough to show that we are no enemies to colonial emancipation; all we require is that when negroes are emancipated, it shall not be at the expense of those who are greater slaves than themselves.'[31]

Female abolitionists developed their own rhetoric, which often focused on the cruel separation of enslaved families. Such ideas could strike a chord with Chartist women, but they were not immune from expressions of racist resentment. In a speech given to a Chartist meeting in Taunton in 1839, a Mrs Frisby used the n-word to wish all black people 'to Old Nick' because the public had been diverted 'by African floggings and cruelties and forgot the English ones'.[32] Such overt racism was less common among female Chartists than expressions of opposition to all oppression. Still, drawing parallels between the chattel slavery of the Caribbean plantations and lack of political freedom or wage exploitation at home could gloss over the former's unique cruelties.[33] In August 1838, the Bristol Female Patriotic Association targeted the

> cunning and designing men who have enlisted our sympathies in favour of the abolition of negro slavery in our colonies: we raised our voices in denunciation of [the slaveowner's] tyranny, and never rested until the dealers in human blood were compelled to abandon their hell-born traffic. But we have learned, by bitter experience, that slavery is not confined to colour or clime – that even in England cruel oppression reigns.[34]

Chartist expressions of anti-abolitionist racism were strongly contested by others within the movement, for whom there were long-standing affinities between the campaigns. Many prominent Chartists were fervent supporters of abolitionism, including William Lovett, John Collins, George Julian Harney, Henry Vincent and Ernest Jones.[35] The relative weight of currents of racism and anti-racism is the subject of some debate.

Historian Ryan Hanley has argued that influential radicals such as William Cobbett consistently promoted ideas of racial superiority.[36] Satnam Virdee, however, has argued that English radicals remained 'relatively free of contamination by the ideology of white supremacy'.[37] The debate within the Chartist movement evolved over time. The creation of the National Charter Association in 1840 democratised the movement and led to a decline in racism, with William Cuffay who was black and the Indo-Scottish Dr John Taylor becoming Chartist leaders in London and Glasgow respectively. The same process also led to a more welcoming attitude to female Chartists.[38] *The Northern Liberator* ceased publication in December 1840.[39] Six years later, the Anti-Slavery League was founded in London by the black American activist Frederick Douglass, Chartist leaders William Lovett and Henry Vincent, and radical Unitarians William and Mary Howitt. Its launch was warmly welcomed in the Chartist press.[40]

Influential abolitionist women began to consider the need for parliamentary reform. When Eliza Wigham and her stepmother, Jane Smeal Wigham, established the Edinburgh Ladies Emancipation Society they found that working women were most supportive. Perhaps it was this contact with efficient and zealous members of the working class which convinced Smeal to become a supporter of universal suffrage.[41]

British Bastilles: The New Poor Law

As we have seen, the New Poor Law provoked mass agitation across the manufacturing districts of northern England led by future Chartist leader Feargus O'Connor, MPs Richard Oastler and John Fielden, and the Reverend Joseph Raynor. *The Times* reported that by 1837 Parliament had received 164 petitions signed by more than 200,000 people demanding repeal. There was some debate about whether including women's signatures on the petitions would discredit them. But in Manchester in February 1838, a large meeting resolved that 'had their petitions been signed by females the signatures would have been increased fourfold ... It was then unanimously decided that it would be better to get up a number of petitions signed exclusively by females.'[42] In the end, women's signatures comprised a very significant proportion of overall signatures on anti–Poor Law petitions.

There were many reasons for the mass opposition to the New Poor Law. The new system replaced the old system of outdoor relief with indoor relief, which was only available to those families prepared to enter a workhouse. The workhouses were popularly known as 'Bastilles' in reference to the Parisian prison which was liberated in the first act of the French Revolution of 1789. They were designed to deter people from claiming relief and so lighten the burden on rate payers. In the workhouses, men, women and children were forcibly separated. Women were not permitted to nurse their sick and dying children. Inmates were subject to a strict regime of gruelling work and a diet so poor there were scandals about cannibalism such as that at the Andover workhouse in August 1845.[43] To the fury of some women, the new law identified poor able-bodied men as the central focus for reform and treated women as dependent wives, even though the majority of recipients of relief were women.[44]

The ideological justification for the New Poor Law lay in the writings of the political economist Reverend Thomas Malthus as laid out in his 1798 essay, 'The Principle of Population'. Malthus argued that the sexual double standard which meant that women experienced 'the superior disgrace which attends a breach of chastity' compared to men may appear to be unjust but was necessary to keep the population down.[45] In industrial societies, the larger the supply of labour became, the lower wages would be. The only solution to this immiseration was for the number of poor people to be decreased by sickness, starvation and death. Malthus's essay spends a surprising amount of time criticising passion, particularly the women who had lots of sex and undermined the recalibration of the population by having too many babies. Malthusianism provided an ideological justification for the withdrawal of all support for the victims of crises in the market, or natural disasters, and it placed women's sexuality and bodies at the centre of political debate. Not surprisingly, women were visible in many anti–Poor Law protests.

In August 1837, *The Times* reported on what it called a 'petticoat victory' in Redruth, Cornwall. Poor Law Guardians ordered inmates from the local workhouse to be relocated to a workhouse some distance away. A 'strong body of about 200 females, commanded by an old weather-beaten female veteran, rushed from behind an embankment and proceeded to contest the removal with the overseers'.[46] The overseers retreated, and the women repaired to a nearby beer shop to celebrate their triumph. In August 1843, some of the most serious anti–Poor Law riots took place in the Carmarthen workhouse. A crowd attacked the workhouse with the aim of liberating those incarcerated within. A large group of women had brought their brooms and declared their intention to sweep away the foundations of the workhouse.[47] One woman who led the crowd, Frances Evans, was seen 'dancing with violent gestures on the table in the hall'.[48] The Carmarthen women took symbols of female domesticity and turned them into instruments of resistance.

Under the old Poor Law, unmarried mothers could claim maintenance from the father of their child simply by naming him, but under the new law women could only claim financial support if they could prove paternity in court. This was a huge attack on the capacity of single mothers to care for their children. Some historians have emphasised how opposition to the Bastardy Clauses encouraged radicals to defend working-class women as virtuous and chaste. Chartist women's addresses, however, suggest that concern with female purity was just one of many more general political worries which were just as, or more, important to them. An address from the Female Radical Association of Leeds published in October 1839 denounced the Poor Law as one element of an oppressive political system:

> We unanimously say – away with the infernal Poor Law (miscalled) Amendment Act. Down with the numerous cotton hells and the murderous transportation system. Such dreadful evils existing, we call on the females of Leeds to come forward and battle for the rights of those who are dear to them – to show their utter detestation of the present brutal Whig government.[49]

This address employed the language of the battlefield and the dungeon rather than the hearth and the home. This is not to suggest that there was no concern with female virtue and respectability in the rhetoric of the anti–Poor Law movement. It is to point out that such ideas were contested by assertions of female agency and female rights.

The New Poor Law was an attempt by Lord Grey's Whig government to refashion cultural attitudes to working-class morality and to work.[50] Enforcing it required a punitive attitude to the bodies of the poor, which were categorised, starved, incarcerated and forced to work. The New Poor Law and the Anatomy Act (1832), which allowed for the bodies of paupers to be dissected by doctors, deprived the poor of the right to mourn and bury the bodies of their loved ones. The authors of the 1834 government report on which the New Poor Law was based identified a 'disease of pauperism' which had infected society.[51] This vision of creeping contagion drew on fears about unmanned husbands unable to support their families and women who had escaped from patriarchal control.[52] Characterisation of pauperism as a disease was opposed by many Chartists. In 1841, John Watkins – a poet, playwright and Chartist from Whitby who wrote regularly for *The Northern Star* – wrote that under the new system of poor relief, 'nor wife, nor mother, she is not deemed a woman; she is called PAUPER; a being degraded far below humanity'.[53] Male Chartists such as Watkins were sensitive to the dehumanising impact that emerging ideas about poverty could have on women. By organising against the New Poor Law, women were asserting their humanity and demonstrating their potential for political agency.

The attitudes to female activism which suffused the anti–Poor Law campaign permeated the early Chartist movement as it began to absorb anti–Poor Law activists in the North.[54] A huge meeting at Hartshead Moor in May 1837 marked the culmination of the popular agitation against the New Poor Law. The gathering was constantly interrupted by calls for universal suffrage and when the meeting ended it was reconvened as a reform meeting.[55] By the summer of 1838, thousands of women had come to believe that only the reform of Parliament could ensure the repeal of the hated act.[56] The campaign against the New Poor Law bridged the gap between older forms of direct protest and newer forms of political organisation.[57] And, unlike the abolitionist campaign, the women involved were exclusively working-class women.

The Chartist movement continued to highlight the malpractices which occurred in the workhouses and their impact on female inmates. In 1841, *The Northern Star* reported on a scandal relating to the treatment of women giving birth at the Sevenoaks workhouse. The women gave birth crammed two or three to a bed, they were moved out of their beds hours after giving birth to make room for more women in labour, and they were denied clean sheets or linen for days afterwards.[58] Reports of this nature foregrounded the usually hidden and sanitised process of giving birth and women's bodily needs. The reports do not refer directly to the blood and sweat of labour, but discussions of the linen and shifts mean that female bodiliness and the physical suffering of childbirth hover around the written words.

Three years later, the *Star* reported on the sexual abuse of women inmates by the master of the Andover workhouse, a Mr M'Dongal.[59] A series of women testified to an official inquiry how M'Dongal had sexually harassed them, put his hands inside their clothes and tried to rape them. Cross-examiners tried to use the women's sexual history to discredit their testimony against M'Dongal. One of the witnesses, Elizabeth Harris, told the inquiry that she had been in and out of the workhouse for seven years and had turned to sex work several times. When the cross-examiner interrogated her about her sexual history, she replied, 'I did not come here to swear I was a virgin. I tell you the plain truth. If I am what I am, that is no reason that Mr M'Dongal should take liberties with me against my will.'[60] These stories publicised the realities of sexual abuse in a government-sanctioned institution and attempts to shame women out of testifying against their abusers. In the pages of *The Northern Star*, exposés of sexual abuse sat next to reports of female organising and campaigning against the New Poor Law.

Towards a political economy of poverty: Elizabeth Hanson and Mary Grassby

Elizabeth Hanson and Mary Grassby were two working women from Elland, near Halifax. In the early months of 1838, these women became unlikely national celebrities. The town of Elland was a centre of woollen textile manufacturing which was insecure work, and the town strongly opposed the New Poor Law. The women of the town took part in rolling a Poor Law commissioner in the snow when he visited in February 1838. It is possible that Elizabeth and Mary took part in this direct action.[61] Such community mobilisations against the Poor Law quickly assumed a more organised form and retained their female leadership.

A 'female public meeting' was held in Elland on Monday 12 February 1838 at the Radical Association Rooms in Dog Lane.[62] Susanna Fearnley was voted to the chair and opened official business by exhorting the women present to take the repeal of the bill into their own hands, and not to rely on others, least of all the House of Commons, 'but at once to assert the dignity and equality of their sex'.[63] This meeting of working women quickly established the idea that women had the power to influence national politics through their own activity, that they had political agency.

A resolution was then proposed by Mary Grassby. Those attending the meeting, Mary argued, might be asked why women should interfere in public matters. She provided an answer: that it was a woman's duty to oppose the bill because they would feel any separation from their children more deeply than men.[64] Mary Grassby's deployment of feelings in this context both played to a conventional view of women as affectionate mothers and subverted it by framing women's maternal feelings as a justification for them to act with firmness and resist the law, whose authors, she suggested, should be exiled in Saint Helena just as Napoleon had been.

Thc resolution was seconded by Elizabeth Hanson. Hanson described how several families in the area had to survive on a penny a day but even this terrible hardship was to be preferred to incarceration in workhouses where the diets were so poor they hastened those imprisoned within to the 'dissector's knife', a reference to the hated Anatomy Act. Female inmates, Elizabeth explained, were subject to gender-based humiliations. Their heads were forcibly shaved and they were given rough 'grogram' gowns to wear.[65] Hanson's speech met with tears and cheers from the audience.[66] She must have been a very effective speaker.

Reports of the meeting began to circulate in the national media, starting with *The Northern Star* and spreading to the *London Evening Standard*, the *Wilts and Gloucestershire Standard*, the *Dover Telegraph* and the *Kendal Mercury*. By 30 April, a report of the meeting in Elland was reprinted in the *Bombay Gazette* in India.[67] This intense press interest lay not so much in the campaign against the Poor Law, which was already familiar to reporters. Rather, the media frenzy was roused by the novelty of working-class women speaking confidently and coherently in a public forum.

A London-based paper, *The Globe,* published its first report of the women's meeting on 20 February 1838. It singled out for derision three aspects of the women's identities: their gender, their class and their geographical location. *The Globe* described the meeting as a rising of 'the old-woman-hood' of Elland, 'wherever that is' and described Susan Fearnley as the 'chair or char-woman flourishing her soap'.[68] The paper quoted Mary Grassby's speech in full, interspersing it with comments on her 'talent for scolding' and speculating about whether she had driven Mr Grassby to drink. *The Globe* demanded to know: Why should others pay rates to keep the Grassbys at home together?[69]

Mary and Elizabeth wrote a spirited defence of their political stance, which was published in the *Halifax Express* and reprinted in *The Globe* on 6 March and *The Northern Star* a few weeks later.[70] *The Globe* argued that it was the expansion of trade and commerce that would address economic hardship not handouts to the poor. Hanson pointed out that commerce had been expanding for the previous forty years, but the massive increase in the production of calico and fustian, 'only enriches a few individuals, and makes slaves of millions'.[71] Elizabeth placed the enrichment of the minority in the context of global competition and of technological developments which increased productivity while degrading human labour:

> We have ransacked the whole habitable globe. If you can find out a way to the moon, we may, perhaps, carry on our competition a little longer; but if you want to better the condition of the productive classes, let our government legislate so as to make machinery go hand in hand with hard labour, and act as an auxiliary, or helpmate, and not a competitor.[72]

Hanson was reflecting the experience of the handloom weavers of West Yorkshire and Lancashire, who had suffered so grievously from the introduction of steam-driven looms in factories.

Hanson and Grassby did not confine their activism to opposition to the New Poor Law. In April 1838, they were among six women from Elland who signed a message of congratulations to the Tolpuddle Martyrs on their return to England.[73] Their broad-based radicalism evolved into support for Chartism. Elizabeth's husband, Abram, was a leading Chartist in West Yorkshire who praised women as the 'best politicians, the best revolutionists, and the best political economists'.[74] Elizabeth's involvement in politics dropped away, perhaps because of the growing demands of her children. Her fourth child, Feargus O'Connor Hanson, was born in 1840. She continued to contribute to Chartist causes until 1852, when she disappeared from historical records.[75]

In 1839, Mary Grassby moved to Hull where she became active in the local Chartist movement. In January 1840, she signed a 'Solemn Appeal to the People' issued by the Association of Female Chartists of Hull.[76] In the census of 1851, Mary was living in Hull with her husband, Richard, their daughter, Rebecca, and their sons Richard and Feargus Roger O'Connor Grassby. Mary Grassby died in Hull on 2 May 1870, aged seventy-one.[77]

Owenism: A feminist alternative to Chartism?

The followers of Charles Fourier, Henri de Saint-Simon and Robert Owen all demanded that private property and the extraction of surplus value from workers should be replaced by collective ownership, which would eradicate cyclical crises. They insisted that human nature was not irrevocably shaped by original sin, but could replace competition, antagonism and hostility with solidarity, friendship and love. They believed that women should be liberated from the family, which was the root of gender inequality. Many Owenites advocated the abolition of marriage, collective provision for social reproduction and birth control with the aim of establishing sexual freedom and gender equality.

Robert Owen was one of very few radical male leaders who explicitly condemned the inferior status of women and their inequality within the family in his *Lectures on the Marriages of the Priesthood* (1835).[78] Owen outlined a new system of living with the despotism of the priestcraft in which an equalisation of knowledge, rights and wealth between the sexes would produce equality, and communal provision would erode the economic foundation of male domination. Owenite socialist women such as Emma Martin and Margaret Chappellsmith created the space to theorise the relationship between women's oppression and the competition and exploitation inherent in the capitalist system.

Some utopian socialists stood apart from what they saw as futile campaigns for reform and concentrated on energetic propaganda campaigns which aimed at nothing less than the total transformation of society. Between 1820 and 1840 some fifty newspapers were disseminating socialist ideas in Britain.[79] Other Owenites engaged enthusiastically with popular movements and mobilisations for trade union rights, for universal suffrage, and for sexual freedom. Eve Taylor noted the British Owenites were so successful that prior to 1850 the term 'socialist' referred exclusively to them.[80]

Many leading Owenite socialists publicly condemned female inequality. It is, therefore, not surprising that many historians often see Owenism as more sympathetic to women's rights than Chartism, whose leaders were divided between those such as

O'Connor, who venerated domesticity, and those such as Lovett, who supported women's political rights. This approach has, however, imposed an artificial division between the two movements and obscured the extent to which they shared a political outlook. A debate about the female franchise was conducted in both the Owenite and the Chartist press. Both organisations believed that women had a special role as the moral regenerators of society and both believed the support of women was crucial to the success of the movement. Demands for women's rights were heard and opposed within both the Owenite and Chartist movements.

Owenites were divided in their attitude to attempts to reform women's social position and some opposed the female franchise, believing that any measure short of the abolition of private property would prove futile.[81] Some Chartists demanded women's rights. In 1842, Chartist lecturer Susanna Inge delivered a message to an audience of women as trenchant as any Owenite demands for women's rights: 'Rouse yourselves to a sense of your merits. Assist those men who will, nay who do, place women on [sic] the equality with themselves in gaining their rights.'[82] Both Chartists and Owenites welcomed women's participation, but in neither movement did women reach the higher echelons of the official movement.[83]

Eileen Yeo described how the Owenites appealed to women:

> In a society where the middle-class wife was little more than a domestic ornament, a decorative piece of personal property, the working-class socialists opened their classes to women, encouraged women to become lecturers in the cause and admitted women on an equal footing to men in traditionally masculine social rituals like the ceremonial dinner.[84]

The same point could be made about Chartism, which also offered women the opportunity to participate in a wide range of educational events, organise their own societies, play a significant role in social gatherings and commemorations, and become lecturers. Owenism included a current of feminist ideas, which advocated collective alternatives to the private family and the female franchise. The Owenite communities, however, often disappointed their female residents, who found themselves responsible for the domestic labour in addition to working on the land.[85] Chartist supporters of women's rights justified women's activism and raised the demand for the female franchise. Both movements were imperfect, but both foregrounded women's activism and degrees of equality.

Female Owenites and Chartists were part of a milieu of female reformers who were debating, theorising, and demonstrating in practice that women could be effective public speakers, writers and organisers. Owenite Emma Martin was a close friend of the Chartist Henry Hetherington. Catherine Barmby was an Owenite and a Chartist, and many Chartist women celebrated prominent Owenite women such as Frances Wright. Currents advocating women's rights and others confirming female domesticity coexisted uneasily and contested each other within both Chartism and Owenism. To depict Owenism as feminist and Chartism as patriarchal is to oversimplify the gender politics of both movements and to marginalise the solidarity women from both movements shared.

Abolitionist legacies

The radicals of the mid-nineteenth century raised questions which will be familiar to those who campaign for the abolition of the penal system and the privatised family today.[86] The state threatened the families of radicals directly through the incarceration of hundreds of Chartist activists. A significant body of correspondence between Chartist couples arose from the separation imposed by prison and the letters testify to the hardships endured by the wives of imprisoned Chartist leaders.[87] The wives of several leading Chartists took over their husbands' business and political affairs while their husbands were in prison. Not surprisingly, demands for penal reform were a consistent theme of Chartist theory and practice.

Chartism is often defined by the three national petitions of 1839, 1842 and 1848. But there was a fourth national petition which demanded a pardon for three Welsh Chartists transported to Van Diemen's Land as a punishment for their role in the Newport Uprising of 1839. *The Northern Star* began a sustained campaign for John Frost, Zephaniah Williams and William Jones to be pardoned and allowed to come home. The paper even suggested that Mary Frost, John's wife, should be granted an audience with Queen Victoria to plead John's case in person.[88] During the spring of 1841, the Chartist movement accumulated 1,339,298 signatures on the petition seeking a pardon. When the petition was presented to Parliament on 25 May, eighteen stonemasons volunteered to carry the huge roll of signatures and a mass demonstration accompanied it from Fleet Street to Parliament. The petition was only rejected on the casting vote of the Speaker. It represented an attempt to intervene in the judicial process, to assert the popular will over the penal system, and to disrupt the power of judges and courts to incarcerate without scrutiny.

Owenites and Chartists began to question the inequalities embedded in the privatised family, and laws which deprived women of the right to their earnings and their children. Opposing the Poor Law necessitated developing critiques of political economy and thinking about ways in which care could be provided, through outdoor relief, higher wages, the redistribution of wealth and the allocation of more resources to social reproduction. The Chartists frequently supported the replacement of the punitive regimes of incarceration in prisons and workhouses with an increased allocation of resources to caregiving.

Many Owenites wanted to create collective alternatives to the family, and the Chartist Land Plan promised an escape from crowded cities to purpose-built rural communities with plots of land for each family. Thompson and Wheeler denounced the family as the seat of 'male despotism'. As a recent manifesto of abolition geography explains, 'Abolition is by necessity speculative, and we ardently embrace its utopian dimension.' Abolitionist movements reject the idea that their demands are 'impractical, unattainable, a dream' because vision and practice are not contradictory but are inseparable.[89] That was as true for the abolitionists of the early nineteenth century as it is for those demanding a better world 200 years later.

'White Slavery' and the Radical Poetics of Mary Hutton

Mary Hutton (1794–1859) was a working-class poet who depended on benefactors and public subscriptions to survive, especially after her husband became incapacitated following an accident.[1] The little that is known about her life comes from scattered reviews and descriptions written by two middle-class male contemporaries.[2] Hutton was one of the most prolific of a very small number of working-class women who published poetry in the mid-nineteenth century.[3] She was also exceptional because of the overtly political nature of her writing. Her first volume of poetry, *Sheffield Manor and Other Poems*, was published in 1830. Her next collection, *The Happy Isle* (1836), contained a poetic critique of the anti–Poor Law Amendment Act of 1834. Her third collection, *Cottage Tales and Poems*, published in 1842, included verses commemorating the Polish uprising of 1830–1. This was a revolt against the Russian occupation of Poland led by young army officers, which was also known as the Cadet Revolution or the November Uprising. Hutton repeatedly used the image of slavery to describe the condition of the defeated Polish nationalists. 'Polish Song' opens with the line, 'No Pole can live a Slave', while 'On the Occupation of Cracow' describes the 'bitter slavery' now chaining the brave Polish patriots.[4]

Literary historians have noted how closely Hutton's poetic works aligned with Chartist critiques of the New Poor Law, child labour and class inequality.[5] Hutton's opposition to the New Poor Laws and chattel slavery were among the most consistent political themes of her writing. There are also echoes of Owenite utopianism in 'The Happy Isle', in which Hutton describes a future utopia:

> No baneful workhouses were there;
> The rich were not alone protected;
> Nor yet the poor sold and dissected;
> No prisons for pale infancy.

Hutton did not merely align with Chartist concerns. She committed herself publicly to the Chartist cause, writing that 'Universal Suffrage was the beacon star'.[6] Hutton also expressed support for the Polish national struggle, which was a very popular cause among Chartists. In the poem 'The Occupation of Cracow', Hutton positioned herself as an instigator of solidarity:

> Let Friends of Freedom now arise,
> Avenge the crying injuries,
> The burning wrongs and agonies,
> That on the Poles await.[7]

Hutton's 1831 poem, 'The Slave', dramatised the plight of a black brother and sister who are sold by their master, and strongly implies that the sister was subjected to sexual violence before she dies under the lash. There is no evidence that Hutton was involved in the very active Sheffield female anti-slavery society but her poetry firmly places her in the abolitionist milieu. She combined denunciations of chattel slavery with criticisms of 'white slavery'. In *The Poor Man's Wrongs* (1839) Hutton identified the limited franchise conceded by the Reform Act of 1832 as the cause of the enslavement of the British working class, a view shared by many Chartists.[8] Hutton also posed the solution to what she called 'political slavery' as universal suffrage, which 'alone can redeem the poor man from his thraldom'.[9] Hutton advocated universal suffrage in works such as *The Poor Man's Wrongs*, which was published in John Cleave's *Gazette of Variety*.[10]

As we have seen, some Chartists chided middle-class abolitionists for their indifference to the exploitation of wage workers in England. In her poem 'On a Poor Little Sweep', Hutton rebuked the

> Britons, all so brave and free,
> Who deeply feel for misery;
> Ye who abhor black slavery,
> With its sad galling chains:-
> Ye who deeply sympathise,
> With human wrongs and agonies:-
> Ye who have both hearts and eyes,
> Behold yon child of pains:-
> Yon shivering, wretched, helpless child,
> On whom contentment never smil'd;
> Compelled to brave the winter wild,
> And wander through the snow.[11]

Ian Haywood, a historian of Chartist literature, observed that Hutton was the only named female author of Chartist poetry. But he argues that she wrote exclusively from the male perspective and expressed little awareness of, or solidarity with, the condition of women. It could also be argued that adopting the persona of male radicals to discuss the direction of the Chartist movement suggested a degree of confidence and of resistance to being restricted to women's issues. Hutton did not want to write 'women's poetry' which focused exclusively on nature or sentimental domestic cliches.

In her preface to *Cottage Tales and Poems*, Hutton devoted a poem to the radical Unitarian and reformer Mary Howitt, and printed an encouraging letter she received from Howitt, a respected author and publisher who had come across Hutton's poems in a copy of the *Sheffield Iris*.[12] This suggests that Hutton identified with radical female authors through a shared concern with both poetry and poverty. Mary Hutton joined the Chartist Women's Rights Association (WRA), established in Sheffield in the winter of 1850–1 by Abiah Higginbottom, which will be discussed below.[13] We do not know why the WRA appealed to

Hutton, when her interest in women's political rights began, or how committed she was to women's right to vote, but she was a member of the organisation which submitted the first collective petition for the female franchise to Parliament in 1851.[14]

Hutton looked beyond domestic spaces towards national and international political issues, and she positioned herself as a prophetic poet and an advocate for the people. Her writing incorporated the political concerns shared by many radical working-class women in the Chartist era. She moved beyond supporting individual campaigns for the abolition of slavery and the New Poor Law to engaging with Chartism as a strategy for resolving a broad range of inequalities and injustices. Mary Hutton's work is important for exploring the ways in which Chartism engaged talented women by presenting them with a strategy for addressing multiple concerns including black slavery, reform of the New Poor Laws, and social inequality through political reform.

3

Insurrection, 1839: 'The Time of War'

Women were central to the Chartist movement when it emerged as a coherent movement in a series of monster rallies in the spring of 1838. The visibility of women at this early stage helps to contest the idea that Chartism was 'a cause undertaken primarily by men on behalf of both themselves and dependent women'.[1] The rhetoric, the culture, and the practices of Chartism were constructed by women as well as by men. One of the earliest events in this wave of reform agitation took place in Birmingham in April 1838 when 12,000 women attended an outdoor rally organised by the veteran campaigner, Thomas Salt. This event preceded the rally of about 150,000 held in a very wet Glasgow in May, which is often identified as the opening act of the Chartist campaign.[2] The women's rally was enthusiastically reported by the most important Chartist publication, *The Northern Star*, under the headline 'Twelve thousand women'. The article began, 'Whigs, Tories, plunderers, usurpers, tyrants and under whatever name you live in breeches, look above and tremble. Petticoat government is a thing you profess to despise, but to which at length you must yield.'[3] The power of the petticoat was established as a valued component of the emerging Chartist movement.

Some Chartist men no doubt believed that women had no business meddling with politics and others thought that the Charter must be won before more controversial questions, such as women's rights, could be addressed. Certainly, the example set by Birmingham was not followed everywhere. Organisers of a 300,000-strong meeting in Sheffield in September justified the lack of women at their procession with the claim that the men could be counted twice because they represented the political interests of the absent women.[4] The women themselves were not required to express their views, still less to act upon them. Other Chartists were less complacent, especially as women began to prove their value as campaigners. Women did turn out in large numbers for the Kersal Moor rally, held on the same day as the Sheffield event.[5] Women demonstrated their capacity to collect signatures on the petitions which were so central to Chartism's identity and political practice. Writing in September, the month that the Kersal Moor and Sheffield rallies took place, Chartist leader Bronterre O'Brien told the readers of *The Northern Star*:

> Depend upon it, my friends, women are sturdier petitioners than the men – wherefore, encourage their Unions by all means and get such of them as have no time for Unions to join you at any rate in signing the National Petition.[6]

O'Brien supported the idea of women creating their own organisations, but, if that was not possible, he wanted men to win women's support for the first great Chartist petition. Some women responded to O'Brien's urging.

In September 1838, a 'very large meeting of females' met in Carlisle to adopt a memorial [petition] to Queen Victoria requesting the repeal of the Poor Law.[7] Just two months later, Carlisle saw the launch of one of the best organised of the early female Chartist organisations.[8] By December 1838, the female Chartists of Carlisle published an address that stated their aim was to follow the example of their sisters in Birmingham, Newcastle, and Glasgow by setting up their own association.[9] Just a few weeks later, 200 members of the Carlisle women's association marched behind their new banner at a 'Grand Demonstration' in Cumberland in support of the People's Charter.[10] The women's organisations adopted different names. The women of Ashton and Newcastle formed female political unions.[11] In Darlington, fifty women enrolled in a Female Charter Association.[12] The names varied, but these groups shared a commitment to wage a determined fight for the Charter.

Women were not automatically welcomed into the Chartist movement as independent activists. At times, they had to be quite creative and bold to assert themselves. In an article titled 'Hurrah for the women', *The Northern Star* described how a Mr Reaves of Sunderland visited Durham to set up a Chartist organisation. Mr Reaves arrived at the room at the appointed time but instead of finding a room full of men, he discovered that 'every part of the large room, window seats and all, was occupied by the canny women of this place'.[13] Reaves had no choice but to address the women, who had locked the door and 'declared he would not leave until he had formed a female association'.[14] *The Northern Star* thoroughly approved of the women's actions.

Within the broad Chartist movement there were tensions between ideas of female domesticity and the demands of care and a recognition of the need for female support and a principled commitment to a greater degree of gender equality. Some women positioned themselves as the instigators of political action, and at times they subverted their domestic role in provocative and mischievous ways. On 22 January 1839, Mrs Williamson, the chairwoman of the Ashton Female Political Union, issued an address to the women of Great Britain and Ireland. In the address, she declared,

> We are determined that no man shall ever enjoy our hands, our hearts, or share our beds, that will not stand forward as the advocate of the rights of man and as the determined enemy of the damnable New Poor Law.[15]

This strategy was particularly audacious as husbands were legally entitled to enforce their conjugial rights and marital rape was not a crime.

Other women were attracted to this intimate form of direct action. In April 1839, the Chartist women of Wandsworth declared in an address,

> Let the females of Surrey follow the noble, the praiseworthy, the truly glorious example of the women of the North. Let them at once declare that no man shall be their sweetheart, that they will take no man for a husband who has not determined to join the campaign for Equal Rights and Equal Laws.[16]

These female Chartists may have been the first women to collectivise their sexuality for a political purpose. Their addresses suggest that the female Chartists developed strategies which were entirely independent of the National Charter Association and stimulated through dialogue with other women.

The Chartist women also engaged with and developed strategies advocated by the National Charter Convention. When the Convention advocated exclusive dealing in May 1839, women responded by organising meetings and urging other women to use their influence among their neighbourhoods and families to build the boycott.[17] The Chartist tactic of exclusive dealing grew out of the abolitionist boycotts, but it involved shunning the unsympathetic shopkeeper rather than the tainted goods. Anti–Poor Law activists used the tactic of exclusive dealing to encourage shopkeepers with a vote to support candidates who opposed the law. During Richard Oastler's election campaign in Huddersfield in 1837, groups of women went from shop-to-shop demanding support for their chosen candidate.[18] Women's influence in the exclusive dealing campaign was widely acknowledged by male Chartists. In a pamphlet advocating exclusive dealing, Chartist Robert Lowery declared: 'Women of Britain! Remember that no woman is worthy of the name of a working-man's wife, who will lay out his hard-earned wages in the shops of those who insult him and deny him his political rights.'[19]

Some historians have suggested that exclusive dealing confirmed women in a secondary role within Chartism because it confined them to the discharge of their domestic duties.[20] Chartists, however, did not see exclusive dealing as a 'peaceful, moral alternative to physical force'.[21] Exclusive dealing was seen as a powerful weapon, capable of winning far-reaching political reform. 'If you abstain from the shops of the Whigs and Tories and support those shopkeepers which are favourable to the

Charter ... the inevitable consequences of your so doing will be the Charter for Great Britain, freedom for Ireland, the repeal of the Corn Law and the obnoxious Poor Law Amendment Act', declared a Chartist prisoner quoted in *The Northern Star*.[22] Working-class women extended the boycott tactic into an interventionist and assertive means of exerting political influence over wealthy electors and shopkeepers. Exclusive dealing was also an 'attempt to exert some form of democratic control over the market and an underlying critique of the deleterious effects of competition on the consumer'.[23] Chartist women were beginning to politicise their personal relationships and weaponised their home-making activities. Their interest in reforming every aspect of their lives would deepen as Chartism progressed.

The Chartists expanded the range of cultural practices, which gave their movement coherence to include flags and banners, hats and caps, ribbons and medals, songs and toasts.[24] The red cap was the most recognisable symbol of Jacobinism and became one of the most prominent symbols of reformers between 1815 and 1820.[25] The frequent hoisting of the red cap at political gatherings was interpreted as a harbinger of revolution and the authorities made considerable efforts to repress its use.[26] The caps adopted by the Chartist movement were often made and presented by women. Historians have interpreted this female contribution as women being used as a symbol of purity and virtue in opposition to aristocratic corruption.[27] An examination of contemporary press reports suggests that the symbolism was more complex. One police spy reported that women in Middleton were going from door-to-door demanding money to make caps of liberty and threatening to murder those who refused to pay up.[28]

The ornate caps of liberty that women made and presented at public gatherings celebrated traditional female skills, but they could appear in contexts which subverted concepts of submissive femininity.[29] Chartist women developed relationships with each other through their addresses, they developed exclusive dealing into a powerful tool for exerting pressure on those who refused to back the Charter, and they contributed to the visual and material culture of the movement. These were all vital to building support for the Charter, but Chartism was at heart a movement organised around petitioning and here, too, women played an important role.

Mass Petitioning and the Creation of Political Communities

The first national Chartist petition was launched by Thomas Attwood in 1838, and he presented it to Parliament in June 1839. The petition had 1,280,000 signatures and was three miles long. Historians have explored the signatures on the Chartists' petitions and how they were presented to Parliament. Not enough attention has been directed to the text of the petitions, which articulated the themes around which the Chartists coalesced. The 1839 petition included this paragraph: 'Our slavery has been exchanged for an apprenticeship to liberty, which has aggravated the painful feeling of our social degradation, by adding to it the sickening of deferred hope.'[30] The petition deployed the idea of political slavery and foregrounded not just physical hardship but also emotional pain. The idea of 'social degradation' was a unifying one, not based on any sectional or gender-based interests. Every member of the labouring community – whatever their occupation, age or gender – could feel the pain of social degradation and of 'hope deferred'. 'Hope deferred' was a powerful biblical reference which spoke to the frustrations of the oppressed whose hopes were aroused, then thwarted. The black American poet Langston Hughes used the phrase to encapsulate the frustrations of African Americans in the civil rights era.[31]

When presenting the first national petition, Thomas Attwood downplayed the number of female signatures on the petition, perhaps fearing that women's names could be used to discredit the petition's legitimacy. He told the Commons that there were 1,300,000 names on the document and that 'there might be some women, but he believed, that some one million men had signed their names'.[32] In fact, between 13 and 20 of those who signed the Chartist petition of 1839 were women.[33] Some female radical associations organised the collection of women's signatures as a separate initiative. The most successful of these local female petitioners in Ashton-under-Lyne, Carlisle and Wednesbury in the Black Country constituted about 20 percent of all signatures collected in the area. Birmingham and Monmouth managed 15 and 13 percent respectively. These figures can be only approximate, but they are broadly consistent with the ratio of specifically female to the otherwise 'male' Chartist associations.[34] Some commentators recognised that this huge support gave the petition moral authority, expressing as it did, 'the desires of certainly the largest mass of men, women and children who have ever appended their names to a single petition before'.[35]

Recent research has found that between 1780 and 1918 more than a million petitions were sent from across Britain to the Houses of Parliament.[36] Petitioning was a central feature of mass campaigning, of collective action and of forging collective identities, both local and national. Petitioning created the possibility of mass participation in politics in the era before democracy. In the early nineteenth century, the London Corresponding Society organised petitions for reform and publicised the names and addresses of those who opened their homes to receive signatures. Such activities were banned under the Unlawful Combinations of Workmen Act of 1799, but petitioning returned as a mass activity in autumn 1816 when near-famine conditions drove thousands to seek political redress. By March 1817, somewhere between 750,000 and a million people had signed petitions. Mass petitioning was a tactic deployed by the abolitionists who laid out their petitions in public spaces or advertised a private house where the petition could be signed. Canvassing was carried out by paid agents. The abolitionist strategy was to flood Parliament with multiple petitions. Very few petitions among the deluge which addressed specifically working-class issues welcomed female support. When the Midlands Framework Knitters petitioned Parliament in 1812, they excluded women from adding their signatures. One exception to this exclusion of women was the anti–Poor Law movement, which encouraged female activism and flowed into the Chartist movement.

The Chartists developed a distinct approach to petitioning. They channelled millions of signatures into three successive national petitions. They actively canvassed for support, an assertive tactic which required face-to-face contact and so created a 'particular claim for legitimacy'.[37] They developed canvassing into a 'major intervention in the political life' of local areas.[38] The Chartists built on the experience of the anti–Poor Law movement and explicitly included women and children in the process of both signing and organising petitions.[39] In 1849, *The Northern Star* carried an obituary for Mary Paris, 'a noble woman who exerted herself for the enactment of the Charter', who had personally collected hundreds of signatures for the 1842 petition and joined the 50,000-strong demonstration which accompanied the petition to Parliament.[40] The Chartists adopted the tactic of petitioning and developed it into a hugely successful mechanism for mass mobilisation, a strategy which depended on their unique approach to family and community involvement.

The Chartists' extraordinarily successful petitioning shaped, articulated and mobilised the politics of the nascent working class. In 1841, a national petition asking for a pardon for the leaders of the Newport Uprising (on which more below) attracted 1.3 million signatures, on a par with the first Chartist petition of 1839. The second big Chartist petition in 1842 carried 3.3 million signatures, which were stitched together into a roll of paper six miles long. Women's signatures made up to 20 percent of the total. Petitioning was at the heart of Chartist ideas about collective action and citizenship, and the tactics created a political community which included women and children.[41]

Chartist leaders envisaged petitioning as a legal and constitutional strategy which would win mass support. They also expected their petitions to be rejected in a process which would educate the masses in the need for 'ulterior measures', such as boycotting the shops owned by those hostile to reform, organising a general strike known as the 'Sacred Month' and military preparations for a possible insurrection. The Chartist Convention was formed to oversee the petition and decide on the tactics of the growing Chartist movement. The first meeting of the Convention took place on 4 February 1839 at a coffee house in central London. The Convention developed into a working-class parliament, which existed in parallel with the Houses of

Parliament, and attracted the attention and allegiance of reformers across Britain.

In Bradford, daily reports of the Convention's deliberations written by local delegate Peter Bussey were read on the doorstep of their beer house by his wife.[42] While the Convention was sitting, nocturnal walkers around Bradford would sometimes disturb groups armed with pikes. Cutlasses and pikes were openly traded in the street markets of industrial Lancashire. At this stage, however, the central strategic thrust of the Convention was ulterior measures and not insurrection. Public demonstrations and assertions of the right to bear arms were designed to increase pressure on Parliament as the presentation of the national petition drew closer.[43] When the petition was rejected, many enraged reformers began to think more seriously about insurrection.

Pussy-foot Chartists and muscular Chartists

The relative merits of moral and physical force were a focal point of debate inside and outside the Chartist movement during these early years. These debates were often couched in gendered terms, with feminine morality, polite persuasion and education placed in opposition to manly fortitude, direct action and militant confrontation. In addition to this gendered language, Moral Force Chartists were explicitly attacked by their opponents for supporting the franchise for women. Feargus O'Connor complained that a leading Unitarian, Dr Bowring, and 'his party sought to outbid us for popularity by declaring for what they called Woman Franchise'.[44] O'Connor opposed votes for women, but he was clearly concerned that support for women's right to vote could boost his opponents' popularity. He denigrated William Fox and the Moral Force Chartists as the 'Pussy foot Chartists'. The Moral Force Chartists were strongly identified with support for women's rights, but it would be a mistake to think that all Physical Force Chartists followed O'Connor's lead and denigrated the idea of women's rights.

The London Democratic Association (LDA), founded in 1837 and with a membership of about 3,000, was the most important of many radical associations formed in London.[45] The LDA was based on what Malcolm Chase has called 'muscular republicanism' and advanced a programme of militant demands including the redistribution of property. LDA leader George Julian Harney, who saw himself as the 'English Marat',[46] believed that female activism was vital to the success of the movement. He told one meeting that men would only emancipate their 'fatherland with the assistance of the females'.[47] Of course, such support could be that offered by subordinate auxiliaries but the federation both allowed women to join on an equal basis with men and supported the establishment of an associated independent women's organisation, the London Female Democratic Association (LFDA).

The LFDA was launched on 8 April 1839 at a meeting held in the Democratic Rooms, Temple Bar. The names of several women involved were recorded. Mary Ireland proposed a motion, which was seconded by Mary Palmer. They resolved to cooperate with their brothers and sisters across the country to establish the People's Charter, to bring an end to the New Poor Law, to cooperate with the women of the North to 'crush the child murdering factory system' and to support any friends of the oppressed who were persecuted by the tyrannical government. It is significant that the women were discussing collaborating with women from the textile districts of Lancashire and Yorkshire to strike at the power of the factory owners. The women's association agreed two rules: members must pay one penny a week and the organisation would be managed by seven officers, plus a president, a treasurer and a secretary. All these roles were filled by women and Elizabeth Neesom was appointed secretary. Mary Warren proposed a second resolution, which was seconded by Sarah Dymmock and resolved that the LFDA should be prepared to 'assist their brethren in any struggle that may arise, in the event of the People's Charter being rejected by the den of thieves in the House of Commons'.[48] Julian Harney and Charles Neesom, Elizabeth's husband, were both present to witness the women committing themselves to 'ulterior measures' in expectation of the petition's rejection.

Just a few days after its launch, the LFDA was mentioned in a trial of thirteen Chartists who were charged with possessing seditious and treasonable inscriptions. The men had been gathering pikes, described as 'formidable weapons', which were produced as evidence in court. Three banners were also offered as evidence against the men. The most 'imposing' carried the word Charter in huge letters and around its border was placed 'Equality of Rights' and 'No Surrender'. In the middle was a picture of a working man armed with a pistol, a sword, and a pike.[49] Among the papers presented in evidence were two placards [leaflets], one announcing a meeting of the London Democratic Association and one advertising a meeting of the LFDA, signed by Elizabeth Neesom. This leaflet announced that LFDA meetings were held weekly and that 'no gentlemen would be admitted after 8 April 1838 except by invitation of the majority of members'.[50] Also included in the evidence was a membership card for the LDA, which had been given to defendant Thomas Ireland by Julian Harney. Thomas Ireland could have been related to Mary Ireland, who had proposed a motion at the inaugural meeting. The presence of Elizabeth Neesom's invitation in the evidence suggests that the men's and women's organisations shared a commitment to winning the Charter by force if necessary.

Within a few months, in January 1840, Charles Neesom was himself on trial for giving a seditious speech after a meeting of about 600 Chartists in Bethnal Green was raided by police.[51] According to the testimony of police spies, Neesom told the crowd that their freedom could not be bought with silver and that the price of the freedom would be blood. He left the meeting 'with a female at his side', probably Elizabeth.[52] Several police officers testified to the presence of women in the crowded meeting and the number could have been as high as 100.[53] Sergeant George King told the court that a woman with a baby, who was very busy running the meeting, immediately identified him as a police spy. She was organising a collection for the room and told a man helping, 'I daresay that policeman will give you a penny' which the policeman promptly did, fearing for his safety.[54]

The LFDA was far from being the only female Chartist society which identified strongly with Physical Force Chartism.

Helen Rogers has documented how the Birmingham Women's Political Union (BWPU) became increasingly frustrated with the cautious approach of Birmingham's male leaders. In November 1838, Mrs Lapworth challenged the Chartist leader and editor of the *Birmingham Journal*, R. K. Douglas, when he argued that it might take years to achieve reform. Lapworth retorted that:

> The women could ill afford to be patient; they had had years enough of misery: they (the women) would have settled affairs in a few months ... They were suffering too much and would again suffer too much in the next winter to wait for years.

The radicals had been sowing the 'seed' of reform for years, Lapworth noted, and the 'harvest' would surely come soon. Mrs Lapworth told the meeting that she did not know, 'if all the gentlemen were as patient as Mr Douglas, but she did know that the women were determined to have their grievances addressed, and speedily too'.[55] Mrs Lapworth was not alone. A Mrs Oxford added she hoped it would take less than a year to win the Charter.

The moderate Chartist John Collins addressed the same meeting. Collins was known as a friend of the BWPU, but on this occasion he had difficulty convincing the meeting that they should not expect too much, too soon. He rather patronisingly advised the women to 'furnish themselves with some of the most necessary articles of daily consumption, for as the winter advanced their price would increase'. One woman shouted, 'That is impossible. We can barely subsist at present.'[56] This exchange suggests that many working women looked to the Charter to deliver immediate relief for the hunger that haunted them. This prompted women to advocate a confrontational and urgent strategy for winning the Charter, which led them into a confrontation with the leading male reformers in their city.

At the same BWPU meeting, a Miss Groves was elected unanimously to the Birmingham Political Council. The Birmingham Political Council was a Chartist organisation set up in November 1838. It was composed of sixty-five elected delegates and planned to work alongside the men's Birmingham Political

Union. Councillors, it stipulated, had to be men of good estimation able to represent the feelings of the town. Perhaps women could also meet this criterion, but I can find no further evidence of Miss Groves' role in the council, which appears to have collapsed amid irreconcilable tensions in April 1839. Her election as a delegate suggests that women were winning respect, which enabled them to prise open the doors previously closed against them in the formal structures of the movement.

In January 1839, Mrs Lapworth observed to a meeting of the BWPU, 'It appeared to her that as they drew near the time of war, their spirit increased.'[57] This martial spirit generated further conflict with the male leaders of Birmingham Chartism. In March 1839, four of the six Birmingham delegates to the National Convention, including Thomas Salt, resigned over the continued use of Physical Force language at the Convention. Salt had, like John Collins, encouraged women's activism but this early support only intensified the women's sense of betrayal over his resignation. Mrs Lapworth told a meeting that she was proud of the National Convention, 'for it far surpassed either the House of Commons or the House of Lords, and there she was most bitterly disappointed when she saw Mr Salt turn round and tell them his feelings'. She had heard many say that Mr Salt was a good man, but he was 'more timid and faint-hearted than many of the women', a remark which excited laughter from the audience.[58] She was particularly annoyed that Salt had previously raised women's expectations of a swift victory: 'In the first instant Mr Salt placarded the town and called the women to come forward and join the great and noble cause, which they imagined they had almost won.' She told the meeting that she would 'never renew her faith in a man who had once deceived her', a phrase which linked political betrayal with more familiar sexual betrayals.[59]

Lapworth's frustration seems to have been shared by other members of the BWPU.[60] When John Donaldson, who had also resigned from the Convention, stood to address the meeting, he was met with cries of, 'We don't want to hear him, he's done enough mischief' and 'Down – we won't hear him, &c.'[61] Miss Groves was in the chair and she intervened to enable

Donaldson to defend his decision to resign. A further article in the *Birmingham Journal* reported that Donaldson

> hoped the ladies of the Union would exercise the influence they possessed to prevent the men who met in the room on Thursday evenings from using such very strong language as they were accustomed to indulge in the National Convention.[62]

Sadly, the women's response to this hope was not recorded. Judging by Donaldson's reception at the meeting, it was unlikely to be popular.

The National Convention moved to Birmingham on 13 May 1839. Harney addressed huge crowds in the city, telling one meeting, 'It might be that if the government began the reign of terror, the people would end it ... it might be that the people should oppose them with the musket and the pike.'[63] Chartists were banned from meeting in the city's central Bull Ring but they defied the ban and marched to the Bull Ring every night. Rumours of bloody revolution were rife. Special constables were drafted into the city and soldiers patrolled the streets. The BWPU's weekly meetings provided an important opportunity for Chartist leaders to intervene in this fraught situation. The meeting on Saturday 25 May was addressed by Dr Taylor, the Anglo-Indian Chartist from Glasgow, as well as Collins and Harney. Mrs Lapworth mocked the occupation of the town. She spoke of the 'extraordinary week' they had just lived through: 'They were all to have been deluged in blood, and either to cause it or prevent it, the town had been crammed full of all sorts and sizes of black and red soldiers'.[64] Lapworth exposed how the vulnerability attributed to women was used to justify the military occupation of the city: 'The worst of it was, that it was saddled upon the women. The men said the women were frightened, and it was to protect them that the army was brought into the town.' Lapworth vehemently denied that women were alarmed by Chartist agitation.[65]

On one procession to the Bull Ring, O'Connor, John Frost and other national leaders stopped off at the women's meeting. Mrs Lapworth took the opportunity to pour scorn on the

Birmingham Journal, which had withdrawn its support from the women when they began to express their support for Physical Force Chartism. Protestations of sympathy for women's activism had given way to mockery and sneers:

> Our great trumpet the *Journal*, no longer sound[s] the note of female fame, but laughs at female virtue and female politicians. It is only by supplication, that our views can now find favour in the eyes of our former friend.[66]

Supplication was not Lapworth's strong point. She advised the Women's Union to turn away from the moderate *Journal* and ally instead with O'Connor and *The Northern Star*. In future, Lapworth said, women would not follow male leaders, but 'would learn the art of speaking for themselves'.[67]

The Nottingham Female Political Union (NFPU) was also aligned with Physical Force Chartism. The first meeting of the union was probably held in December 1838. It was chaired by Mrs Daniels, and debated a motion moved by Mrs Barnett and seconded by Mrs Hunt. The motion committed them to circulating an address written by Mary Savage, the secretary of the NFPU. After describing the suffering of children and expressing solidarity with Chartist men, Savage continued: 'Sisters and women of England, much is still in your power ... Aid your husbands, brothers, friends and children. Let them know that the union of millions is strength and power, is not to be resisted by tyrants.'[68] Her speech moved from familiar concern for the welfare of children, to a sense of solidarity between women and men and a militant assertion of the right to use physical force against tyrants. The Whig-supporting *Nottingham Journal* ridiculed the NFPU address for containing 'absurd and seditious ravings' and mocked its 'appropriately named' secretary, Mary Savage.[69] The *Journal*'s response suggests that Physical Force Chartists were bad enough, but female Physical Force Chartists were infinitely worse.

At least some of the Nottingham women were prepared to put their rhetorical support for physical force into practice. Elizabeth Cresswell, of Mansfield, a town to the north of

Nottingham, had the distinction of being one of the few Chartist women to be sent to prison during the Chartist agitations. She was convicted for unlawful and riotous assembly in the summer of 1839. Forty-three-year-old Elizabeth was arrested with a group of men who marched through Nottingham brandishing weapons. She was arrested in the Black Swan pub and was found to have a loaded gun hidden in her skirts.[70] She claimed to be looking after the gun for a friend, but the jury were not persuaded. In the late 1830s, women associated themselves with Physical Force Chartism. They polemicised for confrontation in their own rhetoric and their own organisations, and some women joined men's attempts to orchestrate an armed threat to the undemocratic institutions of the state.

Women in the Chartist insurrections

Few Chartists had expected the first national petition to make a difference to parliamentary attitudes and in this respect the rejection of the petition did not disappoint. When Thomas Attwood and John Fielden, with a theatrical flourish, rolled the giant cylinder into the Commons chamber it was greeted by laughter. *The Northern Star* pointed to this as evidence to persuade 'all the noodles who hope for favour or amelioration from the wretches who at present rule us ... if there be yet living one working man who is dolt enough to hope for help from these, this must undeceive him'.[71] In the spring of 1839, Chartist agitation generated a remarkable flowering of popular political awareness unparalleled in any previous radical agitation. In the Welsh industrial counties of Glamorganshire and Monmouthshire about one in five of the population were committed Chartists. In Scotland more than fifty new local Charter organisations were formed during this spring campaign.[72] 'There is now more of a political feeling in this country than ever existed, perhaps, in any nation in the world,' declared Henry Vincent's *The Western Vindicator*, 'it would seem that every man has become a politician.'[73]

There is plenty of evidence that women also became politicians. They set up their own societies to collect signatures for the first national petition. But petitioning was only ever seen as a first step towards more militant strategies and there is evidence that women were prepared to support the 'sacred month' [national strike]. When a Chartist asked an audience of female Chartists in Newcastle 'were they ready to make a sacred month of it and take to the hillside?' he was met with repeated shouts of "We will."'[74] Plans for the 'sacred month' were widely supported, but there was also a near-universal conviction that the state would swiftly force strikers back to work and provoke a decisive confrontation.[75] The majority agreed with O'Connor and Lovett that the 'sacred month' should not be prematurely risked against a powerful and repressive government, and the moment passed.[76]

While the national Chartist Convention wavered, rumours of insurrection abounded in some cities. 'Their object in the dead of night is to fire the town at one end,' wrote a Bolton informer, 'take possession of the town and burn the barracks.'[77] George Julian Harney returned to the Chartist Convention in police custody, having been arrested in Newcastle for promising to campaign with a 'musket in one hand and a petition in another'. He tried to convince the magistrates that he had said 'biscuit' not 'musket' and was extolling the virtues of oatcakes to sustain strikers. This claim provided a rare moment of humour in the proceedings.[78]

State repression provoked an angry determination to take up arms for the Charter. Women had to find new ways to assert themselves when men turned to military drilling with pikes and sabres, which were a departure from women's more traditional crowd actions. Women at Trowbridge were reported to be 'particularly violent and outrageous' when the Chartists smashed church windows. Women's perceived inability to bear arms was one of the arguments raised against them being given the vote. Some women defied the weight of convention and joined the men in their military-style manoeuvres. The Female Chartist Association of Cockermouth caused alarm by arming themselves with pikes.[79] Women also found ways to take part in the insurrections which broke out in 1839 and 1840.

The most significant attempt at insurrection took place in Newport, South Wales, on 4 November 1839. Women were well-organised in South Wales. More than a thousand women from Monmouthshire signed their own petition in favour of the Charter. This was despite a distinct lack of support for women's activism from John Frost, the leader of Chartism in Newport. In the summer of 1838, Frost addressed a meeting of the Newport Working Men's Association in which he justified the exclusion of women from the Charter's demand for the franchise as natural because providence had assigned men and women different roles, and because it was the duty of men to attend to the more important affairs of life. 'Indeed', he argued, 'he thought that women had power enough already, and all present who were married would no doubt agree with him; for his own part he would no more think of acting in opposition to his wife, than he would think of burning his fingers over the candle.'[80]

It is impossible to know whether Frost was a patronising critic of his wife Mary's attempts to exercise influence or genuinely respected her. Whatever his views, Mary was an energetic Chartist. She had named her son Henry Hunt, and she and their daughters were among the hundreds of members of the Newport Female Patriotic Society. The society frequently hosted visits by popular Chartist orator Henry Vincent, which attracted hundreds of women who listened to his speeches and then marched through the streets of Newport.[81] In April 1839, Vincent addressed an open-air meeting from the window of the Frosts' house. A women's meeting held two days later was so popular it had to be moved to a bigger room and did not finish until midnight.[82]

This female activism was part of a wider Chartist unrest, which reached such a pitch that soldiers were billeted in the town. In May, a royal proclamation gave local magistrates the power to ban any Chartist meeting at will. A few days later, three Chartists were arrested. A crowd gathered to try to free them, and one woman pelted a special constable with stones and was arrested. Tensions continued to grow throughout the summer months. Vincent was arrested in London and appeared in front of the Newport magistrates with the three local Chartists. He was committed to Monmouth Gaol but later released. On 20 May, some 30,000 people attended a local Chartist rally in the town. Anger grew in July when the national petition was rejected and it escalated further in August when Henry Vincent was sentenced to a year in prison, another victim of arbitrary injustice.

These growing tensions erupted on 4 November, when up to 5,000 Chartist sympathisers from across Monmouthshire marched on Newport under the leadership of John Frost. Chartists were arrested on their way into Newport and were held at the Westgate Hotel in the centre of the town. The Chartists were determined to liberate their comrades and surrounded the hotel. Windows were smashed and the soldiers of the 45th Regiment of Foot, who had been deployed to protect the police, were ordered to open fire. Between ten to twenty-four Chartists were killed and a further fifty injured. Four soldiers and the mayor of Newport were reportedly injured. According to witnesses:

> Some of the women who had joined the crowd kept instigating the men to attack the hotel – one old virago vowing that she would fight till she was knee-deep in blood, sooner than the Cockneys should take their prisoners out of town. She, with others of her sex, gathered large heaps of stones which they subsequently used in defacing and injuring the building which contained the prisoners.[83]

In the repression that followed, women were accused of inciting their husbands to rebel. During one trial, a desperate woman with a baby in her arms whose husband had been shot at the hotel applied to a magistrate, Reverend Coles, for the return of her husband's coat. Coles interrupted her to say:

> My good woman. I do not want to hurt your feelings; but it is owing to the advice of a great many of you women that we owe all this. You had better go home, and tell the other women what I say, 'that if they had given their husbands better advice this would not have happened'.[84]

Hundreds of Chartists were arrested and three of the leaders of the uprising, John Frost, Zephaniah Williams and William

Jones, were convicted of treason and sentenced to be hanged, drawn and quartered, sentences which were commuted to transportation. The women of the Frost family began to fight for John to be pardoned. Sarah Roberts, John's eighty-one-year-old mother, organised a petition to Queen Victoria while John was on a prison ship in York awaiting transportation. This petition was signed by Mary Frost, her daughters, Elizabeth, Sarah, Catharine, Ellen, Anne, and her son, Henry Hunt Frost, and was widely reported in the newspapers.[85] *The Northern Star* advised Mary to appeal to the Queen in person, but I can find no evidence that the two ever met. Chartist children were soon being named after Mary. Edward Woodhead registered his daughter as Mary Frost Woodhead and Allen MacDonald named his daughter Mary Frost.[86] Chartist women did not forget Mary. A decade later, the women of Holbrook, a remote village in Derbyshire, issued an appeal to the Chartists of Great Britain on behalf of Mrs Frost, Mrs Williams and Mrs Jones.[87]

These appeals position Mary as a long-suffering and virtuous wife, a victim of tyranny whose only crime was to be married to a Chartist husband. Such portrayals may have been calculated to win maximum support for Mary, but they served to diminish her own political life and her agency. Mary was not a submissive and dependent wife. She was born in 1782 into a middle-class family. She was a widow with two children when she married John Frost in 1812. In 1839, Mary was in her mid-fifties and had two grown-up children and seven surviving children with John, the youngest of whom, Anne, was twelve. Despite the pressures of childcare, and despite running John's business while he was away at the National Convention, and possibly in defiance of John's wishes, Mary joined the Female Patriotic Society of Newport and took part of Chartist activities in the town.[88] When John Frost was bankrupted by a feud with a local man, Thomas Protheroe, Mary sold all her furniture to keep him out of prison.

In 1841, Mary and her daughters Elizabeth, Ellen and Anne were living in Montpellier Street, Bristol. Mary's biographer claims that Mary was active among the Chartists of Bristol and, although I can find no evidence to support this view, it is consistent with Mary's long association with Chartism. In February 1842, *The Northern Star* reported that Mary was living in straitened circumstances and appealed for financial support for her.[89] Mary spent seventeen years, with the support of her daughters, campaigning for John to be allowed to come home.[90] In March 1853, Mary's daughter Catharine was so confident of success she set off to meet her father in Van Diemen's Land to be ready to bring him home. In July 1854, Catharine and John received news of his conditional pardon, but he had to wait in New York for the unconditional pardon, which was finally granted in May 1856. John was finally reunited with Mary, but they had only just over a year together. Mary died on 2 December 1857 aged seventy-five.[91]

Just a few weeks after the collapse of the Newport Uprising, plans were being laid for an insurrection in South Yorkshire. The Newport Uprising had involved husband and wife John and Mary Frost. The planned uprising in Sheffield revolved around another couple, Samuel and Mary Holberry. Samuel Holberry had served in the army but left in 1835 and found work as a distiller in Sheffield. The Sheffield Working Men's Association was formed in October 1837. Its first act was to boycott celebrations planned for the coronation of Queen Victoria.[92] Mary Holberry was born in 1816 in the Attercliffe area of Sheffield. Her father, John, was a labourer. She married Samuel Holberry in October 1838 when she was twenty-two years old. This was the year the People's Charter was published and the campaign for the Charter shaped the couple's lives. By 1839, Samuel Holberry was among the leaders of the Sheffield Chartists. Plans to launch a 'general uprising' were discussed when official Chartist business was concluded in the Fig Tree Lane Rooms. Holberry toured local towns to mobilise support and returned to Sheffield for the crucial meeting in January 1840. Public buildings were to be captured and turned into 'Chartist forts'. Simultaneous risings were planned in Dewsbury and Barnsley. Unfortunately for the insurrectionists, a publican in a Rotherham pub used by Holberry's group was a police informer. At midnight on 11 January, police raided Samuel and Mary's home and arrested them.[93]

Mary was several months pregnant at the time of her arrest. She was held in solitary confinement for two days and interrogated. Mary refused to talk and was released without charge. Samuel and seven others were charged with sedition and committed for trial. Holberry was sentenced to four years in Northallerton House of Correction. The judge had been ordered to send the 'worse' of men to the prison furthest away from their home, with the worst diet and harshest work regime. Samuel was forced to work on the treadmill and held in solidarity confinement.

There was a huge campaign for the release of the Sheffield prisoners. Chartist organisations also supported Mary whose baby, Samuel John, was born in May 1840. He died at the age of eighteen weeks and was buried in a pauper's grave. Mary was stricken by grief, but she recovered to take an active part in campaigning, petitioning for Samuel's release, writing letters to politicians and the newspapers. Samuel refused to let Mary visit him in prison. He was close to death when he wrote to her:

> My dear, you say you should like to come to York to see me; to that I cannot give my consent. In the first place we should have to look through the odious bars and it would only make you more unhappy.[94]

Samuel died in April 1842 at the age of twenty-seven.

In 1845, Mary married a publican, Charles Pearson, and went on to have five more children, the oldest of which she named Holberry Pearson. In 1845, she was described by a Chartist newspaper:

> After three years of heart corroding activity and mental anguish, she is still a truly fine woman, tall in stature, of graceful deportment, handsome expression and possesses an excellent temper and considering the defects of education, a mind of no mean order.[95]

Mary died at the age of sixty-seven in 1883 and was buried in the same grave as Samuel Holberry.

During the Chartist agitations, Mary Frost was a middle-aged woman, and Mary Holberry was twenty-five years younger. The fact that a respected community leader and a young activist were both caught up in an insurrection and the inevitable repression that followed suggests the breadth of Chartism's appeal. Mary Frost was an engaged Chartist, but in the insurrection itself, she appeared to have waited at home for news of events. Her main public role was to appeal for clemency for her husband, which she did with determination. Mary Holberry was arrested and interrogated, an ordeal she bore with courage, never apologising or justifying her role. She too fought hard for her husband and was not broken by her grief for her husband and child. The experiences of the two Marys, and those of all the audacious women Chartists who protested against the rejection of the national petition, contributed to the continual revision of the Chartist attitudes towards women and their capacity to drive the campaign forward.

1841: *'Where women lead men will follow'*[96]

September 1841 marked two significant events in the history of female Chartism. In York, about seventy delegates were selected to take part in a public meeting, procession and soirée organised to greet Feargus O'Connor when he was released from the city's prison in York Castle. The delegates proposed and debated resolutions and then marched together to the prison. The streets of York were full of delegations of Chartists waving banners. A 'numerous array of flags' was draped from the Castle walls. When O'Connor was released, he mounted a specially made 'triumphal car' (a horse-drawn carriage), covered in velvet and designed to resemble a conch shell. He then paraded around the town to cheers and applause.[97]

Among the list of delegates at the meeting printed in *The Northern Star* were Elizabeth Ellis and Elizabeth Sumper from the Chartist stronghold of Bradford. This is one of the few records of women's organisations being represented at a delegate event, or of women being elected from a mixed-sex Chartist branch. There was a history of female Chartist organising in Bradford. In March 1839, a meeting of the Northern Union of Women of Nelson Street held an open-air meeting. A Mrs Topper was in the chair and the meeting agreed to go door-to-door collecting subscriptions for the imprisoned anti–Poor Law activist Reverend JR Stephens.[98] The two Elizabeths may have responded to this legacy of female activism. There is no record of any male delegates from Bradford, so it is possible that they elected the women to represent them in York. There are no other mentions of Ellis and Sumper in the Chartist press.

In the same month, September 1841, the annual Metropolitan Delegate Meeting of Chartists in London published an appeal to the 'Men and Women of Britain'. One paragraph was directed at encouraging the women of Britain to become active Chartists:

> Women of Britain, you have ever been foremost on every good, in every noble cause, we entreat your assistance. This is pre-eminently your cause. You have to bear the greater burden – the greater share of our misery and distress. You have to endure the insults and contumely of a class of avaricious and unfeeling shop-keepers, who prey upon your indigence and want; you have to bear the thousand varieties of domestic vexations, which to the impatient spirit of man, would be worse than the actual distress. You are then even more interested than ourselves in procuring a fair day's wage for a fair day's work. Lend us then your powerful assistance, animate this glorious struggle, cheer us by your approbation, enliven us with your presence and we cannot, we will not fail of success.[99]

Women's imputed capacity to endure domestic vexations was not advanced as a reason for patience and passivity but as a reason for women to become active Chartists. Women had a shared interest in winning a wage which could alleviate their domestic miseries. The leading figures of London Chartism publicly declared that female support was indispensable to the movement. The signatories to the address included many of the most influential figures of London Chartism, including Phillip M'Grath, Edward Pickersgill, Martin Thomas Wheeler and

John Watkins. The address did not explicitly ascribe to women the capacity to occupy positions of leadership within the movement. The London delegates did, however, articulate ideas of female agency and capacity to lead in other publications.

In the same year the appeal was published, Watkins wrote a letter to *The Northern Star* announcing that 'London is shaking off its sleep and will soon arise like a giant refreshed.' Watkins' letter contained further good news: 'I am also happy to inform you that a Female Chartist Association is being formed in London, so that if the men won't lead the women will, and then see if the men won't follow.'[100] It was also in 1841 that Watkins published his *Address to the Women of England*, which justified the franchise for single women. A new edition of Mary Wollstonecraft's *Vindication of the Rights of Woman* was published by the Chartist publisher John Cleave and advertised as available from his office on Shoe Lane and from 'agents for *The Northern Star* throughout the Kingdom'.[101] The appeal, Watkins' letter and pamphlet and the publication of the *Vindication* suggest that, by 1841, London's male Chartist leaders not only welcomed female activism, they also acknowledged that women were potentially powerful allies who deserved to exercise political rights.

There is some evidence that these debates influenced the actions of women at the grassroots of the Chartist movement and encouraged them to politicise the more personal aspects of their lives. One of the best examples of this process comes from a report in *The Northern Star* from March 1841 which recorded what happened when a Mrs King took her child to be baptised by a magistrate, Mr Webb:

> Mr Webb: 'What is the child to be called?'
> Mrs King: 'James Feargus O'Connor King.'
> Mr Webb: 'Is your husband a Chartist?'
> Mrs King: 'I don't know, but his wife is.'
> Mr Webb: 'Are you the child's mother?'
> Mrs King: 'Yes.'
> Mr Webb: 'You had better go home and consider it again: for if the person that you are naming your child after was to commit high treason and get hanged, what a thing it would be.'

Mrs King: 'If that should be the case, I should then consider it an honour to have my child called after him, so that I shall never have him out of my memory so long as the child lives: I think Feargus O'Connor is a great deal honester [sic] man than those who are punishing him.'

Mr Webb: 'Well, if you are determined to have it named after him, I must name it; but I never met such an obstinate lady as you before.'

Mr Webb then registered the child.[102]

A 'new move'

The National Association for the Improvement of the People was the Chartist organisation most closely associated with support for women's rights. The Association's founding manifesto, *Chartism: A New Organisation for the People*, was written in prison by William Lovett and John Collins and published soon after their release in July 1840, much to the fury of Feargus O'Connor. O'Connor believed Lovett and Collins were proposing a 'New Move' which was a challenge to his authority. Lovett established the National Association for Promoting the Political and Social Improvement of the People in autumn 1841. Historians have cautioned against overestimating the importance of the National Association, which they see as 'feeble' and merely a 'side organisation' of Chartism.[103] Kathryn Gleadle explained how historians of Chartism have dismissed the Association as short-lived and insignificant, while historians of feminism assumed Chartism was unsympathetic to women's rights.[104] The National Association, therefore, has rarely been the subject of systematic historical investigation but a brief exploration of the Association sheds new light on Chartism's gender politics.[105]

Despite its name, the National Association never established a national organisation and drew its support from London, where it became influential among some reforming networks. The Association was not a mass-membership organisation, but it developed a distinctive outlook which permeated the radical culture of London in the early 1840s and helped to establish support for women's rights in the working-class movement. The Association's launch attracted only seventy-three supporters, but the organisation was sufficiently popular to open a 2,000-capacity hall in Holborn by 1842.[106] The Association Hall was planned as a site for 'rational amusements' such as lectures and meetings as well as singing and dancing.[107] The Association gave coherence to a current within Chartism that believed that self-improvement through moral reform and education could perfect individuals and emanate from them to reform society as a whole.[108] Such improvement entailed a rejection of misogynistic cultures of workplace and pub sociability and domestic violence and the development of an alternative culture based on the reform of the environment in which working-class families lived and worked. This focus on personal reform as a precondition for political reform created the space for women to position themselves as crucial agents in the regeneration of society, who could educate themselves and their children and bring their moral influence to bear on recalcitrant or degenerate men.

Within the membership of the National Association there was an alliance between those who believed women's role should be to refine men, beautify the home and devote themselves to their children, and those who saw women's political activities as instrumental to the wider reform of society.[109] In *Chartism: A New Organisation*, Lovett and Collins attempted to bridge these divided opinions of women's role by suggesting that women's vital role as homemakers meant that they needed political rights. They argued that women's capacity to spread 'comfort, cheerfulness and affection' with their 'sympathy and kindness' necessitated the urgent improvement of women's education and the extension of their social and political rights.[110] Women should have a role in framing laws they were subject to, and women educated children and, therefore, should be educated themselves.

The Association made winning female equality its third objective, after a plea for unity and securing the Charter itself. Those joining the Association committed themselves to, 'disseminate such facts and opinions in favour of the political and social rights of women as may lead to their enfranchisement, and the amelioration of their social condition'.[111] To further the acquisition of those rights, the Association was open to, 'All persons, men or women, approving of the Objects of this Association.' Membership for women cost four pence a month, which was cheaper than the eight pence fee for men.[112] The *National Association Gazette*, launched in January 1842, made a clear statement with its masthead: 'The Rights of Man and the Rights of Woman'.[113] The *Gazette* consistently criticised the 'trashy philosophy' which deprived women of education and cramped their faculties.[114] While feminist historians have looked for antecedents among the middle classes, the *Gazette* argued that women's rights were 'more thoroughly understood and more generally recognised among the working classes than among the rest of society'.[115] The National Association was optimistic that both working-class men and women could be won to support the struggle for women's rights.

Among those who joined the Association were influential men who were publicly committed to women's rights. Charles Neesom was the chair of the first branch of the Association, which was established in the City of London in October 1841. Neesom publicly defended women's right to organise and his wife, Elizabeth, was a prominent leader of female Chartism in London. Radical Unitarians Collet Dobson Collet and William Shaen also joined the Association. Shaen was a prominent supporter of women's rights. His daughter recalled, 'It was perhaps on behalf of women that William Shaen undertook the most strenuous of his many labours.'[116] Collet Dobson Collet was the brother of Sophia Dobson Collet, who wrote articles in the radical press under the pen name Panthea and campaigned for votes for women. Dobson Collet's daughter, Clara, campaigned for protections for working women and became a friend of Eleanor Marx.

Prominent among association members was John Collins, who had a strong association with the well-organised female Chartists of Birmingham and maintained friendships with several prominent female activists, including Elizabeth Pease. Henry Hetherington joined the Association, bringing with him a long experience of encouraging female organisations such as the

Friends of the Oppressed, a society of women who wanted to campaign for a free press, which was active in the early 1830s. James Watson, who also joined the Association, published the works of Mary Wollstonecraft, Frances Wright and John Reginald Richardson's the *Rights of Women*. Association member William J. Linton was a consistent supporter of women's suffrage who argued for 'Universal Suffrage and complete equality for both sexes'.[117]

The Association also attracted support from more middle-class supporters of women's rights, including Peter Taylor MP, William Ashurst and James Stansfeld, lawyers who had both supported women's right to attend the World Slavery Convention of 1840. Their later commitment to the campaign to repeal the Contagious Diseases Acts has led one historian to describe them as 'outstanding feminists'.[118] The Association attracted a circle of men who supported women's political rights within Chartism and in other contexts.

Little is known of the women who supported the Association. The wives of male members were enrolled as 'auxiliaries' and it is impossible to gauge the degree of enthusiasm these 'auxiliary' members felt for the organisation. Despite its declarations of female equality and rights, the Association did not have any women in its leadership, and it did not record the names of any female members. Henry Moore, a woodcarver, was a member of both the LWMA and the National Association. In 1836, Moore married Mary Sharp of Malton, Yorkshire, who was James Watson's niece. The Mrs Moore who joined the National Association in September 1842 was probably Henry Moore's wife.[119] It seems likely that Mary Lovett, William's wife, was also involved. Mary Lovett did not give public lectures or write regularly to the press, but this did not mean that she was unwilling or unable to play an authoritative role in public affairs. In 1839, when Lovett was sent to prison, Mary took his place as secretary of the National Convention. This was one of the very few examples of a woman assuming a leadership position in one of Chartism's highest bodies. Mr Carpenter, who had requested that she take on the role, was optimistic that following her appointment, 'women everywhere would be encouraged and excited to do in like manner and the most important consequences would follow'.[120] Mary Lovett also campaigned vigorously to improve her husband's conditions in jail by writing to men of influence and authority. Her letters were included in a collection of memorials and testimonies relating to Lovett's treatment, which were published as a pamphlet by sympathetic MPs in February 1840.[121] When necessary, Mary Lovett was willing and able to exercise authority in a public position.

This brief description of the membership of the Association demonstrates that the class nature of London Chartism was more fluid than elsewhere and the Association attracted members from among middle-class radicals. Also apparent is the extensive support for women's rights which was articulated within its organisations. Chartism incubated support for expanding women's political rights and the ideas developed by female Chartists and their supporters permeated out through other radical circles, while simultaneously absorbing feminist ideas from other networks. This was especially true of the close relationship between the National Association and the radical Unitarians of the South Place Chapel.

The leading figure in the South Place Chapel congregation was William J. Fox, who was described as 'in political opinions a Chartist – and something more'.[122] Fox worked closely with London's Chartists and lectured at Lovett's National Association Hall.[123] Fox encouraged female activism, and the South Place Chapel was 'a breeding ground for feminist ideas and discussion'.[124] The Chartists of the National Association shared the Unitarians' aim of uniting everyone, regardless of class, nation or creed, to promote the social and political improvement of the people. In this milieu, political, religious and cultural identities and allegiances were fluid and multi-layered. William Shaen, William Ashurst, James Stansfeld and William Prideaux were among the Unitarians who supported the Charter. William and Catherine Barmby and William Linton were Unitarians, Owenites and Chartists.[125] William Fox, William Ashurst and Peter Alfred Taylor MP all belonged to London's Radical Club, which voted to support the Charter. Lovett contributed articles on education to *Howitt's Journal*, which was published by prominent

Unitarians William and Mary Howitt, and *The Northern Star* advertised and reprinted articles from *Howitt's Journal*.[126]

William Fox was elected MP for Oldham in December 1852. His victory was both a reflection of and an encouragement of women's activism in this textile district.[127] At a large meeting organised to celebrate Fox's election held at Oldham's Working Men's Club, 'The gallery around the top of the hall was filled with ladies, and there were not a few nursing mothers among them.' When Fox appeared, 'a thousand fair hands above waved a cloud of white handkerchiefs above their heads and matrons tossed their babies till the little creatures began to crow in accordance with the general ecstasy'.[128] The presence of mothers and babies at a political meeting suggests that Fox had either instigated or mobilised a pre-existing gender-inclusive political culture. Fox's support for women's rights was a prominent part of the political stance, which helped him to secure a base of popular support among workers in the textile district of Oldham.

It would be easy to assume that it was the well-educated, literate Unitarians who promoted feminist ideas among the Chartists, but there is evidence of a much more reciprocal relationship between Chartist and Unitarian supporters of women's rights. In 1841, Richardson published 'The Rights of Women' and Watkins published his 'Address to the Women of England' in the *English Chartist Circular*, both of which justified female political activism and advocated for the vote for single women. The Unitarians did not publish any coherent support for women's right to interfere in politics for another decade. Harriet Taylor published 'The Enfranchisement of Women' in 1851. John Stuart Mill did not publish 'The Subjugation of Women' until 1869. The Chartists published tracts and pamphlets defending women's right to engage with politics and to vote before Unitarians had developed and voiced their own views on the female franchise in print.

The Unitarians established the Whittington Club, an adult education and social centre. The Whittington Club voted to support the Charter and it followed the model established by the National Association and several National Association members were also 'Whittingtonites'.[129] The club admitted women and its 'grand feminist ambitions' have been identified as a neglected part of the British women's rights movement.[130] The Whittingtonites' embrace of women's rights was, however, quite cautious. In 1850, the *Whittington Club Gazette* hosted a debate about whether Mary Wollstonecraft should be celebrated or condemned as a disgrace to her sex.[131] The framing of this debate suggests that the members of Lovett's National Association, who had published and celebrated Wollstonecraft's works, were leading rather than following Unitarian support for women's rights. Support for women's rights with Chartism was consistent and persistent, but it failed to convince the leaders of the movement to add women's right to vote to the six points of the Charter. The reasons for that omission were complex, rooted in debates about family division and class unity.

The female franchise and family friction

When women were explicitly excluded from the franchise extension in Lord Grey's Reform Act of 1832, there was no immediate feminist response. It was 1851 before the philosopher and partner of John Stuart Mill, Harriet Taylor, published an article supporting the female franchise and criticising the Chartists' failure to include votes for women in their Charter. Her essay was a response to the activities of Chartist women of Sheffield who had petitioned Parliament for the female franchise a few months earlier. Women did not collectively petition Parliament for the vote until 1851, and that petition was organised by Chartist women. In so far as feminist claims for political rights were heard at all during the two decades following 1832, they were heard among the women and men of the Owenite and Chartist movements.[132]

The celebrated philosopher James Mill, John Stuart Mill's father, set out a foundational argument against women voting in his *Essay on Government* (1820). Mill argued that it was clear that women's claims to the franchise could be 'struck off without inconvenience' because their interests were represented by their fathers or husbands.[133] The female franchise was not just unnecessary, it was also a potential source of domestic conflict at a moment when domestic harmony was becoming a central element of Victorian ideology.[134] The perceived connection between family disruption and the revolutions in eighteenth-century America and France prompted the elevation of domestic harmony to a cultural preoccupation.[135] Victorian domestic ideology was disseminated through political speeches, legal texts, judicial decisions, a vast marriage advice literature and religious literature of various kinds. Marital disputes were increasingly seen as 'a violation of the domestic peace on which so much depended' and were, therefore, to be avoided at all costs.[136] Martial rows over who to vote for could undermine social stability.

Many influential Chartists, including Feargus O'Connor, opposed the female franchise because of these fears it would cause family dissensions. It was family unity rather than female incapacity which prompted O'Connor's opposition. A significant number of leading male Chartists argued that both married and single women had a right to vote because of their contribution to society as mothers and as producers.[137] A list of those advocating the female franchise would include William Lovett and many others in the LWMA, as well as Bronterre O'Brien, George Julian Harney, Henry Vincent, William Cuffay and Ernest Jones. More male Chartists supported the right of single women to vote because they had no one to represent their interests in elections. Richardson argued that the capacity of women to vote was demonstrated by the presence of a female monarch and their right to vote rested on the contribution women made to the wealth of the nation.[138]

Chartism was imbued with the idealisation of domestic unity. For many Chartists, the family unit was not just a private institution but formed a strand within broader community networks.[139] An address issued by Emma Miles, president of the Female Chartist Association of London and published in 1842, articulated how concern for children gave a sense of urgency to political campaigns. She deployed the motif of slavery to articulate her sense of disrupted domesticity and class antagonism:

> How long is man to exist the slave of another? ... How long to hear the cry of their starving children, to bear the sight as bitter as the cry, of seeing their little ones creeping forth to a factory, there to be worked like machines until they are worked out of existence?[140]

Working-class men and women, Emma argued, had been too patient but the Charter was now rousing them from their lethargy and reminding them of the power they possessed to win their rights when they united to obtain them.[141] For Miles, workers and their children were enslaved by their dependence on exploitative employment. She was impatient with fatalism and passivity, which she counterposed to the potential power that gender unity could generate.

Critics of domesticity could be found among middle-class feminists for whom the family meant dependency and confinement, and work outside the home promised independence and fulfilment. Middle-class women compared their political and legal disabilities and their limited cultural opportunities with those of their brothers and husbands, and they sought more equality. For most working-class women, employment constituted a barely tolerable burden performed at the expense of childcare and other domestic responsibilities. Working-class women could not look enviously upon the limited legal powers and political rights enjoyed by their husbands. They had to campaign for men to achieve their rights, while simultaneously creating space to assert their own.

Working-class female Chartists negotiated ideas of domesticity by emphasising how the very people who preached the virtues of domesticity employed women to work in their own factories for lower wages than men and for hours which made it impossible to care for their families. The female Chartists of Newcastle asserted that:

> We have been told that the province of woman is her home, and that the field of politics should be left to men; this we deny; the nature of things renders it impossible, and the conduct of

> those who give the advice is at variance with the principles they assert.[142]

A sense of class unity between husbands and wives was generated by the identification of a common enemy in the hypocritical employing classes. For the establishment, appeals to family harmony justified the exclusion of women from the democratic process. For the Chartists, family unity was distinct from middle-class ideas of domesticity, which were used as a tool to disempower women and divide the working class.

Any potential alliances with middle-class women around a shared desire for domesticity were ruptured by class antagonism. The domestic comforts of wealthy women depended on depriving female servants and factory hands of their ability to enjoy a family life. In 1839, the Birmingham Chartist Mrs Lapworth argued that rich ladies were complicit in the exploitation of working women and had a material interest in procuring more labour for less money.[143] Lapworth's criticisms were specific as well as general. One of the leaders of the male radicals and Moral Force Chartism in Birmingham, Thomas Salt, identified women working as both a symptom and a cause of working-class distress but nevertheless admitted to replacing male workers with women earning half men's wages at his own brass factory.[144] As we have seen, Lapworth supported the Physical Force Chartists in opposition to Salt and her denunciations of the hypocrisy of the wealthy may have been aimed at her political enemies inside the Chartist movement.

Some female Chartists were critical of the whole idea of domesticity itself, which they denounced as a middle-class con to encourage female passivity and benefit the employing class and the government. The women of Keighley argued that the idea of women staying at home was a device used by 'the government and money mongers of this country' to keep women 'ignorant and divided'. They asserted that it was 'the duty of every working man and woman to declare their political sentiments publicly, in order that both the country and the Government may be acquainted with the wants and grievances of the millions of our oppressed country women'.[145] The Keighley women did not frame their demands around ruptured domesticity. They rejected the whole idea of female retreat into the home as one which was detrimental to women's potential collective power. This was a bold stance when practically every Victorian claimed to stand for family unity.

'Bid the Outraged World, Be Free!': Making Common Cause with Elizabeth Pease and Anne Knight

The World Anti-Slavery Convention of June 1840 was commemorated by Benjamin Robert Haydon in this acclaimed painting. Haydon's grand canvas is dominated by the figure of the abolitionist leader Thomas Clarkson and crowded with identifiable portraits of delegates. Yet, only a handful of female faces are visible. Two belong to Quaker abolitionists Anne Knight and Elizabeth Pease, remarkable campaigners who saw in Chartism a movement with the potential to address both social and gender inequalities.

Anne Knight argued that her friend, the prominent abolitionist Lucy Townsend, deserved a place in the painting. Knight wrote to Townsend,

> I am very anxious that the historical picture now in the hand of Haydon should not be performed without the chief lady of the history being there ... [I]n justice to history and posterity the person who established [female societies] has as much right to be there as Thomas Clarkson himself, any perhaps more, as his achievement was in the slave trade; thine was slavery itself, the pervading movement, the still small voice.[1]

Knight understood how women had to negotiate tensions between their desire to fulfil their religious and political duty by making a public stand, and the way they were encouraged to avoid public scrutiny. The conflict between public advocacy and fear of the consequences of public exposure shaped the political experience of Anne Knight and Elizabeth Pease.

Elizabeth Pease's sympathy with the disorganisers

Elizabeth Pease was a member of a prominent Quaker and abolitionist family. She was born in 1807 in Feethams, the grandest mansion in Darlington. Her father, Joseph Pease, was one of the first Quakers elected to Parliament in 1832. Pease embraced a range of radical causes and this activism encouraged her to understand her reluctance to speak out in public, not as the natural state of womanhood but as an increasingly outdated social convention. In December 1840, she wrote to the Birmingham Chartist leader John Collins,

> I believe there are few persons whose natural feelings are so opposed to women appearing prominently before the public as mine – but viewed in the light of principle I see, that prejudice, custom and other feelings which will not stand the test of truth, are at the bottom, and must be laid aside.[2]

Pease developed a more sustained critique of the conventions surrounding female reticence in a pamphlet, *An Address to the Women of Great Britain* (1838), which she co-wrote with Jane Smeal. The address argued that women should set up their own political societies and speak out on political questions. It was one of the first publications in Britain which aimed to encourage women to engage in public political activism.

Chartist agitation helped bring the condition of the working class to the fore and Pease became increasingly concerned with the labouring classes. During the militant strike wave of 1842, Pease met Joseph Sturge and other Birmingham-based reformers with whom she discussed, 'the importance of extending the suffrage to operatives'.[3] Pease argued that class inequality justified Chartist militancy, writing:

> One's whole sympathies go with the 'disorganisers', driven as they are almost to desperation by insult and injury heaped upon them by those, who if actions be interpreters of feelings, consider that they are but chattels made to minister to their luxury and add to their wealth.[4]

Pease was sensitive to how inequality injured the 'feelings' of the labourers and acknowledged that this hurt was important to the workers' overall well-being.

Elizabeth Pease exchanged letters with the leading Chartists of Darlington and helped them to distribute Chartist documents.[5] When Pease expressed her support for Chartism in public, she had to confront the double standards imposed on women. She observed, 'It is thought most unaccountable for a gentleman to say he sees nothing wrong in Chartism – but for a lady to do so is almost outrageous!'[6] Pease's abolitionist activism encouraged her to advocate for women's rights and to become active in the interests of her gender while engaging with political reform which would benefit working-class women and men.

Pease's activism did not decline with the demise of Chartism in the 1850s. She continued supporting internationalist ideals through the Aborigines' Protection Society, which was established in 1837 to promote the welfare of indigenous people living within the British Empire.[7] In July 1839, members of the Aboriginal Protection Society set up the British India Society, which exposed British misrule in India and campaigned for more ethical and humanitarian practices to be introduced in the colony.[8] Elizabeth Pease was fully committed to both organisations.

In 1853, Elizabeth gave the largest donation, £400, towards the building of the £2,300 Mechanics' Institute in Skinnergate, Darlington. The institute had been formed in 1825, in the earliest days of a worldwide movement to provide educational opportunities for the working class. It provided a library, lectures and classes, as well as social facilities for its members. In the same year, Elizabeth married Dr John Pringle Nichol in an independent chapel off Northgate. Dr Nichol was the professor of astronomy at Glasgow University and was considered the greatest astronomer of his day. Nichol was a Presbyterian and it was forbidden for a Quaker to marry outside her faith, so Elizabeth left the Quakers and moved to Edinburgh. Her husband lived just five years after their marriage – 'Alas! Alas! Widow and desolate,' she wrote in her diary.[9]

Despite her grief, Elizabeth threw herself into numerous causes in her new home city of Edinburgh: peace, temperance, anti-vivisection and women's suffrage. She was a founder of the Edinburgh National Society for Women's Suffrage in 1867; she attended the Great Demonstration of Women in Manchester in 1880 with 5,000 other women; she signed a 'letter from the ladies' to MPs in 1884 asking for women who headed households to get the vote. Elizabeth Pease Nichol died in Edinburgh in 1897. Her political development suggests that some politically experienced women active in the radical milieu of the 1830s and 1840s were attracted to Chartism as a potential vehicle for the campaign for women's rights and wider social reform. This was a view Elizabeth shared with her friend, Anne Knight.

Anne Knight's complete anti-slavery

Anne Knight was born in Chelmsford in 1786 into a prosperous Quaker family, one of eight siblings. Knight never held an elected or salaried position and never published anything substantial. But her whole life was devoted to political campaigning, and she deserves a *much* more prominent place in the history of radical politics and female suffrage than she occupies. Anne did not acknowledge any separation between private life and public campaigning. Every one of the many, many letters she sent was an opportunity to make a political point. She often stuck brightly coloured gummed labels carrying political slogans and mottos or snips of poetry on her envelopes to be read by all those who handled the post. She carried political tracts in black, silk purses and pulled them out at social gatherings to brandish them in the face of political opponents.[10]

In 1824, Anne embarked on her first tour of the Continent. Such travels were not unusual in Quaker circles. Back at home in 1825, she joined forces with abolitionists Elizabeth Heyrick, Sarah Wedgewood and Sophia Sturge to launch the Birmingham Ladies Anti-Slavery Society. By 1830, Knight was fully immersed in the anti-slavery movement. She canvassed door-to-door with petitions, collected money and oversaw the printing and distribution of abolitionist tracts. She also travelled frequently to London where she worked with leading abolitionists including Thomas Clarkson and Joseph Sturge, and other women, including Elizabeth Pease. In 1834, Anne returned to France on a speaking tour.

In 1840, Knight was at the centre of the arguments at the Anti-Slavery Convention. Fierce rows erupted when the American women delegates were told they were not recognised as delegates and then instructed to sit out of sight of the male delegates. Anne Knight recognised how, despite their activism, women were excluded from positions of authority. She denounced the way in which abolitionism enlisted women's help 'in the labour of collecting and going from house to house for signatures to petitions', but excluded them from 'the muster role for the counsel-board'.[11] Knight's protests against the exclusion of women from leadership will resonate with women who have confronted similar expectations in radical and socialist organisations in the decades since she first called out such marginalisation.

These attempts to exclude women from the Convention inspired Anne to take up a new cause – the cause of women. She wrote to Maria Weston Chapman of the Boston Female Anti-Slavery Society that women were no longer prepared to 'sit and spin' by the fire or 'distil rosemary and lavender for poor neighbours'.[12] Women had the capacity to instruct men in the conduct of spiritual warfare. In fact, Knight suggested, women's judgement was so mature that they were now superior to men.

In 1843, another delegate who had experienced the arguments at the London Convention, Marion Reid, published *A Plea for Woman: Being a Vindication of the Importance and Extent of Her Natural Sphere of Action: with Remarks on Recent Works on the Subject*. Reid argued that women were entitled to vote to reform unjust laws they were subject to and to challenge their exclusion from 'honourable and useful occupations'.[13] She reassured her readers that such pursuits were entirely compatible with female domesticity.[14] Reid refuted the 'obnoxious charge' that the enlargement of women's domestic sphere was incompatible with the discharge of domestic duties.[15] She sought to enrich female domesticity rather than replace it. Despite her commitment to domesticity, Reid's short book has been described as a 'feminist treatise' and the 'first book by a woman arguing that possession of the vote was crucial to ending gender discrimination'.[16]

Anne Knight kept a copy of Reid's *Plea*, which she annotated and decorated with glued-on political labels and pages from other publications. Her interactions with the pamphlet provide a window into her thinking about women's rights. The two longest insertions in Knight's copy of the *Plea* are from works by Chartists.[17] The first insertion consists of two pages from Richardson's *Rights of Woman*, in which he asserts that women have the natural right, the civil right, the political right and the duty to interfere in politics. The second is an appendix to a book by the French Catholic and socialist Félicité de La Mennais, *On Slavery*, published by the Chartist James Watson in English in 1840. Knight preserved an appendix to the book which was written by the Chartist William Linton in support of women's political rights in which Linton argued, 'Rights have no sex.'[18] Knight's insertions suggest that she wanted to strengthen Reid's plea for political rights with more confident Chartist assertions of women's rights.

In 1847, Anne Knight wrote a letter to Matilda Ashurst Biggs, daughter of William Ashurst, which she then published as a leaflet. This broadside is often credited with being the first leaflet to demand votes for women to be produced in Britain.[19] In it, Knight argued, 'Never will the nations of the earth be well governed, until both sexes, as well as all parties, are fully represented and have an influence, a voice and an enactment of the administration of laws.' A year later, Knight was living in Paris. She embraced the possibility for human liberation she identified in the uprising of spring 1848. The revolution, she argued, was a chance to 'shake off the monster Moloch', a biblical reference to the worship of money: 'We have been too long grubbing and petitioning, and dancing attendance on him, instead of breaking his jaws and plucking the prey from his teeth.' Knight was deeply influenced by the female French utopian socialists Flora Tristan, Clare Lemar and Jeanne Deroin. Knight and Deroin tried to influence the radical Club of the People by sending a letter which argued:

> Brothers, if only your declaration of principles would proclaim loudly the complete abolition of all privileges of sex, of race, of birth, of caste and of fortune you would soon see in your ranks women of spirit and intelligence who would uphold your heroic efforts and help you to triumph.[20]

Knight read and kept clippings from Jeanne Deroin's magazine, *The Opinion of Women*, and became a fervent supporter of Deroin's 1849 election campaign.[21] The two women continued to correspond and campaign together. The progress of their relationship in the early 1850s will be discussed further.

In February 1850, Knight published a robust reply to a Chartist who had argued that unity in the movement should take precedence over women's right to vote. Knight wrote a letter to the *Brighton Herald* in which she pointed out that women were not exempt from hard labour:

> It is justice that we demand for all who bear their share in the burdens of the State, and who does not pay taxes in this miserably tax-bound country? Is she exempt whose part it is to work 18 hours out of the 24, sleep little, and to be too much worn with Labour to think?[22]

Knight herself had independent means but she was sensitive to the hardships faced by working women and understood that labour was an important justification for the female franchise.

A year later, in March 1851, Knight was on the lookout for Feargus O'Connor. She wanted to confront him in person to persuade him to give a firm commitment to supporting the female franchise. *The Northern Star* published a letter from Knight in which she described going twice to the paper's London office in search of O'Connor. Reading Knight's letter conjures up an image of the mighty Feargus hiding somewhere in the *Star*'s offices until he could be reassured that Knight had left.[23] Knight's strong association with the Sheffield Women's Rights Association and the Women's Elevation League will be discussed further. Both associations show that Knight consistently and persistently raised demands and created new organisations capable of promoting women's rights and women's suffrage.

The last few years of Knight's life were spent peacefully in Waldersbach, southwest Strasbourg. Although she was quieter than she had been, Knight never stopped yearning and praying for a social transformation. Two months before her death in November 1862, she recalled the unfulfilled promise of 1848: 'It is 14 years and where are we now? Still heaving our agonised chests under the couchmar of a military despotism. Still dragged at the chariot wheels of the sons of Belial – how long Lord? How Long?'[24] Knight's lifelong commitment to campaigning for equality and political reform drew her to Chartism, which she saw as an imperfect but powerful vehicle for realising her far-reaching political ambitions.

4

General Strike, 1842: 'Every Woman Ought to be a Politician'

The Chartist petition of 1842 was the best supported and most politically ambitious of the three national petitions. It was signed by about a third of the adult population, an extraordinary achievement which could not have been realised without thousands of working-class activists who collected signatures outside factories and mills and among their communities. The petition was presented to Parliament on 3 May 1842 by the Chartist MP Thomas Duncombe with these words:

> I beg respectfully to offer to the acceptance of this House, a petition signed by 3,315,752 of the industrious classes of this country. The petition proceeds from those upon whose toil, upon whose industry, upon whose affection, and upon whose attachment, I may say, every institution, every law, nay, even the very Government, and the whole property and commerce of the country depend.[1]

The petitioners demanded annual parliaments, which would ensure accountability as

> Members elected to serve in Parliament ought to be the servants of the people, and should, at short and stated intervals, return to their constituencies, to ascertain if their conduct is approved of, and to give the people power to reject all who have not acted honestly and justly.[2]

The 1842 petition also raised economic demands, directing the attention of the MPs to the 'great disparity existing between the wages of the producing millions, and the salaries of those whose comparative usefulness ought to be questioned, where riches and luxury prevail among the rulers, and poverty and starvation among the ruled'. The petitioners wanted a rebalancing of the relationship between work and free time, and that between production and social reproduction. They condemned the way working hours were protracted beyond the limits of human endurance and rewarded with wages which were inadequate to sustain bodily strength and supply those comforts so imperative after an excessive waste of physical energy.

When the petition was overwhelmingly rejected by Parliament, workers responded with localised riots and strikes which coalesced into Britain's first general strike. The strike was independent of Chartist organisations, but it was intimately bound up with hopes that the Charter could protect workers from the imposition of wage cuts. In June, colliers from North Staffordshire 'turned out' [went on strike] in protest against a wage cut. Their strike immediately began to spread. Strikers pulled the plug out of steam engines to stop coal production as they marched from pit to pit – their strike became known as the Plug Riots. Strikers processed from town to town, pulling plugs and demanding food from shopkeepers. By August, there was a general strike across large areas of the West Midlands and Lancashire, which reached as far as Dundee in the North and Cornwall in the South.

On Sunday 7 August, strikers from Stalybridge in Lancashire turned out at all the mills still working in Ashton-under-Lyne. About 13,000 strikers then marched on Hyde and Oldham. Strike meetings held that evening resolved to strike until the Charter was law. Gatherings of workers pledged to spread the strike and fight for political rights to end wage cuts. Similar events occurred across Lancashire and West Yorkshire as strikers took over towns and blockaded roads with carts. The demand for 'the Charter or no return to labour' was heard everywhere. Three years earlier, the Chartist leaders had agonised over calling the 'sacred month' and backed off. Now, the sacred month was erupting across the country – and women were at the heart of the movement.

Some three weeks into the strike wave, the *Leeds Times* reported that 'one of the most hideous features of the present insurrection among the working-classes is the turn-out of women.'[3] When many thousands of women, many of whom were mothers, travelled from Lancashire into Yorkshire to spread the strike, they were 'inverting the laws of nature' and had left their natural sphere for the, 'bustle, turmoil, rioting, sabreing, and shooting of this frightful insurrection'. The women reminded the editor of *The Leeds Times* of the early days of the French Revolution, a comparison which was frequently made to emphasise the dangerous consequences of female activism.[4] One witness observed, 'The girls of some of our manufacturing districts are wearing the garb of women, but actuated by the worst passions of men, in very riot and outbreak the women are the leaders and exciters of the young men to violence.'[5]

The images of violent, vengeful women conjured up in the press were not just lurid phantasms. Women did indeed help to drive the strike movement forward with militant tactics. At 5:30 a.m. on 10 August, a crowd of women gathered in Great Ancoats Street, Manchester. They marched through the streets, collecting more women as they went. At the first mill they came to, Mill Street Mill, working people came out and the mill was shut down. When Kennedy's Mill refused to shut the women hurled a volley of stones at the windows and broke in through the main door. *The Northern Star* reported how 'the police charged the people, sparing neither age nor sex, but lying about the right and left with their bludgeons and cutlasses; many were knocked down and beaten till they were unable to rise from the ground.' But the women fought back. It took the intervention of one detachment of dragoons and another of the Rifle Brigade before the women dispersed.[6] The following morning at 6:30 a.m. a meeting took place on a predictably wet Granby Row Fields in Manchester. The *Manchester Guardian* reported that, 'Notwithstanding the wetness of the weather, probably upwards of ten thousand persons of both sexes (the number of women was large) congregated there.'[7] The strike movement in Lancashire and West Yorkshire was a movement of women.

In Preston on 12 August, a crowd including 'a very large number of women and children' began smashing windows at Dawson's Mill. Local magistrates read the Riot Act, and two strikers were shot dead in the ensuing repression.[8] A huge rally in Bradford pledged 'not to work again until the Charter was established' and two columns of demonstrators headed out to Halifax where thousands of female turnouts refused to disperse when the riot act was read and only scattered when the cavalry was brought in. Six people died during the suppression of the rioting. Strikers from Rochdale marched to Bacup and Todmorden and back to Rochdale, closing the mills that were still working: 'Girls, not more than twelve or fourteen years of age, wearing heavy clogs, went along with this party – a distance of at least twenty-one miles, without the least refreshment.'[9] This act of physical endurance was matched by women's boldness and courage in the face of state repression.

At 7 a.m. on Monday 15 August, about 5,000 strikers, including many women, began to march from Manchester to Halifax. One of the women, a 'regular Amazonian', 'harangued the meeting for a considerable time with great vehemence and earnestness'.[10] In Halifax on Tuesday 16 August, the anniversary of the Peterloo Massacre of 1819, crowds of men and women, their aprons filled with stones, ambushed the cavalry and freed strikers who had been arrested. A local paper invited readers to

> Picture the scene on Halifax-heath – the encampment of about 15,000 people on the purple heather, the women collected in groups, singing Chartist songs, and stirring up the men to rescue the prisoners! These women entered Halifax at the head of the crowd. When they reached the North-bridge, where the military were drawn up to oppose their progress, numbers of women ran forward and seized the horses' bridles to turn them aside, exclaiming to the soldiers, 'You wouldn't hurt women, would you?'[11]

Women could try and use their gender to deflect violence, but it was a risky strategy.

When crowds of strikers arrived at Birley Mill in Chorlton, southwest Manchester, they were confronted by the owners of the mill who were determined to resist the strikers' demands and keep their mill open. Elizabeth McQuin, a thirteen-year-old weaver employed at Birley's, was struck on the head when the management of the mill hurled missiles from the roof down on the mass picket below.[12] Eventually, the mill was forced to close. This victory would have been very sweet to the mill workers. Birley's Mill was owned by Sir Hugh Hornby Birley, the notorious captain of the yeomanry who many held responsible for the Peterloo Massacre of 1819. On every anniversary of the massacre, access to St Peter's Fields was blocked by the military so those wishing to remember the dead and injured gathered outside Birley Mill. On the anniversary of Peterloo on 16 August 1842, *The Northern Star* published a list of the yeomanry involved in the massacre with Birley's name at the top.

Women were involved in supporting the strike and the strike supported them to seek redress for their grievances. A meeting of operatives in Todmorden pledged to fight for a return of wages to the 1840 rate, for a ten-hour day and for women with young children to be redeployed away from heavy machinery.[13] The women strikers were prepared to target other women when they threatened to undermine the strike. When Stockport workers marched on Greg's Mill in Styal, the women burnt down the housing set aside for females still working.[14] The *Manchester Guardian* reported that of thirty-nine people arrested in Stafford, nine were women, 'all young and assuming a devil-may-care attitude'.[15] Elizabeth Taylor was charged with calling Ellen Gowan a 'knobstick', a slang word for a strike-breaker. Ellen the knobstick wisely failed to give evidence against Elizabeth, who was acquitted.[16]

By the first days of September, the strike was entering its fourth week. Starving strikers were beginning to return to work, but significant numbers of women stayed out. On Friday 2 September, the *Manchester Guardian* reported:

> In the course of the afternoon (Friday 2nd September 1842) a meeting of female operatives was held in Ashton, when a resolution was passed to the effect that 'they would neither go to work themselves, nor allow their husbands to do so, until they get their price as agreed'.

The women adopted an assertive stance in relation to their husbands. The 'ladies also had a procession in the evening; but fortunately, they did nothing except talk very largely'.[17] The women were not violent but women talking 'largely' together, free from the supervision or scrutiny of men, has always suggested the possibility of subversion and insubordination.

In early September, Manchester police officers attacked strikers waiting for their relief payments. One of the forty-four strikers arrested was Alice Kershaw, who was heard 'calling the police all sorts of names' as the police took their prisoners to the lock-up.[18] Alice was ordered to keep the peace for three months. Six women – Sarah Massey, Esther Anderson, Jane Fletcher, Jane Hannay, Dinah Yates and Ann Scott – were charged with being among a crowd of females who gathered to free the prisoners. They were all discharged.[19] In the Oxford Road area of Manchester, windows were broken at a mill belonging to Messrs George Wooley, Marsland and James. The most active assailants were women with aprons full of stones.[20] In October, a specially convened court sentenced many strikers for rioting and disturbing the peace. Among the defendants was Anne Lewis, sentenced to eight months hard labour, and Hannah Boon and 'several women' who were sentenced to two months' imprisonment with hard labour.[21]

The 1842 General Strike was one of the first and most extensive exercises of working-class power in nineteenth-century Britain. The Chartist women used economic power to propel political reform forward, and they expected political reform to open the path to economic change. The geographical spread and political focus of the strikes suggested imminent revolution to many contemporaries. These fears were reflected in the extent of the repression that followed, which was unmatched in the nineteenth century. The numbers arrested and imprisoned had no equal until the next General Strike of 1926. In the North-west alone, more than 1,500 strikers were brought to trial. Some Chartists had tried to spread, deepen and organise the movement, but others preached restraint and feared the danger of confrontation with the state. This ambivalent stance did not protect the Chartists from the wave of repression. Feargus O'Connor and fifty-eight other delegates to the Chartist National Convention went on trial at Lancaster Assizes in the notorious 'monster indictment'. They were charged with inciting riots, risings and strikes.

Establishing the full extent of female militant activism in the strike is important for understanding the broad support enjoyed by the 'turn-outs'. However visible women's role in the strike, their presence alone cannot justify a claim that the strike led to an enhanced role for women in the Chartist movement. Their acts of militancy during the strike could be dismissed as eruptions of traditional community violence which lacked any broader political understanding. There is, however, evidence that the pre-existing networks of support for women's rights were significantly strengthened by the example set by the striking women. Chartists who had previously patronised women as auxiliaries to their cause now began to see them more as comrades whose contribution was vital to the success of the movement. Demonstrating such a shift in attitudes to women in the aftermath of the 1842 strike requires an exploration of how male Chartists appealed to women with a new urgency and how women responded to those appeals.

On 10 September 1842, the Chartist Metropolitan Delegate Meeting in London issued an address. Unlike the address they published a year earlier, the 1842 address was directed exclusively at women and its tone registered a shift in attitudes towards female activism. In the autumn of 1842, when Chartism had to regroup after the defeat of the strike movement, women could provide a potential source of recruitment, of energy and of support:

> Dear sisters in bondage – we address you at this important juncture, feeling it to be a duty incumbent upon us to take the most active and vigorous steps to secure your valuable co-operation

> in the great and glorious cause of liberty whereby to emancipate ourselves and you from political and social slavery.

The authors of the address stated that it was no 'disparagement to accept, nay solicit your aid in our political struggle'. The address also appealed to women as reluctant and unhappy workers, who slaved for sixteen or twenty hours a day, for the most scanty subsistence, in 'circumstances so repugnant to your feelings that life itself becomes unbearable'.[22] Feelings were as important as long hours and low pay in this critique of working conditions.

This second appeal also struck a new note of sensitivity to the barriers women had to overcome before they could engage with Chartism. Women could feel too self-conscious and lacking in the confidence necessary to attend a public meeting alone. The address suggested that they might feel more comfortable going to meetings with their husbands, sweethearts or other relatives, but such support should not define women's access to Chartist events. The address spoke to 'those who have no relatives who are members' advising them, 'to take courage and introduce yourselves, and we can confidently assure you that you will never have cause to repent doing so, for all our acts are legal and lawful, and your attendance at our meetings so far from being inconsistent with your sex and duty, as some would make it appear, we can incontestably prove to be a duty of paramount importance'. The London Chartist leaders wanted women's support but they were also offering something in return. The address suggested that attending meetings would place women 'on a better, more equal footing with men'.[23] This implied that the leaders of London Chartism thought that women wanted greater equality and that involvement with Chartism would help them to establish that greater equality. London leaders presented a version of Chartism which appealed to women by rejecting notions of female retreat and subservience to acknowledge their role as waged workers, and to offer greater gender equality. Male Chartists renewed their efforts to engage women in response to their militant role in the strike wave and because the need for movement's renewal was urgent.

The London Female Charter Association was launched a month after this second appeal was published. This organisation was to have a dramatic effect on how female Chartism was understood by wider society in the aftermath of the strike wave. The meeting which really launched the association took place on 17 October 1842, just weeks after the strike movement was defeated. This meeting was described above, in a discussion which focused on how rapidly Susanna Inge and Mary Ann Walker caught the public imagination and how personal abuse was directed against them to intimidate them, and all other women, out of political life.

Mary Ann Walker and Susanna Inge were catapulted to prominence in the aftermath of the 1842 strikes in which women's roles had shocked and scared the Establishment. This was a moment when working-class women had asserted themselves in national political debate, but it was also the moment when opportunities for female activism were beginning to decline. Historians have argued that the masculinisation of popular politics in the 1840s was the fault of working-class men and, in particular, artisans who were either misogynistic or held to a code of chivalry which undermined women's independence.[24] Chartist enthusiasm for women's activism was encouraged and deepened by the experience of petitioning, organising insurrections and striking together. The experience of defeat and the imperative of keeping the hope of reform alive were far more important in shaping the direction of Chartism in the mid-1840s than working men's desire to put women back in their place.

The price of defeat

The defeat of the second petition and the general strike closed off the immediate possibility of radical reform and posed sharp questions about how to survive in the unreformed system. For many working people that survival depended on the care and support provided by the family. The family was under enormous pressure because of rapid industrialisation and the growth of factory production, which meant women had to work outside their homes. Women had always performed arduous tasks and worked for long hours, but their work was made both visible and incompatible with social reproduction when it moved from the home to the workplace.[25] Commentators criticised factory girls for lacking domestic skills and assumed that paid employment rendered women unfit to be wives and mothers.[26]

In the textile mills of Lancashire, large numbers of women and children were employed to replace male workers, and this prompted a public debate about the 'inversion' of gender roles. The female Chartists of Upper Honley and Smallthorne used the rhetoric of inversion in their address of 1839: 'You who have seen the order of nature inverted, the female driven to the factory labour for her offspring and her husband unwillingly idle at home, dependant [sic] alike on female and infantile labour for his own existence.'[27] The employment of women and children outside the home prompted fears of the imminent breakup of the family. Factory labour also had implications for the health and well-being of women. Rigid routines made breastfeeding and managing menstruation very difficult and harsh discipline increased the possibility of sexual harassment by overseers.

Paid employment outside the home was fundamentally incompatible with childcare. This issue overshadowed radical politics but is downplayed in histories of female Chartism.[28] This omission is more surprising given that debates about childcare were a constant theme in mid-nineteenth-century literature and aired frequently in the press and parliamentary debates. Scandals developed around the number of children poisoned by unscrupulous childminders or neglected while in the care of baby farmers or inexperienced siblings. A government report published in 1844 found that many women worked in textile mills from 5:30 a.m. until 8 p.m., with fifteen minutes for breakfast and forty-five minutes for dinner.[29] One factory inspector reported that around a third of the women working from 6 a.m. to midnight were married, and husbands brought their babies to the mills to be breastfed at the looms.[30] Childcare was dangerous. Mary and William Lovett's baby daughter, Kezia, died when she fell from a childminder's knee. The crisis of childcare formed a crucial element of the political outlook of female Chartists and was a recurrent theme in their speeches and addresses.

In 1838, the female Chartists of Newcastle described having their children with them in the factories: 'We have seen that because the husband's earnings could not support his family, the wife has been compelled to leave her home neglected and, with her infant children, work at a soul and body degrading toil.'[31] Many Chartist autobiographies described the miseries of child labour from first-hand experience. John Leatherland recalled: 'One of the most sorrowful of scenes witnessed under the sun is that of a sickly youth worn down with pain and disease on his way to a factory on a cold, dark winter's morning.'[32] The Chartist women had to find ways to defy the right of employers to exploit the labour of whole families in conditions which undermined their ability to provide adequate care. Working-class families had to support children, older people and people with physical disabilities caused by workplace injuries and unhealthy work practices. Lung problems, eyesight loss, amputations and back pain were endemic among textile workers and artisans. The defeat of the strike movement, the end of immediate hopes for parliamentary reform and higher wages, and the crisis in the family provided the context for Chartist women to turn to the land as a possible way of providing the care required by their dependents.

Escape to the country

The Chartist Land Plan involved settling families on plots of land acquired through a centralised ballot scheme. The plan promised a new life of independence and health in Chartist communities well-equipped with leisure facilities and health care. The plan has been identified as a key moment in a trajectory that led Chartism away from female activism and gender egalitarianism towards male dominance and female subordination. One historian remarked that the Land Plan was 'resolutely patriarchal' with opposition to the paid employment of women at its core.[33] But this patriarchal plan won widespread enthusiasm from Chartist women and historians generally agree with the Chartists' own assessments that women's support was crucial to the success of the scheme.[34] The Chartists aimed their Land Plan propaganda at women and women responded in large numbers. Chartist women were not simply making the best of a set of bad choices or surrendering their independence in return for freedom from the factories. They supported the Land Plan because it offered them the prospect of exercising more control over their lives and of regenerating their communities.

The idea of returning to the land was a recurrent theme within the broad currents of radical thought in the early nineteenth century. Access to land offered the possibility of addressing multiple working-class concerns, including poor sanitation, adulterated food, overcrowded housing, the rigid discipline and danger of the workplace and vulnerability to the fluctuations of the market. Most importantly, access to land was seen as a guarantee against 'hunger in a land of plenty'. The idea of returning to the land drew strength from multiple traditions, which included agrarian millenarianism and Owenite communalism, as well as nostalgia for the patriarchal, preindustrial family.

The radical agrarian tradition took organisational form within Chartism as early as 1840, when Feargus O'Connor had proposed the creation of Chartist agricultural associations.[35] This emphasis on the land was temporarily submerged beneath the great agitation for the 1842 petition, but it resurfaced with renewed power after Parliament's dismissal of that petition and the defeat of the general strike. In 1843, the National Charter Association adopted a new constitution, which pledged to provide the 'means of support for those who are desirous to locate upon the land'.[36] The NCA Convention of 1845 launched the Chartist Co-operative Land Society, which was unprecedented among other radical land schemes in scope and ambition.[37] At its height, the Land Plan attracted 70,000 weekly subscribers.[38]

The Land Plan was part of a shift away from militant confrontation towards a focus on education and personal improvement, which involved moral regeneration centred on the home.[39] This focus on personal reform could reinforce ideas of female domesticity, but it also politicised the family and afforded women a central role in social regeneration. Working-class reformers who were demoralised or frustrated by the failure of the 1842 petition could take heart from the establishment of the settlements, which offered the prospect of immediate relief and radical change. Women were attracted to the promise of a solution which saved their children from neglect and factory labour, and which could recalibrate their relationship with nature as a source of collective wealth not individual profit.

In December 1847, Feargus O'Connor issued an appeal to the women of England in which he acknowledged their activism and the influence of the wives who 'have induced their husbands to embark in our Glorious Land Plan! ... To your open and virtuous support of the Land Plan, I attribute its astounding success.'[40] Support for the Land Plan may have been seen as more respectable than petitioning and rioting, framed as it was by a sense of moral and familial improvement, but it was an alternative that could not be realised without independent working-class action. And that action could not be sustained without the active support of the women.[41] In an emotionally charged address given at O'Connorville on May Day 1847, O'Connor asked the crowd, 'Who can look upon those mothers, accustomed to being dragged by the waking light of morn from those little babes now nestling to their breasts?' At this point, O'Connor, ever the showman, was apparently so overcome that he had to sit down and weep openly. O'Connor finished his address amid loud cheers with an affirmation of domesticity, 'Let the father nourish, and the fond mother nurture, their own offspring and then we shall have a generation of FREE CHRISTIANS.'[42] O'Connor appealed to patriarchal traditions, but he also articulated women's hopes that they could find immediate release from poverty, hunger and confinement in the factory system.[43]

It is difficult to find anything but enthusiasm for the Land Plan among Chartist women, although the number of addresses published by female Chartists during these years was lower than it had been during the highpoints of 1839 and 1842. In September 1847, *The Northern Star* reported on a soirée organised by the female Chartists of Bradford in honour of Feargus O'Connor, who had just been elected as MP for Nottingham. The main address was delivered by Mrs Leek, who combined the rhetoric of domesticity with the language of radicalism, patriotism and constitutionalism. She appealed to women 'to aid and encourage their husbands, brothers, sons, fathers and all good men in their patriotic exertions to restore their lost political rights'.[44] The restoration of these rights, Leek suggested, could bring 'comfort to the cot, contentment to the wife, and plenty for all'. This could be interpreted as a downplaying of women's agency; they were only to encourage men and bring comfort to their homes. The next sentence, however, recentred female activism:

> Sisters, you who have thought politics belongs to men only, say to your husbands, 'Is there no way whereby this brand of slavery can be removed? What is the cause that in the midst of plenty there is starvation?' If the law is to blame, be up and aid in the removal of the law.

Leek called on women to 'obtain the franchise by joining the patriotic band', an ambiguous appeal which could include votes for women themselves. Leek advocated 'militant domesticity', but she expressed it within the idiom of radical constitutionalism: 'Will British women longer be the mothers of a race of slaves, will they remain passive spectators, while governments fritter away the rights and privileges their forefathers bled for?'[45] Women were reproducing both children and the social slavery that ensnared them, and they had to take collective action to break the cycle. Leek generalised from domestic preoccupations to the evils of factory production, the 'tender mercies of the poor law skilly commission' and calamitous 'class legislation'. Leek also spoke of the 'degeneration of the operatives' who sat back and allowed their historic rights to be stolen from them. They needed to fight for the Charter not just to reclaim their political rights, but to restore their pride and self-respect.

At the end of her speech, she declared: 'Let the Charter, the Land and the Cottage be our rallying cry.'[46] The cottage could be an idealised symbol of female retreat, but it could also be seen as one of the only available means by which women could establish control over their lives, and create an alternative to unhealthy, overcrowded and unsanitary urban living. For many working women the shortage of and adulteration of food and industrial pollution created a shared sense of a political ecology. The private ownership of the land was seen as unnatural, as were methods of production which led to the destruction of resources and artificial shortages of natural resources such as clean air and water. The land was a source of natural abundance, but that plenty was denied by those seeking to profit from the hunger of others by taxation and rent. Within the intellectual culture of Chartism, moral improvement was dependent on physical improvement and moral and physical health were inextricably linked, and both depended on finding more natural ways of living.[47] Leek's address succinctly expressed some of the complex themes of later female Chartist rhetoric, which both acknowledged and resisted attempts to marginalise women's voices within the veneration of cottage and the land, and raised demands for greater female independence. A closer look at the women who subscribed to the Land Plan supports this analysis.

Nottingham was a centre of female support for the Land Plan. The city was also home to a radical tradition of female organisation. In 1834, labouring women organised the Nottingham Female Political Union (NFPU) of women trade unionists to protest the treatment of the Tolpuddle Martyrs. They sent a petition to Parliament signed by some 2,200 women.[48] Mary Savage and the NFPU were in the Physical-Force camp of Chartism. They were also assertive in the national structures of the movement. In the spring of 1843, the women of Nottingham nominated seven of their members to represent the town on the General Council of the National Charter Association. The women delegated were Mrs Francis Wright, Martha Sweet, Caroline Blatherwick, Mary Ann Ellis, Jane Abbott and Mary Ann Abbott.[49] It is not clear if the women were able to attend National Association meetings, but the list of nominees was sufficiently serious to be published in *The Northern Star*. The NFPU mobilised women to carry out exclusive dealing, a tactic widely used to support Feargus O'Connor's successful election campaign in Nottingham in 1847.[50] Women in Nottingham were employed in the lacemaking industry, where they tended to be relatively independent of male relatives but endured terrible conditions. They were not dependent on male relatives, but they were dependent on male and female 'middlemen', and their work was insecure. They worked at home in damp, humid rooms and had their eyesight and fingers ruined. Both political traditions and work patterns generated female support for the escape and independence offered by the Land Plan.[51]

Matthew Roberts has identified 142 of the 243 women enrolled as shareholders of the Land Plan from Nottingham. They were overwhelmingly working class and more likely to have jobs than samples from elsewhere.[52] More women from Nottingham worked in textile industries and clothing trades than elsewhere, and more were recorded as heads of their households. Fewer women in Nottingham had children than in other studies. Only 16 percent of Nottingham's female subscribers had male relatives who were also members of the Land Plan.[53] This suggests that women did not enrol simply to support their husbands. In Nottingham, the plan engaged the support of women who wanted the independence and freedom from sweatshop conditions and the better health offered by ownership of land. The Land Plan ultimately failed, with only 250 of the 42,000 shareholders settled in any of the communities before the plan was wound up by Act of Parliament in 1851.[54] It was a victim of its own popularity and could not supply enough plots of land to meet the expectations of its many shareholders.

Inhabiting a female body in the conditions imposed by urbanisation and industrialisation, and organising childcare around factory work, meant a constant struggle. Working women looked to the Land Plan as a tangible and achievable way to create alternatives to the factory system for themselves and their children, alternatives which offered freedom, autonomy and the prospect of living harmoniously with nature. The Chartist Land Plan contained elements of nostalgia for a more 'natural' pre-capitalist, patriarchal society, but it was less a reassertion of male control and more an attempt to construct an achievable alternative to destructive capitalist methods of production. The

Chartist movement was not a conduit through which middle-class ideas of domesticity deprived women of any effective means of exerting any influence over the forces shaping their lives.[55] Middle-class and evangelical ideas of women's natural domestic role could chime with working-class women's desire to escape the factory, but they did not overwhelm working women's belief that their labour was vital to their families, communities and class, or their confidence that they could play an indispensable role in the success of Chartism and the moral regeneration of society. Many Chartist women responded to the difficult political situation of 1846 and 1847 by seeking a new life in the Chartist communities. Others used different strategies to sustain and influence the movement and to popularise its democratic core values.

The 'Red-Hot Radical' Eliza Cook

Eliza Cook was by far the most popular female writer associated with Chartism.[1] Cook was the youngest of eleven children born to a brass worker in Southwark. She was encouraged to educate herself by her mother and published her first poems when she was seventeen years old. By 1845, a reviewer in the *London Journal* described how Cook, 'was as well-known wherever English language is spoken, as that of any poet or poetess whose lubrications have enriched our national literature'.[2] At the peak of her popularity between 1830 and 1860, Cook was a household name in both England and America. *Eliza Cook's Journal* was published from 1849–54. It was the first British journal named after a woman and it reached a circulation of 50,000–60,000 copies a week in 1849, surpassing Charles Dickens' *Household Words*.[3] Cook became an important figure in the internationalist and education-focused London milieu comprised of Chartists and Unitarians. She publicly backed the Kentish Town library when it opened its doors to women.[4] *The Northern Star* reported that Eliza Cook and her partner, Charlotte Cushman, contributed to a fund-raising appeal for the Italian republic in the summer of 1849.[5]

Cook was deeply concerned with both representing and being accessible to 'The People'. Her poems frequently reinforced the idea that England's wealth depended not on landowners and industrialists but on labour.[6] Her 'Songs of Labour' expressed a radical vision of a democratic England which fused her belief in the dignity of labour, whether performed by women or men, with the advocacy of workers 'levelling up' through education and cultural pursuits. Her poems were published regularly in *The Northern Star* from 1839 through to the end of the 1840s.[7] In 1844, the editor of the *Star* joked that a Chartist poet, James Cowen, was in love with Cook because his poetic tribute to her was so appreciative.[8] Her relationship with the organised Chartist movement was not based exclusively on the reproduction of her poems. She led a campaign to erect a memorial to the Chartist poet Thomas Hood and she took part in debates about how to maximise the influence of democratic ideas.[9]

In 1847, Eliza had a public argument with the irascible Feargus O'Connor when she supported a rival candidate for the Nottingham constituency in the general election. O'Connor wrote to *The Northern Star* calling Cook an 'amphibious thing spitting venom' at his campaign, in a barely veiled reference to her lesbianism.[10] Undaunted by O'Connor's hostility, Cook continued to try to influence the direction of Chartism. Her poem, 'A Song: To the People of England', was written to both celebrate and intervene in the Chartist resurgence of 1848. In the poem, Cook calls on the Chartists to be determined but responsible revolutionaries:

> Show that you have sense and feeling,
> Fit to gain and guard your place;
> Let your own determined dealing
> Meet Oppression, face to face!
> Not with weapons red and reeking;
> Not with Anarchy's wild flame;
> But with love and open speaking,
> In 'The People's' mighty name!

Cook's 'A Song for The Workers' was written to commemorate the movement for shorter working hours. Cook gives poetic expression to the idea of 'property in skill' expounded by the Chartists. Cook extends the idea to include the labour of women, which poses an alternative to the rhetoric frequently used to describe women's labour in terms of degradation and the inversion of nature:

Though her hand grows hard with duty,
Filling up the common Fate;
Let fair Woman's cheek of beauty
Never blush to own its state.
Let fond Woman's heart of feeling
Never be ashamed to spread
Industry and honest dealing,
As a barter for her bread.

Cook personally subverted conventions which governed female appearance and sexuality.[11] She cut her hair short and styled it like a man, and she dressed in masculine clothes and lived with her lover, the actor Charlotte Cushman, for many years. During her editorship of her journal, Cook became more open about her relationship with Cushman:

> We were good, earnest friends at first, and now
> Where is the hand by which could be unbound
> The mingled threads of Feeling's fairest hues,
> That hold us captive in Affection's thrall?[12]

During the radical years of the 1840s, Cook could combine literary success with open support for working-class activism and heterodox sexuality. As the high point of Chartism receded after 1848, Cook's public persona and her poetry became subject to intense scrutiny. In 1852, reviewer John Dix published two scathing portraits of Cook, noting that her poetry was 'highly popular amongst a certain class of readers, who do not care for "high art" in poetry, but are content to have commonplace subjects dished up for their not over fastidious palates, in pretty smooth rhyme'.[13] His second profile attacked her in a more personal way, describing her as a 'hybrid-looking individual', who 'looked essentially mannish, and but for an amplitude of petticoat' could be taken for 'one of the Lords of Creation'.[14] These attacks took place in the context of a decline in working-class radicalism. Her last volume of poetry was published in 1864.

Cook fell out of favour with the public and literary historians have done little to restore her reputation. This radical, gay, female poet of the people was dismissed as a purveyor of risible Victorian sentimentality. The eclipsing of Cook's reputation suggests that Chartism and associated radical networks created a space for heterodox women to achieve literary success, a space which disappeared when the movement receded. *The Northern Star* helped to cement Cook's popularity among workers and found an independent voice within the Chartist movement, but, when Chartism went into retreat, she lost that platform. Cook has not been included in any studies of Chartist poetry so the implications of her popularity among Chartists have been overlooked.[15] The prominence of her writing in Chartist publications helps to challenge the idea that the movement reinforced conventional attitudes towards gender.

5

Revolution, 1848: 'Breaking the Chains of Women'

As the new year of 1848 dawned, just four families – the Hanovers, Habsburgs, Bourbons and Romanoffs – ruled over millions of Europeans of diverse nationalities. In January 1848, a succession of huge, spontaneous revolts cascaded across Europe from a starting point in Sicily. Within a month the French monarchy had been toppled and revolutions had broken out in south-west Germany, Bavaria, Berlin, Vienna, Hungary and Milan. Women's militancy in the 1848 revolts continued the traditions of rioting and community mobilisation established during the eighteenth century. In 1848, however, women also began to join and create new political formations and demand that the female franchise be incorporated into the newly established democratic structures. Malwida von Meysenbug was in Frankfurt when she watched newly elected delegates gathering to draw up a democratic constitution. She later observed: 'The thought of bringing about woman's full freedom for intellectual development, economic independence and all civil rights was in the process of becoming a reality; this thought could never again die out.'[1]

By May and June, initial euphoria and popular unity against the old order were being eroded by latent political and social divisions between middle-class democrats, who wanted only constitutional reform, and socialists and radicals, who demanded more fundamental social and economic change. These tensions erupted into open conflict, which culminated in the June Days in Paris when about 3,000 insurgents were killed, including at least 300 women, and thousands more were arrested. By the autumn of 1848, counterrevolutions had taken place in Berlin, Prague, the Kingdom of Naples and Vienna. New uprisings in the southern German states and in Rome were quickly crushed. The democratic revolts were extinguished by military force but not before women had inserted themselves into the political sphere.

The female activists of 1848 drew on pre-existing international networks which connected radical women through printed material, political organisations and personal contact. Jeanne Deroin's *An Appeal to Women* was published in France in 1832. It was translated into English by the Anglo-Irish Owenite and writer Anna Wheeler and published in Robert Owen's paper *The Crisis* in 1833.[2] Desirée Gay, a French seamstress and utopian socialist, lived in England in the 1830s where she met Robert Owen and Anna Wheeler. She went on to play a significant role in the revolution in Paris in 1848.[3] Ernestine Rose, a Polish Jewish woman, arrived in England in 1830 and cooperated with Robert Owen to establish his Association of All Classes of All Nations. She then travelled to America where she became a founding figure in the American women's movement. Two decades later, in 1852, *The Northern Star* celebrated the support Rose gave to the Hungarian nationalist Lajos Kossuth when she enabled him to address fifty meetings in New York on the fight for 'liberty and freedom'.[4] Female socialists created transnational networks of organisational and personal connections which continued for decades. The early socialists of Britain, France and the US shared a belief that the progress of the socialist cause depended on the involvement of women. These ideas permeated London radical circles and shaped the outlook of many who went on to create the theoretical and organisational foundations of the Chartist movement.[5]

Springtime of the women

Historians from a range of political traditions have characterised the revolutions of 1848 as a missed opportunity to set Europe on a democratic, constitutional path, a turning point during which history failed to turn.[6] For Marxist historian Eric Hobsbawm, a writer generally sympathetic to the potential for revolutionary social change, the revolutions 'failed, universally, rapidly and – though this was not realised for several years by the political refugees – definitively'.[7] More recently, Christopher Clark has identified 1848 as a historical moment when political ideas fused or fragmented and produced showers of new entities whose trails can be traced through the decades that followed.[8] This chapter will investigate one component of this ferment of ideas: the emergence of women, not only as members of the insurgent crowd, but as actors in the political sphere.

Historians have attributed the failure of 1848 to the impatience of the revolutionaries who challenged emerging democracies to address economic demands before they had the opportunity to establish themselves, thus making them vulnerable to resurgent monarchies. Exploring the stance adopted by radical women in 1848 contests this narrative by demonstrating the indivisibility of political and social demands. Working-class women could not enjoy political liberty or freedom without a transformation of family structures and the redistribution of wealth. Mothers without means to feed their families were hardly able to participate in public life as citizens of a new republic.

Large numbers of women participated in the uprisings in multiple ways – as democrats, nationalists, socialists and feminists – and they did so despite their exclusion from the new liberal political manifestos and elected legislatures. Mike Rapport has argued that persistently misogynistic attitudes towards women constituted a serious limitation to the 'Springtime of the Peoples', which did little to emancipate women and failed to grant them the vote anywhere in Europe.[9] Rapport is right to point to the deeply embedded conservative ideas about women's role in society which prevailed across Europe. He underestimates, however, the extent to which women's courageous and energetic activities within nationalist and democratic movements began to undermine those ideas.

Exploring the events of 1848 presents a challenge to a long-established consensus among historians that the decline of female Chartism after 1839 was an 'incontrovertible' fact.[10] A small number of scholars have pointed to the female Chartist associations (FCAs) which continued to exist and the continued relevance of exclusive dealings which involved women.[11] Elizabeth Neesom's LFDA, for example, was still in existence in 1848 with a new secretary, Charlotte Rees, a female chairman [sic] and a claimed membership of some 1,500.[12] Matthew Roberts has recently discovered the existence of previously unrecorded FCAs, one third of which existed during the period of late Chartism. There was a marked upsurge in female societies in 1848–9 when twenty-five separate FCAs were recorded and more were probably in existence.[13] In June 1848, *The Northern Star* reported on a meeting of the female Chartists in Leicester, which attracted an audience of about 4,000. The meeting was chaired by Mrs Cully and resolved to set up a female Chartist association. It also resolved to establish a defence fund for procuring justice for the victims of violence by special constables who had been on a rampage against the town's unemployed, beating people and dragging women from their beds.[14] The meeting was addressed by Mrs White and Mrs Simpson, who told the crowd how she had been sacked from her job because of her Chartist sympathies.[15] This meeting suggests that large numbers of women were engaging with Chartism as late as the summer of 1848.

The existence of the FCAs was an important measure of female activism, but it is not the only one. Women were allowed to join the National Charter Association in the early 1840s and this opening up of membership to women could explain any decline in the number of FCAs.[16] In an address to Feargus O'Connor published in May 1842, the male and female Chartists of Birmingham referred to themselves as 'male and female members of the National Charter Association resident in the borough of Birmingham', an area with a strong tradition of female organisation.[17] The National Charter Association may have offered women a louder voice in the national movement than local women's organisations. The number of separate women's organisations may have shrunk not because women were in retreat but because they were playing an increasingly assertive role in the National Chartist Association.

Women, refugees and London Chartism

By 1848, London was the organisational and political centre of Chartism. The National Charter Association and *The Northern Star* had both moved south from Leeds to London. London was also the destination of thousands of political exiles as Belgium, France and Switzerland all became more hostile to refugees by the late 1840s.[18] Internationalism was deeply ingrained in London Chartism and connections between refugees and Chartism were readily established in London's radical spaces and communities. The nationalist revolutionary Giuseppe Mazzini ran a school for poor Italian boys situated opposite William Lovett's coffee shop, a proximity which led to a strong friendship between the two men.[19] Many French socialist exiles brought with them a strong commitment to women's rights. The French utopian socialist Étienne Cabet lived in London from 1834 to 1839 and associated with Robert Owen. Cabet's most influential and popular novel, *The Voyage to Icaria*, had a strong feminist component expressed through ideas of women's participation in the democratic structures of the future. The book was translated into English and published by the Chartist Henry Hetherington.[20]

Internationalism provided a cohesive political and organisational current within London's radical circles, but it was by no means the only preoccupation of the capital's activists. One historian has described the political culture associated with London radicalism in the late 1840s as

> dotted with lectures and classes involving such men as Holyoake, Cooper, Barmby, Lovett, Hetherington, Fox, Howitt, the radical M.P. Bowring, Mazzini, Linton, all sharing in a common Enlightenment rationalism and humanitarianism and international causes, often promoting medical and religious reform, feminism, vegetarianism, and the rejection of cruelty.[21]

This description captures the breadth of concerns shared by radicals, but by focusing exclusively on public speaking it excludes the women who were also present in these circles but did not lecture in public; women such as Eliza Cook, Mary Howitt and Eliza Meteyard. Chartist and Owenite Catherine Barmby contributed articles to the Owenite press and was prominent in the Communist Church. Sophia Dobson Collet was a member of Fox's congregation and contributed feminist articles to Holyoake's *The Reasoner*. The only women in this milieu who addressed public meetings were Chartist women such as Elizabeth Neesom and Miss Simmonds in Bethnal Green.[22] Chartism provided women with access to a public platform, which was extremely rare even in radical circles.

Internationalism was most closely associated with the more left-wing Chartists, such as George Julian Harney and Ernest Jones. Harney became the leader of the London Democratic Association and editor of *The Northern Star* in late 1845. In September that year, he launched the Fraternal Democrats which became one of the most important multinational organisations in radical London. Harney appealed to European exiles and Chartists of both genders to engage with radical politics. On 11 March 1848, he published Robert Owen's address to the 'Men and Women of France' in *The Northern Star* in which Owen advocated 'local self-government' by divisions of both men and women.[23] By publishing this address, Harney positioned *The Northern Star* within an international debate about the legitimacy of female legislators at a point when French socialist Pauline Roland tried to claim her right to vote in a mayoral election and Jeanne Deroin put herself forward as a candidate for the Legislative Assembly.[24]

The internationalist currents within London's radical networks were transformed by the arrival of waves of political refugees from Europe throughout the 1830s and 1840s. Only a small minority of these exiles were women and only a small number of these women became prominent within Chartist circles. One of the few who did was Marta Schell Viettinghoff. Viettinghoff and her husband, Jan, had fought on the barricades during the battle for Warsaw in the winter of 1830–1. Forced into exile, the couple arrived in London in 1836 and immersed themselves in London's radical politics. They joined the East London Democratic Association in the spring of 1837, just a few weeks after it was formed, attracted by the association's militant stance and commitment to working-class independence. A year later, the organisation re-established itself as the London Democratic Association (LDA). The LDA offered radical Londoners a militant alternative to William Lovett's London Working Men's Association, which favoured alliances with middle-class sympathisers.[25] This stance helped the LDA grow into the largest and most militant Chartist organisation in the capital. *The London Democrat* and *The Operative* were both London-based newspapers closely associated with the LDA. Under the leadership of Julian Harney, the LDA developed a close relationship with European revolutionaries. Veterans of Poland's 1830–1 revolution against reviled Russian domination were afforded great respect in the LDA. Jan Viettinghoff and Major Beniowski, a military leader and advocate of armed insurrection, spoke at large events held to commemorate the tenth anniversary of the Warsaw Uprising in 1841.

Marta Viettinghoff developed her public profile by writing letters to Chartist newspapers. In one letter published in *The Operative,* Viettinghoff defended Major Beniowski's right to receive a government pension awarded to Polish exiles which the prime minister, Lord John Russell, had withdrawn. Viettinghoff criticised the 'blasphemous alliance' between the 'miserable government of England' and the 'Russian Dukes'. This letter is significant for two reasons. Marta Viettinghoff did not apologise for, or attempt to justify, her intrusion in public affairs. She assumed her right to comment on politics and politicians, and on national and international affairs. Secondly, she signed her letter, 'Martha Schell-Viettinghoff, Member of the London Democratic Association, 51 Clarendon Square, Somers-town, June 12, 1839'.[26] This signature suggests that she was presenting herself not as an individual but as a member of a political party or even as a representative of the LDA.

Another of Marta's letters demonstrated why she attracted hostility for her 'loud espousal of Jacobinism'.[27] In May 1839, she wrote to the *London Democrat* to encourage support for Physical Force Chartism and revolutionary violence:

> If the cities of my ill-fated country – preserved in safety by the traitors, for the shelter of the enemies, had been burned or destroyed by the revolutionary movement, they would quickly have been rebuilt by the unfettered hands of a free and happy people.

This letter was not just rhetoric. It was published at the height of the agitation for the first national petition. Marta emphasised her revolutionary credentials by signing her letter, 'Yes, hail spirit of Robespierre and Marat.'[28] The LDA afforded Marta a platform in London's Chartist press, which she used to polemicise against the government and to advocate for insurrectionary violence.

It seems likely that Marta was the breadwinner in the family, although this was less a statement of female independence than an enforced necessity. In October 1837, she was employed on railway construction around King's Cross and complained that her husband's 'idleness imposed upon me the necessity of very hard labour'.[29] The marital tensions caused by Jan Viettinghoff's lack of interest in work deepened. By September 1840, Marta was complaining to friends that her husband was a 'tirant' [sic] and she eventually left him, taking their son to live in France in 1848, when she disappeared from public view. Although few women played such a prominent role in mixed-sex Chartist organisations, Marta's position within London Chartism suggests that male Chartists were open to women with political experience playing a prominent role.

Following the defeat of the European revolutions, London's international communities grew in size and influence. The largest number of political refugees came from Germany and France, and each national group brought with it its own distinct attitude towards and experience of female activism. The influence of German refugees Karl Marx and Friedrich Engels over the radical wing of Chartism has been well-documented. Engels and Julian Harney became friends in 1843, and they remained friends for fifty-two years. Engels lived with working-class Irish radical Mary Burns and, following her death, with her sister, Lizzie, an Irish nationalist. Harney was one of many radicals to recognise their relationship and accord it the status of a marriage. Marx began his friendship with the Chartist Ernest Jones in 1850 when Jones was released from a two-year sentence. Jones was born in Berlin and had grown up there and could converse freely with Marx in German. Marx called Jones 'the most talented, consistent and energetic representative of Chartism' and offered himself as a contributor when Jones launched a weekly paper, *Notes to the People*, in May 1851.[30] The influence exerted by a third member of the Marx circle – Karl's wife, Jenny Marx – has been overlooked by historians who have tended to emphasise her domestic miseries.

The Marx family were living in Belgium in early March 1848 when *The Northern Star* reported from that country that great excitement had greeted news of the February revolution in Paris. The *Star* also noted the 'uncompromising' attitude of German democrats exiled in the city. Karl Marx was ordered to leave Brussels and then arrested at his home. Jenny Marx was also arrested, forced to leave her three young children at home with a servant and put in a prison cell with what the paper described as 'the lowest order of prostitute'.[31] Jenny Marx was indicted for 'vagabondage' because she failed to produce her passport when stopped by police. The report in *The Northern Star* may have emphasised the degradation of Jenny Marx's cellmates to excite maximum sympathy for her situation but the idea of respectable womanhood contrasted with degraded sex workers in the report sits uneasily with the paper's generally sympathetic approach to women forced into sex work.

From Belgium, the Marxes fled to Republican Paris. In the summer, they headed for Cologne to take part in an uprising in the city, but they were expelled when the uprising was defeated. They moved back to Paris, but by then the city was in the grip of a counterrevolution and, in August 1849, Marx was told to leave. He sailed to England and, two weeks later, a heavily pregnant Jenny, Helene Demuth, the Marx family servant and friend, and their three young children set off to join him. Marx was too ill to meet them at the dock. He sent a German friend, Georg Weerth, to escort them to their new home in a boarding house in the German community of Leicester Square. Weerth was an exiled German radical and poet, and a prominent figure within

Julian Harney's Fraternal Democrats.[32] He was mentioned frequently in the Chartist press as a friend of Chartism and the English working classes.[33] Weerth provided one of the first connections between Jenny and London Chartism.

Jenny was both a witness to and a participant in the great stream of political refugees who swept into London, and she attempted to earn a living and create new organisations. Jenny described in her memoirs the dual nature of émigré life in London, which involved both a constant struggle to survive and a perpetual forming and fracturing of new political organisations:

> Thousands of fugitives arrived daily; they were all more or less in dire straits, few had any means, all were dependent on others and in need of help. Emigrant committees were organised to assist the emigres, meetings were arranged, appeals made, programs drawn up, and great demonstrations were prepared. In all the emigrant circles dissensions broke out. The various parties gradually split up completely.[34]

Jenny acted as secretary to an organisation established to aid refugees, led by Marx, Weerth and Heinrich Bauer.[35] She also contributed to the frustrating work of creating new political networks. She sent copies of the radical paper Marx edited to Engels, asking him to forward copies to Helen Macfarlane, who will be discussed. Jenny Marx was deeply engaged in the sociability which was a key aspect of both reforming culture and life as a refugee. When the Marx family moved from Soho to the relative peace of Hampstead Heath, she wrote:

> I missed my long walks in the crowded West End streets after my meetings, our clubs and the familiar public houses with the cosy conversations which had so often helped me to forget my worries for a while. Luckily, I still had to copy out an article for *The Tribune* twice a week, and that helped to keep me *au courant* with world events.[36]

Jenny's political engagement was circumscribed by the demands of her young children, and her difficulties were intensified by poverty and ill health. She was, however, an active participant in the political and social life of London Chartism. The German activists accepted women's right to organise, to write and to engage in radical political movements, but any distinctly feminist perspective was marginal among German refugees. The situation was different in the Parisian heart of the 1848 revolt.

France: A theatre of female revolt

Popular reaction to the news of the revolution in Paris in February 1848 was extraordinarily enthusiastic, especially in London.[37] The Chartists sent a delegation to Paris to greet the provisional government and issued a public address 'To the Men and Women of France'.[38] The euphoria did not last. Following the second uprising against the new government in June, thousands of French radicals began to flee from Paris. About 5,000 French refugees arrived in London in the winter of 1851–2, when Louis Bonaparte overthrew the Second Republic.[39] One of these exiles was the utopian socialist Jeanne Deroin, who was a source of political inspiration to Chartist women. Deroin was born in Paris in 1805. She was a seamstress when she became involved in the early socialist movement. She qualified as a schoolteacher in 1834 while bringing up her three children – one of whom was severely disabled – and coping with an alcoholic husband. Pauline Roland moved to Paris and shared in Deroin's socialist feminist publishing and organising projects. During the insurgency in Paris in the spring of 1848, Roland and Deroin participated in radical clubs and contributed to the burgeoning radical press, which included publications such as Eugénie Niboyet's *The Voice of Women* and Desirée Gay's paper *The Politics of Women*, which was orientated towards working-class women.[40]

The newly elected National Assembly initially supported workers' organisations and the right to work and was responsive to women's demands for work and for nationalised restaurants and laundries, in which Desirée Gay and Pauline Roland were prominent.[41] Roland was a historian and writer who had lived for twelve years in a free union with her partner, the painter Jean Aicard. She campaigned for both women's and workers' rights by helping to establish a trade union for women teachers and playing a key role in convening the Union of Workers' Associations.

The political advances spearheaded by these women were reversed during March and April. A petition for the female franchise was overwhelmingly rejected by the newly elected legislative assembly. Women were then excluded from the national workshop organisation and Desirée Gay lost her position. In May 1849, Jeanne Deroin attempted to stand as a candidate in elections for the national legislature. In her election address, Deroin linked the question of gender with that of class, a connection which would have resonated with Chartist feminists: 'A legislative assembly entirely composed of men is no more qualified to legislate for all than would be an assembly of the privileged to decide on matters concerning working people.'[42] Deroin failed in her bid to be elected to the assembly, but in October 1849, Deroin and Roland were elected to the leadership of another organisation, the Fraternal Association of Democratic Socialists of Both Sexes. In April 1850, their offices were raided and forty-nine people, including Jeanne Deroin, Pauline Roland and five other women were arrested.

Deroin and Roland were imprisoned for conspiracy and sedition. In May 1851, Jeanne and Pauline were sharing a cell in Paris's Saint-Lazare Prison. They found the opportunity to issue what was, under the circumstances, an extraordinarily courageous appeal from their cell. Deroin and Roland voiced their concern that the 1848 revolution was sidelining women, that 'the storm which is overthrowing the throne and the scaffold, breaking the chains of the black slave, had forgotten to break the chains of women'.[43] Deroin and Roland publicly restated their belief that unity between working-class men and women was a precondition for winning both women's rights and wider social reform:

> Your socialist sisters of France are united with you in the vindication of the right of women to civil and political equality.

> We have moreover, the profound conviction that only by the power of association based on solidarity and by the union of the working-classes of both sexes to organise labour can be acquired, completely and pacifically, the civil and political equality of women and the social right of all.[44]

The women were in prison, facing trial and custodial sentences, but they never stopped trying to influence other women to join the movement for equality and for socialism.

The activities of the French socialist women were known to English radicals, through personal relationships and reports in the British press.[45] In November 1848, a Welsh newspaper reported that Desirée Gay, an 'authoress of some repute', had addressed a banquet for 'Lady Socialists' which attracted some 1,200 women.[46] British newspapers circulated reports of Deroin's decision to stand for the Constituent Assembly in April 1849.[47] *The Northern Star* published Deroin and Rolands' appeal and other articles about the French women were published in the *Reynolds's Weekly Newspaper*, which was edited by George W. M. Reynolds, a major figure in the later Chartist movement.[48] Deroin and Roland could simultaneously activate and stimulate the creation of new international networks of female solidarity. These networks were not, however, powerful enough to protect the women. Roland was sentenced to transportation to a French penal colony in Algeria and died on her way back to France to be reunited with her children in December 1852. Deroin was sent to prison for two years and when she was released, fearing rearrest, she fled to London with her three children. Settled in West London, she and her daughter ran a school for the children of French refugees. Deroin joined the International Working Men's Association and later the Socialist League, alongside William Morris and Eleanor Marx.[49]

Deroin and Roland were among the most visible of the female political activists who rose to prominence in the European insurgencies of 1848, but they were far from being the only women to assume a public role. The multiple examples set by female democrats and socialists were celebrated by other women and deployed as symbols of heroic nationalism and reform agitation.

To radicals, women such as Deroin and Roland were examples to be applauded and emulated. To reactionaries, they were a warning of the social chaos which could erupt if working-class women were allowed to meddle with politics. Female involvement in insurgent movements, military confrontations and radical journalism during the European revolutions of 1848 prompted a public debate on women's political rights.

Politics and poverty: Mary Ann and William Cuffay

Radical London was shaped by the exiles from Europe and Ireland, and by the city's historical role as the nexus of the transatlantic slave trade. London's radical circles included black activists such as Catherine Despard, the Jamaican-born wife of Irish revolutionary Edward Despard, the tailor and publisher Robert Wedderburn and Cato Street conspirator William Davidson. In the 1830s, William Cuffay, the son of an enslaved man from the island of Saint Kitts, won a following among London radicals through his involvement in solidarity actions with the Tolpuddle Martyrs and a large strike of London's tailors in 1834. These experiences led him to embrace Chartism and he became a leading figure among London Chartists. Cuffay was one of the organisers of the Chartist rally at Kennington on 10 April 1848, convened to mark the presentation of the third national petition to Parliament. When the Chartists found their routes to Parliament blocked by the police, Cuffay spoke passionately against O'Connor's plea to the crowd to disperse peacefully. The crowd did disperse and, despite some continued resistance waged by Chartists, this marked the last high point of the Chartist movement.

Cuffay's enthusiasm for Chartism was shared by his wife, Mary Ann, a hatmaker who married Cuffay in 1827 and settled with him in the working-class district of Lambeth in South London. Cuffay was black and disabled, and a particular target of the mainstream media. Mary Ann was more representative of most Chartist women than Mary Ann Walker or Susanna Inge because records of her life only exist because she was married to a famous male Chartist. Mary Ann Cuffay's experiences reveal many aspects of the difficulties working-class women had when negotiating a public presence. We know little of Mary Ann's activities before her marriage, and after her marriage she was seen exclusively through the eyes of others.

In November 1842, *The Northern Star* reported that Mrs Cuffay had received a round of applause in acknowledgement of her hard work raising money for Chartist prisoners.[50] In the spring of 1848, Mary Ann was seen making bullets out of old printers' type alongside her husband. Cuffay was betrayed by a government spy, arrested, charged with preparing an armed insurrection and sentenced to twenty-one years penal transportation. *The Times* reported: 'Mrs Cuffay was among the crowd in the body of the court during part of the examination but having ventured to express her views of the proceedings in too audible terms, she had to be put out by an officer.'[51] There is some evidence that Mary Ann Cuffay did have a reputation as an orator and supporter of women's rights. In March 1853, five months after she left England to join her husband in Tasmania, the *Morning Post* commented:

> Mrs Cuffey [sic] and other female orators on this and the other side of the Atlantic have enlightened us as to what ought to be the rights of women, we are afraid that as to what their rights *are*, they have been left in a safely benighted state.[52]

I can find no archival evidence that Mary Ann addressed public meetings. This may have been lost, or the *Post*'s comment may have been an expression of the close connections between female Chartism and the public advocacy of women's rights in the public imagination.

Mary Ann Cuffay's presence in the mainstream and radical press demonstrated how permeable the boundaries between the home and the political arena could become. In a speech to the Chartist Convention in April 1848, Cuffay described how his own lack of work meant that Mary Ann had to go out charring. When her employer discovered her identity, she was dismissed. Cuffay's speech drew attention from mainstream reporters who were titillated by his public admission of poverty and wifely employment.[53] The *Birmingham Journal* exploited the comic possibilities of Cuffay's revelation:

> He being short of work, Mrs Cuffay went out to do a little washing, but on hearing what a terrible revolutionist her husband was, her employers banished her from the suds, and packed her off in a lather of indignation to the frothing Cuffay who now had double reason to cry, 'Down with the upper classes, and no aristocratic soap'.[54]

Press reports of Cuffay's speech projected Mary Ann into the public gaze as a comic figure to be mocked. When describing a new portrait of the Prince of Wales, one reviewer commented on the Prince's 'white unwhisperables as spotless as if Mrs Cuffay herself had an extra half pound of brown Windsor [soap] to them'.[55]

The Cuffays' predicament attracted scrutiny because it brought into the public gaze an uncomfortable contradiction between ideas of female respectability and domesticity and the female labourers and servants who performed the intimate duties on which the upper- and middle-class domestic comfort depended. In 1850, the satirical *Punch* magazine suggested charwomen were 'the lowest trade of domestic – even lower than the maid of all work'. Charwomen were employed for short-term work and so were always an outsider compared to the other servants and were rarely able to complete all the tasks the mistress demanded of them. As *Punch* pointed out, 'She slaves, but never gives satisfaction. She is expected to do the work of six days in one. She pleases no-one.' Charwomen such as Mary Ann Cuffay were privy to the uncomfortable truth that, behind the perfume, lace, satin and silk, the bodies of the rich exuded the same smells and stains as the bodies of the poor. Or, as *Punch* put it, 'as you sit in the parlour, there she is accumulating evidence against you under your very feet.'[56]

When William Cuffay was deported, Mary Ann Cuffay spent three years in poverty campaigning for the funds to join her husband in Tasmania and actively fundraising for all the

Chartist prisoners' families. *The Northern Star* reported that at one auction, Mrs Cuffay donated two maps and a painting of Chartist lecturer Mary Ann Walker to the cause. Her ownership of this portrait suggests that she identified with a tradition of Chartist female activism. Donations from other supporters included political books and domestic items, including a pair of scissors, a pair of braces, a silk waistcoat and children's books and pocketbooks.[57] The public auctioning of these intimate, personal items to support Chartist prisoners, points again to the permeability of the divide between the domestic and the political worlds.

In 1851, Mary Ann Cuffay was forced to enter the Chatham workhouse where she had to surrender her domestic privacy entirely. For Mary Ann, the threat of the hated 'Poor Law Bastilles', so common in radical rhetoric, was a lived experience. In November 1852, *Reynolds's Newspaper* reported that Mary Ann had finally been granted government assistance to join her husband, and she made the long and arduous journey alone, arriving in Hobart in April 1853.[58] Mary Ann Cuffay was subjected to intense public scrutiny. Her domestic life was disrupted by poverty and by judicial processes. Like many working-class women, Mary Ann found within Chartism the means to campaign against a political, economic and judicial system which confined her to menial labour and economic vulnerability.

The 'Women's Charter'

In the summer of 1848 *Punch*, which had so mercilessly satirised the female Chartists in 1842, mocked what they understood to be a new women's rights movement. The magazine published its own Women's Charter, a title which reflected the way in which female political ambitions were associated with the Chartist movement and older radical demands for charters of rights. *Punch*'s Women's Charter mockingly observed, 'At length women are beginning to know their own strength – at length the hour of equality is about to strike', because women have resolved upon a 'triple charter for maid, wife and widow'. The

Women's Charter reduced women's fight for political rights to absurdities, such as unlimited pocket money for maids and wives demanding that husbands smoke in the garden. What is remarkable about this facetious anti-feminist satire is just how widely it was circulated. Throughout June and July 1848, these few paragraphs were republished multiple times.[59] The Women's Charter belittled increasingly visible female assertiveness and working-class demands for the Charter, both of which intensified the disturbing nature of the other.

The Chartist press responded very differently to demands for women's rights. The rhetoric of women's rights became more visible within Chartist speeches and addresses, and the Chartist press provided a platform from which women could demand the vote. A letter published in *Reynolds's Weekly* on 23 March 1851 from a correspondent named 'Omega' made a lengthy and explicit demand for women's rights. Omega's letter concluded:

> In the name, then, of justice, of common and universal right, and of humanity, that is the same now as it ever was, and ever will be. We demand an agitation of the question in order that women shall have a recognised right to partake of that which an extension of the franchise is intended to give.[60]

The events of 1848 gave confidence to Chartist women's rights advocates such as Omega to renew their demands for women's right to vote within the Chartist movement. Chartism became an organisational vehicle, which they sought to shape into a collective movement capable of securing their rights.

The revolutions of 1848 created unprecedented opportunities for tens of thousands of European women to participate in military actions, popular uprisings against authoritarian states and short-lived democratic forms of government. Women whose lives had been confined to repetitive and exhausting domestic labour and arduous and badly paid employment found their horizons expanded to include questions of revolutionary strategy, political theorising and new ways of living. Women demonstrated that they were capable of political organisation and leadership. The third national Chartist petition and the European revolutions of 1848 were defeated, and that defeat led to an intense political debate within Chartism. The movement embraced a more comprehensive and radical programme, central to which was the demand for secular, state-funded education. Historians have noted that, while the organisational structures of Chartism fractured and began to wither, the ideas Chartism advanced and, in particular, the demand for secular education, gained increasing traction within the broader labour movement.[61] Support for the female franchise also spread and was sustained through a number of informal personal, political and geographical networks, which could respond to new opportunities to campaign for the female franchise which emerged in the 1850s and 1860s.

Irish Nationalism, Chartism and the 'Lady Insurrectionist'

Sarah Theobald

The possibility of Irish revolutionaries making common cause with a Chartist uprising in Britain haunted the British authorities in 1848. The unfolding horror of the Irish Famine propelled Irish national movement towards demands for social reform and alliances with British radicals. Solidarities between Chartists and Irish nationalists were one pillar of the British working class's resistance to nationalism. Irish immigrants were prominent in every tier of the Chartist movement. Leading Chartists John Cleave, Bronterre O'Brien and Feargus O'Connor were all born in Ireland. Although many Irish organisations discouraged their followers from associating with Chartism, Dorothy Thompson argued that Irish immigrants constituted 'a very considerable presence in the Chartist movement'.[1] In areas such as Manchester and Liverpool, Malcolm Chase observed, the 'convergence of Chartism and Confederates [as the Irish nationalists were known] was effectively total'.[2] Mary Ann Walker was called many things by mainstream journalists: one name invented for her was 'she-O'Connell', a reference to Daniel O'Connell, the leader of the Irish nationalists.[3]

Feargus O'Connor was not a leading proponent of Chartist internationalism, which tended to be associated with the left wing of the movement, but he embodied many of the international connections which animated late Chartism in London. O'Connor's father, Roger, was an Irish nationalist lawyer who defended members of the United Irishmen accused of insurrection in 1796. O'Connor's uncle, Arthur O'Connor, was an agent for the revolutionary Irish nationalist, Robert Emmett, and the United Irishmen. One of Mary Ann Walker's most widely reported speeches was given at an event to commemorate Emmett's life.[4] In 1807, Arthur O'Connor married Elisa de Condorcet, the daughter of French revolutionaries Sophie and Nicolas de Condorcet, who had translated the writings of Thomas Paine into French and supported the political rights of women.[5] In 1819, Feargus O'Connor's brother, Francis O'Connor, enlisted in the Latin American independence army led by Simón Bolívar.[6] O'Connor's family history suggests that internationalism was not merely a political principle but was also a lived experience which shaped and was shaped by the personal histories of Chartist men and women.

The most celebrated female Chartist lecturer of 1848 was Sarah Theobald, a woman of Irish descent who advocated unity between the Chartists and the Irish Confederates. Theobald was the only woman employed as a lecturer by the national Chartist Movement. She began her lecturing career towards the end of 1848 when the experience of the European revolutions had expanded ideas of what constituted appropriate activism for women. Theobald barely features in the histories of female Chartism.[7] Her career as a Chartist lecturer, however, demonstrates some important aspects of the gender politics of later Chartism. Theobald's rhetoric drew on that used by Chartist women at the high points of 1839 and 1842. She invoked the idea that female activism was legitimised by the republican ideal of liberty.

Theobald also repeated the familiar idea that female activism was justified by male failure, telling one meeting that:

> If the men were not prepared to do their duty, and hurl back the insults they had received from their oppressor, she could tell them that the women, though the 'weaker vessel', were determined in

the name of God to do their duty and one and all to raise the standard of Liberty (loud cheers and laughter).[8]

Theobald continued the long-standing radical critique of the Poor Laws when she told a meeting in July 1848, 'it was more glorious and godlike, however, to die for their country than to go into yonder Bastille and solicit arms'.[9] Continuities with earlier female Chartist rhetoric can be identified in Theobald's speeches, but there were also significant differences which made Theobald a particularly unsettling and subversive figure for the authorities.

Theobald was frequently described in newspaper reports as an 'Irish woman', an identity strongly associated with the persistent fear that the Irish and the Chartists would launch a united uprising. The unease Theobald provoked was evident from the authorities' responses to her lectures. In early August 1848, Theobald addressed an open-air meeting in Greek Street, Stockport. Local magistrates were so fearful of the impact of her speech, they allowed the meeting to proceed only if organisers guaranteed that no violent language was used. Newspapers reported that Theobald 'detailed Ireland's wrongs and England's miseries, commenting upon them with the view of effecting a practical fraternisation between the disaffected of both countries'.[10] This female advocacy of common cause between the working people of Ireland and Britan was threatening to the British government. Several press reports identified Theobald as a 'Lady Insurrectionist', who warned the government that 100,000 women were ready to march on Prime Minister Lord John Russell.[11]

In August 1848, the *Halifax Guardian* reported that Theobald's claim was 'the first open exhibition of that new system of organisation, projected originally by the Irish Confederates, but adopted by the violent portion of the English Chartists'.[12] The *Guardian* noted that it was Ernest Jones who 'encouraged the London Chartists by the story of 90,000 Yorkshire men ready to march on Downing Street. And a Mrs Theobald is now reversing the story, by assuring the Lancashire Chartists that there are 100,000 women in London ready to rise, we suppose, "like a man".'[13] Theobald 'reversed' expectations, suggesting that the threat to the government came not from Yorkshire men but from London women, executing a double geographical and gender shift. In June 1848, Theobald delivered a militant speech in Birmingham, which was published in several Irish newspapers under the headline, 'Hurrah for Mrs Theobald'.[14] The papers located her female activism within the context of the European revolutions, asserting that if Theobald, 'were at Berlin, Naples, or any of the towns in Italy, where women displayed such fearlessness of death, she would probably have been found fighting amongst the foremost'.[15] This positioning of Theobald as a brave German or Italian insurrectionist reveals both the impact those women had made on the radical imagination and the esteem in which Theobald was held among Irish nationalists.

There are no records of exactly when Theobald began lecturing but the reports above suggest she was well-known by the summer of 1848. She was on the West Yorkshire Chartist lecturing circuit by January 1849, when she delivered her first lecture in Keighley's Working Men's Hall. *The Northern Star* reported on her exhausting schedule of meetings as she crisscrossed West Yorkshire, speaking on temperance, 'The Rights of Man', and 'Woman's duty, and her position in society at the present crisis'. At the end of this lecture a female Chartist Association was formed with thirty-four women enrolling.[16] Reports of her speaking engagements continued throughout the year, with lectures given in West Yorkshire, South Yorkshire, the Midlands and the North East.[17]

In the summer of 1849, *The Northern Star* reported that Theobald 'delivered a lecture on the Rights of Man and the People's Charter, in the Chartist Room, which gave unbounded satisfaction to an overflowing assembly'.[18] There are no reports which satirise Theobald as a 'hen Chartist' and no debates about her right to interfere in politics. She did not have to defend herself like Walker and Inge had done in 1842. This suggests that women's right to speak on political matters was more accepted in 1848 and 1849 than it had been when Walker and Inge ascended the public platform six years earlier.

Theobald spoke as a woman of the working class with the authority of experience. Women, she said, 'wanted to be liberated from the horrid slavery they were now suffering from under their oppressors; and she, as one of the slaves of the system had known what it was to be roused by the sound of the bell in the morning'.[19] Theobald appealed to women whether her subject directly related to women's concerns or wider political questions. In August 1848, the *Bradford Observer* reported on a meeting of the Female Chartists Association held to celebrate the twenty-ninth anniversary of the Peterloo Massacre in the People's Institute, Ancoats, Manchester, addressed by Theobald. The building was 'completely crowded' with a 'large number of females being present'.[20]

Throughout 1848 and into 1849, Theobald continued to address large gatherings and recruit new members to female Chartist organisations. Press reports suggest that she continued to lecture on temperance and women's rights as the organised Chartist movement declined.[21] In Blyth in 1855, Theobald described how women were leading the temperance fight and advocated '"Women's Right" in general'.[22] Mary Ann Walker and Susanna Inge disappeared from public life as Chartist militancy went into retreat following the defeat of the 1842 petition. In 1848, Theobald sustained her position as a female lecturer despite the demise of Chartism as an organised movement. The 1848 revolutions had helped women to establish their right to a place on the public platform created by Chartism and, for Theobald at least, left a legacy of public lecturing.

6

Resistance, 1850s: 'The Strong-Minded Women of the Party'

On Monday 15 September 1856, a Chartist demonstration gathered in London to welcome John Frost home from his long exile. Behind a carriage carrying Frost and other Chartist leaders came a procession of pedestrians carrying red caps of liberty and banners bearing slogans such as 'The sovereignty of the people' and 'Disobedience to a tyrant is an honour to God'. As it passed through Leicester Square, the procession was joined by a contingent of exiled German socialists who raised their own banner, which proclaimed 'Long Live the Universal Social Democratic Republic'. The crowd had swelled to about 20,000 in number by the time it reached its destination on Primrose Hill, where the marchers sang songs and listened to speeches until 6 p.m.

Contemporary newspaper reports commented on the large number of women present and many remarked on the two young women who led the procession.[1] One report observed that flags, caps of liberty and banners 'were triumphantly borne aloft by the strong-minded women of the party'.[2] This chapter will explore why these strong-minded women were still marching, alongside European socialists and Chartists, years after Chartism had supposedly subsided into a moderate shadow of its former self. The Chartism which endured into the 1850s had reconciled itself to finding spaces to work within the system and was more of a pressure group than a mass movement.[3] It could, however, still play a significant role in stimulating working-class resistance which involved women.

As Chartism subsided in the 1850s, it left behind a residual radical culture among the working classes who were increasingly looking for new ways to extricate themselves from their 'degraded state'. Ideas of class confrontation gave way to education and moral reform as more realisable pathways to a better life.[4] By the 1850s many middle-class commentators saw the residential qualification for voters as an essential 'guarantee of moral fitness'.[5] The idea of 'respectability' and associated ideas of abstinence, self-control and duty emanated from the middle classes and gained significant traction inside the working class. Within these general developments, however, some ex-Chartists found ways to continue their campaigns for social as well as personal reform. Trade unions, friendly societies and cooperative societies all provided forums within which middle-class hegemony could be resisted and democratic and egalitarian values could be promoted in evolving ways.[6] This chapter will explore how women continued to organise for their rights into the 1850s.

Late Chartism in Steel City

One of the most significant women's organisations which emerged after 1848 was the Sheffield Women's Rights Association (WRA). The formidable campaigner Anne Knight has been identified as its instigator.[7] Knight contacted Sheffield's Chartists to ask for the names of women who would join a campaign to persuade Chartist leaders to include votes for women in the Charter. The leader of the Sheffield Chartists, Isaac Ironside, supported female suffrage because, as one historian suggested, 'his commitment to Owenism rendered him sensitive and sympathetic to this issue'.[8] Ironside supplied the names of like-minded local women and Knight wrote to them in January 1851. The WRA held an inaugural meeting in February 1851 and agreed to support a petition calling for female suffrage, the first collective petition for votes for women submitted to Parliament.[9] That is the accepted story of the WRA, one which fits neatly into a narrative which places middle-class women in the vanguard of all women's organisations.

New research by Matthew Roberts challenges this view. The WRA did not, in fact, owe its existence to Anne Knight, he argues. The Sheffield women planned their association a few months before Knight first wrote to them. Knight initially approached Ironside to supply contacts, but he then became peripheral to the WRA and his wife, Elizabeth, did not join. The women of the WRA expressed sharp political disagreements with Ironside, which focused on his refusal to vote in council meetings.[10] Exploring the history of the WRA also prompts a revision of those histories which attribute any identifiable women's rights current within Chartism to the influence of Owenism.[11] The women most strongly associated with the WRA were Abiah Higginbottom, Eliza Rooke, Ann Thornhill, Eliza Bartholomew, Mary Brooke, Mary Hutton, Kate Ash, Henrietta Holmshaw, Eliza Cavill and Ann Higginbottom. They were not members of the Owenite branch in Sheffield, nor were their husbands. The WRA did not meet in the Owenite Hall of Science; it met in the Chartist venue, the Democratic Temperance Hall. Roberts argues persuasively that 'the roots of the WRA were not to be found in Owenism or middle-class feminism; they were to be found in Chartism itself'.[12]

The women of the WRA were not dependent on Knight or Ironside, but both did make an important contribution to the organisation, and it would be a mistake to underestimate this. Internationalism was a central concern for the WRA, and it was Knight and Ironside who connected the women of Sheffield with Jeanne Deroin and Pauline Roland. Knight was a friend of Deroin's and Ironside went to France to deliver an address to the provisional government, which hailed the 'greatest revolution ever known'.[13] He led a march of about 12,000 Sheffield Chartists, which congratulated the French Provisional Government.[14] Whatever the WRA's differences with Ironside, in April 1851 it celebrated its association with a ball and soirée, and Ironside presided 'at the unanimous request of the committee'. A letter from Anne Knight was read out, along with passages from Frances Wright's *England, the Civilizer*, read by Ironside, and a poem by Mary Hutton. Abiah Higginbottom delivered a speech on the 'Industry and Independence of Women' before the dancing began at 9 p.m.[15] Knight had not actually met any of the Sheffield women and their relationship was based exclusively on correspondence. She praised them for 'planting the tree of liberty' and advised them to nurture its growth and help it to spread to other towns.[16] Either in response to Knight's prompting or from their own initiative, in the same month that Knight's letter was read out the Sheffield WRA established a plan for a National Women's Rights Association and appointed Anne Knight as its first president.[17]

The WRA, developed within Sheffield's Chartist networks, was led by working-class and artisan women and placed the idea of women's right to political representation 'front and centre'.[18] The WRA's opening address, published in February 1851, outlined women's lack of rights, not merely within Parliament but reform organisations themselves, pointing out that women 'perform all the drudgery of his political societies and never to possess a single political right'.[19] This echoes the complaints made by Knight at the anti-slavery convention a decade earlier. *The Northern Star*'s second report of a WRA meeting included an address by Abiah Higginbottom and Mary Brooks, which was read out to the meeting. In the address, they argued: 'There are some who will say, would you have women to enjoy all the political, social, and moral rights of man? To this we most emphatically answer yes.'[20] The WRA address became the basis for a petition which demanded women's suffrage. It became only the second women's suffrage petition to be considered, and overwhelmingly rejected, by Parliament.

The WRA did not confine itself to campaigning for female suffrage. At one of its regular meetings held at the Democratic Temperance Hotel, Sheffield, in June 1851, Mrs Abiah Higginbottom read out Deroin and Roland's prison appeal to 'great acclamation'.[21] In August, *The Northern Star* reported that a second letter had been sent by Deroin and Roland to the Sheffield Chartist Council. This letter argued that the Charter should include the demand for the female franchise and was printed on the front page of *The Northern Star*, which suggests that the newspaper was more prepared to give prominence to the issue of the female franchise than when former editor Feargus O'Connor was in charge.[22] The WRA also extended solidarity to Teresa Kossuth, wife of Hungarian national hero Lajos Kossuth, and raised funds for European refugees.[23] In March 1852, the WRA launched a petition against the expansion of the militias, which it placed in an internationalist rhetoric: 'Your petitioners also beg to observe that they have no fear about any other invasion than that which the government and honourable members are at present engaged in – namely, the invasion of our own hearths and liberties.'[24] The women of the WRA countered anti-French jingoism with a protest against the repression they faced at the hands of the British state. The WRA's demands for political rights were far more comprehensive and assertive than those advanced by later Victorian feminists.

The WRA adopted a strategy of exerting pressure on the leadership of the Chartist movement, in particular, Feargus O'Connor, to support women's right to vote. In November 1851, a Chartist meeting was held in Sheffield in honour of O'Connor. It could not have been a very relaxing evening for him. The women in attendance attempted to bounce him into supporting votes for women. They began by praising O'Connor's 'continued and unflinching advocacy in the cause of freedom'.[25] They then claimed to speak for their sisters in Glasgow, Leeds, Edinburgh and other towns, who they had emboldened 'to speak out for universal suffrage, in which they solicited his powerful aid'. O'Connor's only reported response was to return the thanks.[26] The WRA campaign was probably the last attempt by Chartist women to push for the female franchise to be included in the Charter, but it was not the last attempt by working-class women to influence radical politics.

The story of the WRA is the story of working-class women's political commitment and the breadth of their political concerns in the final years of the Chartist movement. Some historians have identified the early 1850s as the point when the leadership of the campaign for female suffrage passed from working-class women to middle-class women. In July 1851, Harriet Taylor published her famous essay, 'The Enfranchisement of Women', in the *Westminster Review*. In the article, Taylor criticised the Chartists for excluding women from the demand for universal suffrage, but she did not assume leadership of any women's campaign. In fact, Taylor acknowledged the influence of the WRA. 'On 13th of February 1851', she wrote, 'a petition of women, agreed to by a public meeting at Sheffield, and claiming the elective franchise, was presented to the House of Lords by the Earl of Carlisle.'[27] Taylor criticised male Chartists, but she knew the initiative for establishing a serious campaign for the female franchise came from the working-class women of Sheffield and the only practical strategy she envisaged was to influence Chartism.

A new organisation blooms in Camden

In May 1852, Anne Knight was among a group of female reformers who established the Women's Elevation League in Camden, London.[28] The WRA fell out of public view after 1852 as the Elevation League was established. Some historians have identified this shift from one organisation to another as more evidence that working-class women ceded the leadership of the women's rights movement to middle-class women. The League was a small and insignificant organisation compared with the WRA and appeared only briefly in press reports. The League's stated aim was to raise the social, moral, professional, pecuniary and political condition of women, which sounds much more restrained than the demands of the WRA. One of the organisation's demands was that women be allowed to enter any calling or profession for which they were physically or intellectually suited. The demand for equal access to work was usually associated with middle-class women as working-class women had plenty of work. The League has been seen as 'predominantly middle class in tone and social composition'.[29] It did not, however, mark the emergence of an exclusively middle-class female leadership.

The social composition of the League is difficult to establish because only eight board members were named and most of their life stories remain unknown. We know Anne Knight had an independent income. Other members of the League's leadership body were Caroline Dexter, who was born in Nottingham and educated in France, and her husband William, who worked as a painter in a Derbyshire pottery factory. In January 1849, *The Northern Star* reported on a radical gathering in Nottingham which was chaired by a William Dexter. At the meeting there were many social and democratic songs, speeches, citations and toasts, including one to Doctor McDouall and the rest of the victims of Whig tyranny and one 'to the brave men of Paris, who died defending the social and democratic republic – the insurgents of June.'[30] The Dexters sound a lot more like Chartist artisans than middle-class radicals. There is some evidence that other members of the Women's Elevation League had links with Chartism in Nottingham and nearby Sheffield.[31]

The first report on the formation of the Women's Elevation League appeared in *The Northern Star* on 5 May 1852. A second article printed a month later reported that league members had gathered to further 'elucidate the principles of the organisation'. The meeting was addressed by two men, Mr King and Mr Naylor, and then by Caroline Dexter. *The Northern Star* reporter described Dexter as 'possessed of talent, enthusiasm and energy and admired for her moral worth, the cause of Woman's Elevation can have no more efficient advocate'.[32] Caroline Dexter would have been familiar to readers of *The Northern Star* as an advocate of female dress reform. The previous year, the Bloomer movement arrived in England from America, where the 'Bloomer Craze' had attracted public interest and controversy. The feminist, abolitionist and journalist Hannah Tracy Cutler brought reform dress to England when she reported from the Great Exhibition of 1851 wearing a divided, shortened skirt. Caroline Dexter was one of the first to embrace the dress reform movement in Britain. She became well-known to the public during a nationwide speaking tour to promote Bloomerism, which attracted extensive press coverage and huge and unruly audiences. On one occasion, *The Northern Star* reported, Dexter was to address a meeting at the British Institute in Finsbury. The venue had capacity for 1,500 people but became so overcrowded that people were trampled and fainted in the crush, and Dexter refused to appear.[33]

Bloomerism touched on sensitive and highly contested issues. Women's clothes signified social status and moral standing in multiple and often subtle ways. Female dress could also confirm women's position as decorative ornaments at the cost of their physical comfort and bodily health. Many supporters of Bloomerism were middle-class women, who were to some degree shielded from the consequences of public disapproval. Yet, aspects of Bloomerism also chimed with the counterculture associated with Chartism, with a focus on making an active contribution to political and economic life, as well as the perfectibility of body and mind.[34] Chartists rejected the degradation of industrialisation and urban living conditions and increasingly advocated the reform of approaches to health, medicine and the body.[35] These ideas were deeply embedded in the culture of Chartism and would have made the women of the WRA more receptive to reforming codes of dress to promote physical health and female independence.

The Northern Star did not dismiss or satirise Bloomerism as a middle-class indulgence or a threat to manliness as other radical papers did. In fact, the paper published approving reports of Bloomerism in the US.[36] In September 1851, *The Northern Star* observed that Bloomerism had arrived in Britain when two women dressed in loose, grey silk trousers walked around Piccadilly handing out handbills advertising the Association of Bloomers, which was led by Caroline Dexter.[37] A week later, the *Star* reported that Caroline Dexter had addressed a huge crowd at the Literary Institute, Fitzroy Square, London and reported her speech at some length.[38] Dexter compared the fashionable dress adopted by Englishwomen to the practice of foot binding in China and other 'absurdities'. She identified a fissure in the justifications for British colonialism, which rested in part on the idea of liberating women from backward cultural practices. The apologists for colonialism maintained a deafening silence on the health-destroying fashions followed in Britain. Dexter pointed out how tight lacing damaged women's health and long skirts made walking in the countryside or the rain impossible. Such themes were common to Bloomerism but Dexter introduced a distinctive class dimension to her argument. 'No custom', she argued, 'was too absurd to be followed, provided the example was set by the affluent.'[39] Dexter inserted an element of class antagonism into her critique of how the wealthy set the tone for fashion which undermined women's health. This dimension of Dexter's critique would have appealed to the Chartists.

In May 1852, *The Northern Star* reported that 'the feminine heroes of the Women's Rights Association are alive and stirring in the noble cause of women's emancipation'. This praise was a response to news that the WRA had engaged the services of Hannah Tracy Cutler for three lectures on dress reform and women's political rights. The WRA also planned a tea meeting at which the 'indefatigable and true Knight of this new chivalry – Miss Anne Knight – is to be present'.[40] The WRA's interest in dress reform and *The Northern Star*'s expressions of support for the movement are significant because support for this women's rights protest could not be taken for granted. Predictably, *Punch* magazine satirised the dress reformers in terms reminiscent of their attacks on the female Chartists a decade earlier, portraying the Bloomerists as hideous spinsters who wanted to emasculate men and reverse gender roles.[41] The Chartist-supporting *Reynolds's Weekly* also mocked Dexter and the Bloomerists. When Dexter objected to a play which depicted the Bloomerists in a derogatory way, *Reynolds's Weekly* advised her to 'retire to a convenient spot and there to convert herself back again to the similitude of a woman. If she would claim the privileges of her sex, let her not sail under false colours.'[42] *The Northern Star* adopted a much more positive approach to female dress reform, perhaps because of the influence of support for women's rights in later Chartism and the links between bodily and political reform in Chartist thought.

Chartism did not require the intervention of middle-class feminists or Owenites to inspire female activism and organisation; it grew organically from within the movement. Nevertheless, Anne Knight encouraged organisational developments and, as a highly respected veteran of many progressive campaigns, she contributed both status and experience and acted as a vital link between Sheffield and the female insurgents in France. The Women's Elevation League was not an exclusively middle-class organisation which filled the space left by the retreating working-class women of the WRA. The two organisations coexisted and were linked through the involvement of Anne Knight and Caroline Dexter, and the issue of dress reform, which engaged both middle-class and working-class women. The existence of these two organisations suggests that in the 1850s, women were still trying to find collective ways to assert themselves. And other women were trying to establish new ways of caring and living within a system which was proving to be deeply hostile to their interests.

Knob-sticks and broom-sticks: Deserving domesticity

The rise of the factory system led to a catastrophe for the working-class family. Women could no longer care for their children and infant mortality soared. By the mid-nineteenth century, opposition to the employment of married women and children coalesced around the demand for a family wage, that men would be paid enough to support their wives and children in the home. Widespread support for the family wage has frequently been interpreted as a demand which reinforced and accelerated female subordination and dependence inside the British working class. Demands for a family wage have been interpreted as a rhetorical ploy to gain sympathy by presenting male trade unionists as chivalrous protectors of dependent women and children.[43] The unifying Chartist slogan of 'a fair day's work for a fair day's pay', popularised during the 1842 strike wave, was replaced by the divisive demand for a family wage which cemented male control over women.[44] But this characterisation fails to capture the complex reality of Chartist attitudes towards women and work. There is, for example, some evidence that women continued to demand fair pay for their labours. At a mass meeting of female Chartists held in Leicester in June 1848, the question of fair pay for women was raised from the platform. Mrs White described the miseries endured by mothers and explained that the women did not want charity, but rather their rights – 'a fair day's wages for a fair day's work'.[45] In Mrs White's rhetoric, fair pay for women was one of the reforms which would enable women to care for their children. Women such as Mrs White explicitly rejected the idea that they were objects of pity: they were demanding what they considered to be their rights.[46]

Exploring how working women themselves framed the demand for the family wage suggests that it did not imply subordination or retreat but could involve an assertion of their rights. The idea of a family wage offered a realisable alternative to the burden of factory labour and an opportunity for women to assert their distinct aspirations. The working-class family was a source of inequality because women who stayed at home were dependent on men's wages. But the family could also provide physical and emotional comfort and security, and it was by far the popular way to meet the needs of non-workers within a capitalist environment. Historian Jane Humphries pointed out that at a time when men, women and children were being forced to work to survive, the family became one of the few sources of working-class control over the supply of labour power.[47] Withdrawing children and women from the labour market could limit the supply of labourers and potentially force wages to rise.[48] The demand for the family wage was a collective response to Malthusian attacks on the right of the poor to have children.

The demand for the family wage featured strongly in the rhetoric of the female leaders of the Preston Lockout of 1853–4, which involved thousands of female and male textile workers. The strike began with a series of small-scale strikes at Preston's textile mills in the late summer of 1853. Workers demanded a 10-percent pay rise to compensate for years of pay cuts. In October, the mill owners conspired to lock the workers out until they dropped their pay claim. In March 1854, the workers responded with a general strike across the extensive textile industry of Preston and surrounding areas. They stayed out until May. The demand of the strike was popularised in the slogan 'Ten Percent and No Surrender', which echoed the Chartist cry of 'The Charter and No Surrender' from the previous decade.

Estimates of the number of strikers varied, but the most

accurate records suggest there were about 18,000 altogether, including about 11,800 females, about half of whom were adult women and about half teenage girls.[49] Women played an active role during the strike. They set up their own solidarity committees, and some women went 'on the cadge', travelling to neighbouring towns to win solidarity from other workers. One union organiser reported how appeals for solidarity met with a warm reception from women: 'The women especially had been most enthusiastic, declaring that they would "carry the flag" as the women of Preston had carried it.'[50] A report of a strikers' procession through Manchester, led by a band and a banner inscribed 'Ten Percent and No Surrender', noted that a large proportion of marchers were young women.[51] Chartists helped to initiate the strike, and Ernest Jones campaigned for solidarity with the strikers in his *People's Paper*.[52] Female Chartism had a long-standing presence in the Lancashire town of Preston, where women had organised petitions for Chartists transported to Australia and attended Chartist meetings in significant numbers.[53] It seems likely that some of these Chartist women were textile workers who participated in the lockout.

It has been suggested that the textile strikers were more interested in securing the right for women not to work than in expressing any interest in gender equality.[54] Recent research by Janet Greenlees paints a more complex picture, one which involves mutual respect, wage equality and a shared concern for providing care for dependents. All weavers were given four shillings a week, and there were reports that women queued for the four shillings every Monday morning, so it appears that women got equal strike pay.[55] The experience of the strike also began to reshape the working-class family. Married women's sustained support for the strike led to a decrease in male drunkenness and domestic violence.[56] Thousands of the women working in the mills had infants under five years old. In the six months before the strike, the number of infant deaths among Preston's weaving families was 594. During the six months of the strike, the number of child deaths fell to 497.[57] When women were not working, their children had a much better chance of surviving their infancy. The demand for a family wage reflected the reality that a lack of childcare put children at severe risk, and the rhetoric of working-class women reflected that deep concern.

Two of the most prominent female strike leaders were sisters Ann and Margaret Fletcher, two textile workers who established themselves as witty, authoritative and respected public speakers. The Fletcher sisters expressed the contradictory aspects of the family wage. They positioned themselves as auxiliaries to the men's strike movement and demanded the family wage using the language of female rights. In November 1853 a widely reported strike rally attracted between 7,000 and 10,000 people. Margaret Fletcher climbed on to a cart to propose a resolution to the vast crowd. She argued that if capital had its rights, so did labour and, 'if capital had a dozen servants, surely the working man had a right to keep his wife at home to wait upon him'.[58] She advised unmarried women to send any suitors 'about their business' if they could not support a wife at home.[59] Fletcher's proposal committed the married women of Preston to refuse to work until their husbands were 'fully and fairly renumerated for their labour', and the women themselves were brought from an 'unnatural to a natural state'.[60] Margaret positioned women as subordinate to their husbands and suggested that female employment was unnatural. She also, however, called on women to exercise their authority over their husbands and make demands on men.

When Ann seconded the resolution, she reminded the crowd how women had to take their young children out of their warm beds in the morning and drag them through the frost and snow: 'How many infants and young children had come to an untimely death through that?' she demanded. 'The men had not done their duty by them,' she told the crowd.[61] Ann continued in this assertive tone when she advised the women present that it was high time they looked after their rights. She was greeted with laughter and cheers when she told them, 'We have let men manage our affairs long enough and a pretty position they have brought us into.'[62] The chair of the meeting requested that only females vote for the Fletcher sisters' resolution, which was carried 'amid great cheering and considerable laughter'.[63] The Fletcher sisters' renunciation of their rights was carried through the exercise of those rights.

The Fletcher sisters both described going 'through the country on the cadge'. In December 1853, Margaret Fletcher spoke at a meeting in Burnley. This time she did not characterise women working outside the home as unnatural. She opposed women working because women were being used to undercut men's wages to the detriment of the whole workforce.[64] The Fletcher sisters deployed a contradictory rhetoric. They argued that women's natural place was in the home, but they argued this in front of thousands of people and they represented the strikers to audiences across Lancashire. For some historians, the family wage was the banner under which radical men turned away from fighting for wage equality and towards imposing domesticity on women.[65] Fighting for gender equality at work would have been very difficult for trade unions engaged in defensive battles against pay cuts, and even if women won better or equal pay, they would still not have been able to care for their families. The problem imposed by factory labour was one of physical distance as well as the level of wages. In theory, wage equality could have opened the possibility of men staying at home to care for children. But 200 years later, that remains a largely unfulfilled vision of equality. It is wrong to assume that the family wage involved an uncomplicated assertion of male dominance and female submission. Such an approach risks erasing the militant, assertive dimensions of the demand and the intense class hostility they aroused.

Domesticity was frequently seen as a privilege reserved for those who could afford it. Evangelicals and commentators elevated domesticity to the status of women's rightful destiny, but it was not to be available for all women. Newspaper reports used satire and ridicule to portray the demand for a family wage as an impertinent challenge to the rights of employers. *The Morning Post* suggested that the workers were seeking

> permanent support, not from wages from labour done, but from the confiscation of capital and are henceforth to regulate their mode of living not from what their wages will earn but from their own fancies and desires and for this delightful consummation the owners of capital are to find the means.[66]

One Lancashire newspaper mocked the domestic aspirations of working women, suggesting that '*Madam Weaver*' 'intends to sit at Chimney corner, getting up her Sunday finery, and teaching the young how to carry home the beer and cook the beefsteaks for dinner'.[67] The paper denied that working-class women released from the discipline of paid labour would be capable of 'useful and virtuous occupation'.[68] Radicals fiercely opposed the idea that working-class women were too degraded and immoral to be worthy of domesticity. By claiming their right to domesticity, working-class women were asserting their right to the respect afforded to their wealthier sisters.

Demands for the family wage implied the redistribution of wealth both from the employers to the workers and from male workers to their wives. The family wage was a rational response to the reorganisation of productive and reproductive labour by hostile forces, a response which placed female activism in the interests of working-class families at its centre.[69] The strike began to crumble in March 1854, as workers began to question whether they could win a 10-percent pay rise and employment for all the weavers and spinners who had turned out. The local authorities and the police began to obstruct and harass strikers when they tried to hold rallies and appeal for solidarity. The drift back to work became a flood in the previously solid mills of Blackburn. On May Day 1854, 10,000 striking workers gathered on Walton Bridge to accept defeat and end the strike together.[70] The next flashpoint in the working class's struggle to sustain their food security, a share of the social wealth and the capacity to reproduce themselves came the next year, and it broke out 220 miles to the south, in London.

Beer, bread and riots

The year after the Preston Lockout ended, crowds of London labourers took to the streets to protest an attack on their ability to provide for themselves and their families. The Victorian political establishment may have been congratulating itself on the demise of the Chartist challenge. The Sunday trading riots of 1855, however, highlighted how little they understood the mood of the urban poor.[71] The riots also showed that the political power of the voteless was real despite its lack of permanent institutional expression. Riots were one way in which the disenfranchised could exercise political power.

Two measures provoked the riots. First, the Wilson-Patten Act closed English drinking places between 2:30 p.m. and 6 p.m. and after 10 p.m. on Sundays. This measure was the culmination of piecemeal attempts at Sunday closing made in several English cities from 1839 onwards. On 13 August 1854, when the new restrictions came into force, there were violent scenes when pub-goers refused to leave at the earlier hour and had to be ejected by the police. The second ingredient for discontent was the Sunday Trading Bill, introduced by the evangelical Lord Robert Grosvenor, which banned all Sunday trading in London with a few exceptions. This show of power by evangelical Christians exasperated London radicals. George Holyoake regarded the Sunday Trading Bill as 'a mere Church monopoly act, for the protection of religion from competition'.[72] The recent religious census showed that a surprisingly small proportion of the population attended Sunday service. Ernest Jones indignantly contested the evangelical monopoly of elevating the brain of man, purifying his heart and ennobling his soul.[73] More practically, London's labourers were seldom paid before Saturday evening, and the bill would mean they would go hungry or access only stale and rotten food.

The mass movement against the Sunday Trading Bill began when posters went up around London advertising a meeting planned for the afternoon of Sunday 24 June. The gathering was going to occupy the spaces in Hyde Park where the fashionable rich were accustomed to parade in their carriages on Sunday afternoons. The posters encouraged Londoners to 'see how religiously the aristocracy is observing the Sabbath'.[74] The poor were to be compelled to go to church while the rich enjoyed their fun. This was a movement in defence of access to food and drink, but it was also a movement of intense hostility to London's ruling elite. Karl Marx, who was present, estimated that at least 200,000 people attended the first protest. The next day, Marx rather optimistically declared, 'The English Revolution began yesterday in Hyde Park.' The police tried to disrupt the gathering and interrupted a speech being given by 'Bligh the Chartist' as the carriages of the wealthy began to arrive. The crowd lined the Serpentine carriageway, and Marx described how 'a babel of jeering, taunting, discordant ejaculations, in which no language is as rich as English', bore down upon the carriage occupants, who were urged to 'go to Church'. 'The spectacle lasted three hours', Marx reported; 'only English lungs could perform such a feat'.[75]

During the following week, more posters appeared, urging attendance at the park on Sunday 1 July. On Saturday, Sir Richard Mayne, Metropolitan Police commissioner, issued notices forbidding any such meeting. In the evening, Lord Robert, who had been subjected to personal threats, prudently fled to the country in a hired carriage. According to *The Times*, by 2:30 p.m. on Sunday, nearly 150,000 people had ignored the police and gathered in the park. The police could not restrain themselves, especially after a large eel was fished out of the Serpentine, passed over the heads of the crowd and thrown at a police detachment.[76] The police decided to clear the carriageway using their truncheons. As 'mobs of men and women' were pouring into the park, policemen dived under the rails and began striking about them like 'rovers in the midst of a herd of oxen, sending the few men and many women and children rushing before them'.[77] Women were mentioned in all the accounts of police violence, which documented how the police had poked their staves into women's stomachs and that women were treated with the upmost 'Ruffianism'.[78]

Monday's press echoed the crowd's indignation at the police brutality. Lord Robert withdrew his measure, complaining that he had been 'mobbed and bullied'. The erstwhile Chartist MP Thomas Duncombe and others induced the government to appoint a royal commission of inquiry into events on 1 July. Now that the original grievance had been removed, the press hoped there would be no more violence in the park on the third Sunday, 8 July. Crowds gathered at the park, however, and sections of the crowd suddenly wheeled into Belgravia and broke

749 windowpanes. The protest, reported *The Manchester Guardian* on 11 July, had passed from its 'original and well-meaning' organisers into the hands of a 'set of ne'er-do-wells for whom there is no expostulation so suitable as a thick stick'.[79] The crowd, which was young and drawn overwhelmingly from London's slums, was no longer portrayed sympathetically.

Chartists were involved in the leadership of the riots, such as it was. G. W. M. Reynolds sold the posters which summoned people to the park in his shop, and the only London papers to applaud the popular coercion of Parliament were *Reynolds's Newspaper* and Ernest Jones's *The People's Paper.* Several Chartists and radicals denounced the aristocracy before the Hyde Park meetings. On the first Sunday, Marx saw 'zealous Chartists, men and women' distributing leaflets advertising one of their meetings. One witness saw leaflets headed 'Arise, O England' and attacking the aristocracy being circulated. Chartists had always attacked class legislation and a centralised government which depended on a police force. The demonstrators on the third Sunday were probably led by East End radicals anxious to take vengeance on the police. Chartist Thomas Frost said that many of those making for the park on 8 July carried sticks and made 'many remarks as to the use that was to be made of them'. Foreign émigrés were prominent in the riots, not as victims, as they had been in earlier riots, but as instigators: 'Just as the British ruling classes sought to educate Europe in parliamentary government, so continental refugees sought to educate British working men in making a revolution.'[80] Two Frenchmen were arrested on 1 July for encouraging a mob with shouts of 'Bravo, Englishmen! A republic! a republic!', and a well-dressed foreigner led the 100–200 youths who broke the Belgravia windows a week later. The refugees, radicals and Chartists had forged relationships during the revolutions of 1848. The riots showed how the London poor could exercise collective power to influence politics and defend their ability to eat and drink and enjoy some leisure time.

Chartism and Communism in the Life of Helen Macfarlane

Helen Macfarlane witnessed the revolution in Vienna in 1848, reported for the radical press and intervened in the direction Chartism took in the early 1850s. Helen was also a philosopher who popularised the ideas of Georg Hegel and Karl Marx among British radicals.[1] Helen was born into a family of mill owners in Renfrewshire, Scotland. Her family's cotton mills went bankrupt in 1842 and she found work as a governess. She was well-educated and fluent in German. By 1845, Helen was living in London with her sister Mary in the home of some wealthy relatives. Helen was working as a governess. Her four other brothers and sisters were living in Burnley and Manchester, in Lancashire. Their father, John Macfarlane, found work as the Manchester agent for the Natal Emigration and Colonisation Company. The company was licensed to buy plots of land at cheap rates and sell them to emigrants. Between 1849 and 1851, the company sent 1,300 emigrants as part of the colonisation of Natal. Helen's family were factory owners and colonialists, but she embraced women's rights, Chartism and Communism.

Helen's writings from Vienna in 1848 suggest that she was in the city in March, when an uprising against the Austrian Prince Metternich forced Emperor Ferdinand to concede a democratic constitution. In September, Karl Marx visited the city and addressed the Vienna Workers' Association, which was led by an Englishman, Alfred Julius Becher, and his lover, Karoline von Perin, who was the president of the Women's Democratic Association.[2] The Austrian Habsburg Empire launched a counterrevolution in October and by November the old empire was back in charge of Vienna. This experience of revolution and counterrevolution shaped Helen's political outlook. She became convinced that introducing formal democratic institutions would not be sufficient to transform life for the poor and she began to consider strategies for establishing fundamental economic change.

George Julian Harney resigned from the editorship of *The Northern Star* in 1850, following the failure of the British attempt at insurrection in April 1848. He then launched two new periodicals, the monthly *Democratic Review of British Politics and Literature*, followed by the weekly *Red Republican*. Helen's socialist political outlook was closely aligned with Harney's. She contributed thirteen articles to these publications between April and December 1850, under her own name and under the pseudonym 'Howard Morton'. Helen also produced the first British translation of Marx and Engels' *Communist Manifesto* for Harney's *Red Republican*. Published in four parts in November 1850, Macfarlane's translation of *The Communist Manifesto* proved to be controversial. Criticism has focused on Macfarlane's use of the word 'hobgoblin' instead of the more familiar 'spectre' to describe the entity haunting Europe. Recent scholarship, however, invites a new respect for Macfarlane's work, which related in creative ways to the language of her contemporary radicals. The translation was sufficiently influential to attract the hostility of *The Times* reviewer, who was alarmed by this apparent 'appeal from the lower orders', who lived physically close to the wealthy, but inhabited a different country.

Helen's experiences in Europe gave her journalism authenticity and originality. Looking back to 1848, she wrote in the *Red Republican* of 'the double rows of cannon placed on the ramparts of Vienna, so as to rake the town on one side, and the suburbs on the other'. This image of the cannon expressed a deeper political truth, which Helen drew out by speculation: 'If the Habsburgs were to disband any portion of their colossal standing army, how long would it be before the Hungarians,

Italians, Croats and Poles would reassert their independence, and the Viennese people plant the red flag on the dome of St. Stephen?'[3] The colossal armies of the emperors, tsars and archdukes of Europe proved decisive in crushing the democratic dreams of spring 1848. The middle classes may have aspired to democratic and civil rights, and wanted a constitutional government, but they were not prepared to put themselves at the head of the legions of labourers. They dare not mobilise the masses and were left with no means to challenge the colossal armies of the ancient regime.

Helen's writings combined sharp polemics on the important political questions facing socialists and democrats with theoretical depth and clarity. Two of her most important targets were the political establishment and the moderate reformers who were an obstacle to radical change. Macfarlane published a scathing criticism of Thomas Carlyle, the influential Victorian essayist, racist and anti-democrat. Carlyle was horrified by the spectacle of the 1848 revolutions in Europe. The experiments in democracy ended, he wrote, with a 'massacre not of the innocents ... but a universal tumbling of imposters and impostures into the street'. For Carlyle, the democrats were the imposters who had been rightly tumbled. Macfarlane skilfully turned Carlyle's words back on him:

> I am free to confess that, for me the most joyful of all spectacles possible in these times is the one which Mr Carlyle laments; one which I enjoyed tremendously at Vienna in March 1848, i.e., 'a universal tumbling of impostors'. For it amounts to this, that men are determined to live no longer in lies.[4]

Macfarlane's imposters were the dictatorial heads of Empire, their ministers and priests who were tumbled from power.

Helen Macfarlane also polemicised against the moderate Christian socialist paper, *The Leader*. A correspondent for *The Leader* referred to the journalists of the *Red Republican* as 'too angry and wedded to the cause of reform'. Macfarlane replied in an article called, 'Fine words – Household or otherwise – Butter no Parsnips.' She wrote:

> It has lately been said by the *Leader* that the writers in the *Red Republican* are 'violent, audacious and wrathfully earnest ...' I should think we are. Just about as much in earnest as our precursor, 'the Sansculotte [sic] Jesus' was when He scourged the usurers and money-lenders and thimble-rigging stockbrokers of Jerusalem out of the temple they had made a 'den of thieves'.[5]

Macfarlane again turned her opponents' words and professed ideas against them to great effect.

Macfarlane's politics combined a robust defence of the role of working-class activism in shaping history with opposition to oppression. She believed that overcoming racism and sexism were a precondition for the establishment of a truly democratic society. This meant that true democracy did not exist anywhere in the world and democracy remained, in Helen's words, a 'soul in want of a body'.[6] Many Chartists emigrated to America, which was widely seen as a place where democrats and republicans could live free from the yoke of monarchs and aristocrats. Macfarlane, however, identified two 'disgusting facts' about American political institutions which undermined their democracy: 'American negro [sic] slavery, and American exclusion of white women from the exercises of all political, and many social rights – are both things opposed to freedom and fraternity, as Russian serfdom, Austrian military despotism and English class legislation.'[7] In an article called 'The Red Flag in 1850', she expanded this critique: 'In America, women generally and coloured people [sic] are enslaved and used up by the citizens of that sham republican.' Macfarlane's focus on the intertwinements of racism, sexism and class inequality can be seen as a continuity of the social critiques advanced by Frances Wright and Elizabeth Pease a few years earlier. Macfarlane, however, developed her understanding of how racism and sexism intersected by placing it in the changed landscape of post-1848 Chartism.

Chartism in the 1850s was a 'different thing from Chartism in 1840', Helen observed. 'English proletarians proved they are the true democrats and had progressed from the idea of simple political reform to the idea of Social Revolution.'[8] Helen described how, having lately returned to this country after an absence of some years, she was 'agreeably surprised by the fact'.[9] She used her platform in the radical press to deepen and accelerate this move towards social revolution and win support for Julian Harney's attempt to turn the National Charter Association into a socialist organisation.[10] Theoretical responses to the events of 1848 are most associated with Karl Marx's *The Civil War in France* but Macfarlane also contributed to socialist understandings of the relationship between political and economic revolutions.

Macfarlane saw the advance of historical enlightenment in the growing political maturity of the Chartists. The alliance between working-class people and the middle classes was unstable and had fractured under the pressure exerted by the old regimes of Europe. This led Macfarlane to conclude that only working-class organisations which remained independent of middle-class leadership could succeed in changing social conditions. Writing in 1850, Macfarlane advanced a critique of the British 1832 Reform Act that looked forward as well as backward:

> We want no merely political reforms ... Did the Reform Bill give us abundant food and airy gardens and clean, well-ordered homes instead of starvation in filthy cellars ... We, the veritable people, the Proletarians, desire a Social Revolution: that *is,* a radical change in our social condition, because we produce the boasted fabric of English greatness and English civilisation.[11]

In this article, Helen echoed the long-standing demand that workers, who produce the wealth, should have a share in it. She historicised the demand by placing it in the context of 1832 and 1848.

Macfarlane also observed how the years of European revolution had deepened internationalist currents among British workers. She did not see an opposition between national freedom and internationalism. Rather, the two were dialectically connected. An aspiration to national freedom, she argued, could be a step on the path to international solidarity:

We will not pause till we have freed our own beloved country from the aristocratic despotism under which it groans; not until the rose, the shamrock and the thistle, be woven into one wreath for the alter of liberty; not until Saxon and Celt – forgetting their senseless feuds and animosities – rally round the Red Banner to the battle-cry of the new epoch, *Vive la Republique, Democratique et Sociale!*' Helen signed this powerful and radical appeal in her own name.[12]

In her political outlook, socialism could both complete and transcend nationalist aspirations.

Macfarlane's journalism reveals affinities with her friends and comrades, Karl Marx and Frederich Engels. Like them, she combined polemical support for workers' activity with theoretical insights that penetrated beneath the superficial appearances of society. Macfarlane defended militant workers and used that defence to develop and popularise the philosophical ideas of Georg Hegel and his conception of history as the unfolding of enlightened ideas. In September 1850, the Austrian General Baron Haynau visited London on a semi-official visit. Haynau was infamous for his role in crushing the Hungarian Revolution of 1848, and for having female insurgents publicly stripped and whipped. A militant crowd led by women tried to lynch Haynau at the Barclay and Perkins brewery on London's South Bank. They chased him down Borough High Street pelting him with horse manure and chanting, 'Down with the Austrian Butcher'. Many were arrested and Julian Harney's Fraternal Democrats launched a campaign to defend workers, mostly draymen, who were prosecuted.

The *Morning Chronicle* reported on a 600-strong meeting held in Farringdon, central London, in support of the Barclay and Perkins draymen. The hall was 'crowded with a mixed assemblage of labourers and artisans, with here and there a small group of females, apparently connected with the same classes'. The *Red Republican* was being sold around the room, and Harney gave a rousing speech. David Black suggests that Helen may have been at this meeting, and we do know that she defended the protesters with her pen:

> Some of the Austro-Russian press gang have expressed their surprise that low people, like draymen, coalheavers, and so forth, should understand anything about continental affairs ... The events of the last two years have done more to enlighten the people than centuries of preaching. Universal history is the best Enlightener. Its lessons, you see, have reached the coalheavers, draymen and costermongers – about whose humanity the enlightened press have entertained doubts. Yet they are men and thinking men too. I honour them and congratulate them from the bottom of my heart.[13]

Macfarlane's writing was imbued with a Hegelian sense of reason developing through the process of historical change which was deepened and accelerated by the actions of the masses. Helen participated in the ferment of ideas among the Chartists who were urgently seeking effective ways to respond to the failures of 1848. She stood unequivocally with those who drew a sharper distinction between political demands which left living conditions unchanged and more thorough-going economic demands. This outlook shaped the radical document adopted by the Chartist Convention of 1851, which called for the nationalisation of land and mines, state education and price controls. By supporting this programme, the delegates including Ernest Jones, G. W. Reynolds and George Julian Harney, voted to transform Chartism into an openly socialist movement.

By the time the Convention met, Macfarlane had left the Chartist Movement. At New Year 1850, she ended her connection with the *Red Republican* after an argument with Harney's wife Mary at a party.[14] Karl Marx criticised Harney for losing one of his sharpest and most original journalists. Macfarlane married a French revolutionary called Francis Proust and in 1853 she gave birth to a daughter, Consuela Pauline Roland. Consuela was the title of a novel by the women's rights campaigner George Sand, which was serialised in Harney's *Friend of the People*.[15] Macfarlane's daughter was also named after the French utopian socialist and women's rights activist Pauline Roland. Macfarlane and her family sailed to South Africa, perhaps with the support of her father, but a year later she sailed home alone after her husband and baby both died. In 1856, McFarlane married a widowed clergyman, Reverend John Edwards, who had eleven children. She settled in Nantwich and had two children of her own. Helen died in 1860 aged forty-one after making the extraordinary transition from Chartist and Communist to country vicar's wife.

Macfarlane's life history suggests that the experience of 1848 both radicalised and politicised female participants and opened new spaces for women to write both polemical journalism and more theoretical articles. For a few years, she provided the theoretical basis for the shift towards 'The Charter and Something More'. That moment of possibility, when both democratic and social change seemed not only possible but imminent, did not survive for long. The new constitutional governments were overthrown, radicals were imprisoned and executed. Women had to find new ways to live within the system while honouring and preserving the hopes for change awakened in the Chartist decade.

7

Suffrage, 1866: 'Dangerous, Go-ahead, Revolutionary' Women

A general election was held in Britain in the summer of 1841. Henry Vincent was one of only eight Chartist candidates standing across the country. He contested the parliamentary seat of Banbury, Oxfordshire. Vincent was a member of the London Working Men's Association and a Moral Force Chartist. He had a national reputation as an orator, and his popularity among women was noted by both contemporaries and historians. He treated women with respect and valued their contribution to Chartism. He was also flirtatious and rather proud of his amorous adventures. Among the crowds who flocked to hear him speak was Mary Smith, a non-conformist schoolteacher. She later recalled her fascination with Vincent's 'captivating' oratory.[1] Some twenty-five years later, Smith became a supporter of the Manchester National Society for Women's Suffrage, led by prominent female suffrage campaigners including Lydia Becker, Elizabeth Wolstenholme-Elmy and Richard Pankhurst. Smith established her own female suffrage society in Carlisle, where she gave pro-suffrage lectures and petitioned in favour of the female franchise.[2] Smith was one of the few working women of the period to publish an autobiography, but her journey from Chartist to suffragist was one travelled by other women. Chartist women made a unique contribution to the emerging women's suffrage campaign.

Excavating the legacy of female Chartism requires a revision of the idea that Chartism's deep veneration of domesticity and patriarchal attitudes left the movement vulnerable to incorporation into a hierarchical and pacified labour movement.[3] The narrative of patriarchal exclusion has obscured working-class women's efforts to continue their resistance to both exploitation and political marginalisation, and to raise wider questions of inequality. One source which provides evidence of female Chartists' continuing support for women's political rights is the women's suffrage petition of 1866, the focus of this chapter.

There were no other working-class women whose presence had attracted as much attention as the Chartist women. When Chartism declined and its female supporters left the public stage, no other working-class women took their place as advocates of women's rights. When middle-class feminists did take tentative steps into political life, they took care to differentiate themselves from their working-class antecedents. The *English Woman's Journal* was launched in 1858 by a group of influential feminists including Barbara Bodichon, Bessie Rayner Parkes and Matilda Mary Hays to campaign for employment opportunities for women. The journal reported on the proceedings of the Social Science Association, commenting:

> There is no fear of English women flinging themselves recklessly into the arena of public speaking ... There is no fear of a woman who has gained a right to be heard on any social question, speaking out in a public assembly except on the rare occasions when womanly tact will advise her of the wisdom and duty of such a course.[4]

In 1870, Katherine Stanley, the president of the West of England branch of the National Society for Women's Suffrage, gave a lecture on 'The Claims of Women'. Queen Victoria joined a chorus of voices condemning Stanley for speaking in public, writing that she deserved a 'good whipping'.[5] These acknowledged feminists were far more cautious about exposing themselves to the public gaze than the Chartist women who preceded them.

This experience of public speaking was one of the distinct experiences Chartist women brought to the emerging women's suffrage movement which emerged in the 1860s. The Chartist women certainly knew how to petition and some female Chartist associations organised the collection of women's signatures.[6] The organisers of the 1866 suffrage petition were much less confident of their ability to collect signatures. Correspondence between the petition organisers shows how carefully they considered the various networks they could approach for support and discussed the best tactics to adopt.[7] They posted their petition out to potential supporters who they already knew. The signatures of those who did agree to sign were posted back and stuck on to the document at the home of Mentia Taylor. Even the women who organised the petition feared the hostility it might provoke. Emily Davies, one of the main organisers, decided to focus on girls' education to 'avoid the odium attaching to the claim for women's vote'.[8] The Chartists encouraged children as young as ten to sign their petitions, which created a broad-based community of petitioners. The organisers of the 1866 petition were intensely aware of the opposition they faced and, possibly to avoid undermining the authority of the petition, did not allow younger women to sign. Millicent Garrett, who was then aged nineteen, canvassed for the petition but was considered too young to sign it herself.[9]

The Chartist women who signed the 1866 women's suffrage petition abandoned the demand for universal male suffrage in favour of the franchise for propertied women, women who they may once have considered to be the class enemy. Granting the vote to propertied women would strengthen the forces in Parliament who would be likely to oppose the granting of suffrage to working-class men and women. These ex-Chartist women were not swept along on a wave of popular agitation. Support for the petition reflected close relationships between neighbours, family members, workmates, friends and lovers. They were clearly prepared to support a political reform which would benefit better-off women. Perhaps they thought this more limited demand was the best that could be achieved in the changed landscape of the 1860s.

The existence of local traditions was important in incubating and sustaining female Chartist activity. The 1866 petition demonstrates the fragility of such traditions. The revival of suffrage among women was contingent on the existence of a female catalyst or group of women who instigated support. Some areas which had strong female Chartist organisations provided very few signatures on the 1866 petition. Only one woman signed the petition from Sheffield, home of the adventurous Women's Rights Association, and only four signed in Birmingham, the home of Mrs Lapworth and the Birmingham Female Political Union.

One might assume that women who later became prominent in the women's suffrage movement were responsible for canvassing their towns, but this would obscure other possibilities. In the 1860s, the Suffolk town of Aldeburgh had fewer than 2,000 inhabitants, but nineteen women from Aldeburgh signed the petition.[10] Newson Garrett was the head of one of the pre-eminent families in the town.[11] In 1865, Garrett's second daughter, Elizabeth Garrett, had just become the first woman to qualify as a doctor. Elizabeth helped to organise the 1866 petition and added her signature from her home in Upper Berkeley Square. In Aldeburgh, her mother, Louisa Newson Garrett, signed the petition, as did her two sisters-in-law, Gertrude and Kate. Elizabeth Crawford speculates that it was Elizabeth's younger sisters, Agnes and Millicent, who so successfully canvassed Aldeburgh.[12] Certainly, the Aldeburgh signatures included women who may have been in the Garretts' social circle, such as Mrs Thelluson, a 'member of Aldeburgh's aristocracy', Mrs Hamilton Begbie, wife of a headmaster, and Mrs H. T. Dowler, wife of the town's vicar and bailiff.[13] It looks obvious that the Garrett family organised the petition in Aldeburgh, but there were other women who could have helped with organising the petition in the town.

One signatory from Aldeburgh, Mary Anne Garrard, was the wife of brewer William Garrard. Garrard had been known as the 'Ipswich Chartist' because he distributed Chartist publications and was a member of the Charter Convention's General Council.[14] Garrard was also a member of the Communist Propaganda Society, established by John Goodwyn and Catherine Barmby.[15] When she signed the 1866 petition, Mary Anne Garrard gave her address simply as Aldeburgh, but she lived on

Church Hill, very near Mrs Henry Culver, wife of a plumber, and Mrs Hunt, wife of a boat builder. It may have been Mary who got her neighbours to sign the petition. Mary Anne Garrard was a seasoned campaigner familiar with the radical movements of the 1840s. Women like her are too often overshadowed by the well-connected and more visible campaigners of the late nineteenth century, but their contributions complete the story of female suffrage.

'An oft told tale': The origins of the women's suffrage petition

The 1866 petition marked the coming together of several political developments. The Liberal Party proposed a new reform bill, which would extend the franchise to male householders whose property was worth £10 or more annually. This provided an opportunity to raise the question of women's suffrage in Parliament. John Stuart Mill had been elected to Parliament in 1865 and his public support for female enfranchisement encouraged campaigners.[16] In the same year, members of the Kensington Ladies Discussion Society committed themselves to support female suffrage and began to consider ways to achieve it. Their strategy relied on their familial and political connections. In May 1866, Barbara Bodichon wrote to Helen Taylor asking if her stepfather, John Stuart Mill, would present a petition to Parliament proposing the extension of the vote to women on the same basis of men. Taylor replied,

> I think also that it is utterly out of the question to suppose that there is the slightest chance of anything whatever being now obtained. Still, if a tolerably numerous petition can be got up, my father will gladly undertake to present it.[17]

The petition's most fervent supporters knew that it stood no chance of being passed by Parliament. It was an act of political drama, which was successful in making marginalised women visible and galvanising a movement for female suffrage.

The 1866 petition was mythologised in early histories of the women's suffrage movement as the first act on the long road to the Representation of the People Acts of 1918 and 1928. Suffrage campaigner Millicent Fawcett referred to the story of the petition and its presentation to Parliament as an 'oft told tale'.[18] More recently, however, the petition has faded from historical accounts.[19] This has contributed to a sense of a rupture in the campaign for women's rights, which assumes that the women of the 1830s and 1840s failed to establish a continuing tradition. It distorts the political identity of the later feminist movement by dividing it from its radical origins.

The leaders of the later women's suffrage movement may have frowned upon their more radical and unconventional antecedents.[20] Petition organisers Elizabeth Garrett Anderson, Emily Davies, Barbara Bodichon and Bessie Parkes have entered the canon of feminist icons. The more radical Clementia (known as Mentia) Taylor and Helen Taylor were later erased from the history of female suffrage.[21] The 1866 petition is an overlooked source, which can support the excavation of the missing links between the women of Chartism and the more radical voices of the Victorian female suffrage campaigners.[22]

One of those radical voices belonged to Helen Taylor, a socialist who supported a wide range of progressive causes including land reform in Ireland. She was elected to the London School Board in 1876 and joined the first Marxist organisation in Britain, the Social Democratic Federation, when it was established in 1881. Taylor's relationship with John Stuart Mill gave her access to London's radical intellectuals. Her friend Harriet Grote was a historian and biographer whose works included *The Philosophical Radicals of 1832, Some Incidents Connected with the Reform Movement from 1832 to 1842* (1866).[23] The Philosophical Radicals came to prominence in the 1820s when they campaigned for universal suffrage, secret ballots and the abolition of the House of Lords and the monarchy. Harriet's husband, George Grote, as well as John Stuart Mill, Joseph Parkes (Bessie's father) and Francis Place, a member of the London Working Men's Association, were all members. George Grote was also a member of William Lovett's National Association.[24] In 1865, Harriet Grote introduced Helen Taylor to

Katherine Stanley, wife of Viscount Amberley and mother to the socialist, pacifist philosopher Bertrand Russell.[25] Both Katherine Amberley and Harriet Grote signed the 1866 petition, and both cemented a familial and philosophical link between the radicals of the 1830s and the radicals of the Edwardian period.

Mentia Taylor shared Helen Taylor's broad reforming outlook. Her friend Caroline Ashurst Biggs called her 'The Mother of the Suffrage Movement', but not all her contemporaries shared Biggs' assessment.[26] Mentia Taylor wrote to Helen Taylor that some of the other petition organisers thought her a 'dangerous, go-ahead, revolutionary person' and that she felt like a 'pariah' among them.[27] Her position at the centre of London's radical Unitarian networks was reinforced by her own extensive network of family relationships.

Clementia Doughty was born into a Unitarian family and in 1842 she married Peter Alfred Taylor, another Unitarian who was elected as a member of Parliament for Leicester in 1862. Peter Alfred was the nephew of Samuel Courtauld, silk manufacturer, philanthropist and art collector. Mentia Taylor's sister-in-law, Sophia Courtauld, and her mother-in-law, Mrs Samuel Courtauld, both signed the 1866 suffrage petition. Mentia Taylor's sister, Caroline Taylor, signed the petition from her address in Bridgwater, Somerset. Caroline and her husband, William Taylor, joined the Birmingham Women's Suffrage Society.[28] Their daughter, Catherine Courtauld Taylor, became president of the Birmingham Women's Suffrage Society in 1903. By then, Caroline Taylor had been widowed and married Alfred Ostler. Their son, Julian Ostler, joined the Men's League for Women's Suffrage and their daughters, Nellie and Dorothy, were members of the National Union of Women's Suffrage Societies.[29]

Peter Taylor's cousin, Louisa McKee, signed the 1866 suffrage petition from her home in Shrewsbury, as did her daughter, Ellen. When the Shrewsbury Suffrage Committee was formed in 1871, Louisa became a member and Ellen became its secretary.[30] Family relationships also interacted with working relationships. Mary Merryweather worked as a nurse at the Courtaulds' mill, where she ran a clinic for the female workers. In 1862,

Merryweather moved to Liverpool, where she trained nurses and she signed the petition from her new address at Dover Street, Liverpool.[31]

The Taylor-Courtauld family created intergenerational networks and friendships, which must have offered women practical, emotional and political support as they risked ridicule and derision for campaigning for the vote. The women's suffrage campaigners were masters of political networking and mixing politics with parties.[32] The personal dimensions of these relationships, however, should not obscure the political choices made by the signatories of the 1866 petition. Among the Garretts and the Taylors, there were women who chose to raise families or devote themselves to philanthropic causes rather than campaign for suffrage. The women's choices were just as political as those made by their husbands, brothers and sons.

The ability of the petitioners to attract the support of an older generation of female activists has been identified as one of the petition's 'most remarkable features'.[33] The oldest signatories were Mary Somerville, mathematician and astronomer, born in 1780, and Maria Burrows, wife of a plumber, born in 1787. Among the older signatories was Marion Reid, author of *A Plea for Woman,* who was born in 1815 and was then living in Bayswater, London. The fifty-seven signatures from Edinburgh were probably the result of the efforts of an older generation of Quakers, Elizabeth Pease and Jane Smeal Wigham, and Jane's daughter-in-law, Eliza Wigham. The Wighams established both the Edinburgh Ladies' Emancipation Society and the Edinburgh branch of the National Union of Suffrage Societies. They both signed the 1866 suffrage petition from 5 South Grey Street, Edinburgh. Evidence from the petition suggests that similar, though less well-documented, politicised familial relationships also existed among working women. Sisters Isabella, Elizabeth and Mary Ann Lamb, milliners working from George Street, below Edinburgh Castle, all signed the petition.

Far away on the Isle of Wight, meanwhile, sisters Ellen Cantelo and Elizabeth Thompson both signed the petition. Their father, William Cantelo, had been a Chartist who worked as a publican and a brush-maker on the island.[34] Ellen was in her forties when she signed the petition and was making a living as a painter and pioneering female photographer. Her connections with the London art world make her the most likely petition organiser on the Isle of Wight. The third signatory from the Isle of Wight was Sarah James, Ellen and Elizabeth's maternal aunt, a milliner who had no home of her own and lodged with a succession of different families on the island.[35] Ellen found a way to engage with new technological possibilities and secure a life different from that of her father or that of her aunt, who appeared to remain trapped in the low-paid, insecure work available to poorer women.

The Chartist signatories

The Chartist women who signed the 1866 petition belonged to an older generation. I can find no birth date for Mary Lovett, who signed from 137 Euston Road, London, the home she shared with William. She married William in 1826, so Mary was probably in her sixties when she signed the petition.[36] The Lovett's forty-year relationship has divided historians, with William Lovett being described as both patronising and paternalistic towards his wife and supportive and respectful.[37] Whatever the dynamics of their relationship, Mary Lovett was more than capable of playing an important public role within the Chartist movement when called upon and Mary ran a series of generally unsuccessful businesses. She might have been largely hidden behind a hardening divide between public and private worlds, but she was a courageous, capable and intelligent woman, who coped with the arrest of her husband and the seizure of all their household goods.[38] Her signature on the 1866 petition suggests that she may have been more assertive in the pursuit of her own rights than either her husband or historians have acknowledged.

One of the Lovett's neighbours, Mrs Amelia Tansley from 185 Euston Road, also signed the female suffrage petition. In 1863, Amelia had married George Tansley who was one of the founding members of the Working Men's College, established in 1854.[39] Amelia was involved in the associated Working Women's

College, established in 1864, along with Elizabeth Malleson, a member of a very well-connected Unitarian family, who also signed the 1866 petition and joined the London Society for Women's Suffrage. We do not know if Mary Lovett knew Amelia Tansley, a much younger woman of more comfortable means, or if one woman influenced the other, but the proximity of their homes and their shared support for the petition suggests a relationship. Tansley's commitment to adult education would have resonated with both radical Unitarians and Moral Force Chartists.

Another signatory from this older generation of Chartist women was Eleanor B. Watson, of 4 Gipsy Hill, West Norwood. Her husband, James Watson, was one of the respected members of London Chartism's older generation of leaders. He was a publisher of radical texts, a free-press campaigner, a founding member of the LWMA and a member of Lovett's National Association. There is reason to think that Watson respected women's political capacities. He was brought up by a single mother who taught him to read and write. In his autobiography, he recalled how his mother introduced him to radical ideas by reading William Cobbett's *Register* to him.[40] Watson was imprisoned for selling banned books in 1823. Undaunted, he published the works of Thomas Paine, Percy Bysshe Shelley, Mary Wollstonecraft and Frances Wright. In June 1834, Eleanor Byerley and James Watson got married. They moved to Norwood in 1865 to be near the green space of Crystal Palace, which is the address given by Eleanor B. Watson when she signed the 1866 petition.[41]

The fact that both Mary Lovett and Eleanor Watson signed the 1866 petition indicates that support for women's political rights was embedded within a political culture which was developed in the free-press movement of the 1820s and helped to shape London Chartism in the 1840s. Another Chartist signatory, Eliza Lynn Linton, was also a wife of leading LWMA member and prominent Chartist William Linton. But Eliza Lynn Linton cultivated the public profile and controversy that other Chartist wives shunned. Eliza Lynn Linton signed the 1866 petition from her hometown in Coniston, in the Lake District. Her extraordinary literary and political career will be discussed below.

Mary Lovett, Eleanor Watson and Eliza Lynn Linton were all married to members of the LWMA and of the National Association. They all had strong connections to London, either living in the city permanently or during the period of their engagement with Chartism. The petition reveals how other networks connected Chartism and 1860s feminism in towns and cities outside London. Ada Barmby and her stepdaughter, Julia, signed the 1866 petition from their home in Wakefield. Other signatories from Wakefield included Annie O'Dwyer and Elizabeth Roach, who both ran schools and lived near the Barmbys' address in Westgate. Ada was the second wife of John Goodwyn Barmby, who was a Chartist, utopian socialist and a correspondent of both William Linton and Friedrich Engels. In the 1820s, Goodwyn Barmby travelled to Paris to meet French socialists. He is widely credited with introducing the term 'Communist' into English.[42]

When Goodwyn's first wife, Catherine, died in 1853, he took the post of minister of Wakefield Unitarian Chapel. In 1861, he married Ada Shepard, the daughter of the governor of Wakefield Gaol, and the couple were active in progressive movements throughout the decade.[43] Most accounts of Goodwyn Barmby's life refer only to Catherine but there is evidence that Ada was also a political activist. Not only did she sign the 1866 petition, but she was also a member of the National Society for Women's Suffrage in the 1860s, along with Goodwyn and his daughter, Julia. Julia later became the secretary of the Wakefield National Society for Women's Suffrage.[44]

Women who were predisposed to support suffrage reform knew each other through the Chartist campaign. Helen Taylor's stepfather, John Stuart Mill, had collaborated with William Lovett in the 1840s and contributed to the National Association library in 1842. This may have brought Helen into contact with women such as Fanny and Jane King, who signed the petition from 9 Eden Grove, Holloway. They were the wife and daughter of John King, a pianoforte maker and old friend of William Lovett. King was a long-standing member of the National Association and named one of his sons after Lovett.[45]

A radical network can be identified in Hackney, East London, home to Mary Anne Plummer. Taylor must have known Plummer because she wrote asking her to help collect signatures for the petition. Taylor reassured Plummer that the petition was not intended to delay the extension of the franchise to more men, but was 'a quiet expression of our wish to be included in the common rights of citizens' in the future.[46] Taylor's sensitivity to the accusation that demanding votes for women would delay the extension of the vote to working-class men was reminiscent of the debates within Chartism. Mary Anne was born in Kettering in 1839 and worked as a milliner before she married John Plummer, a stay-maker, in 1860. As a teenager, John Plummer had been inspired by Chartism and made a name as a poet and trade unionist.[47] The Plummers moved to Hackney, where Plummer's role as a newspaper editor brought him into contact with John Stuart Mill, who praised him as one of the most 'inspiring examples of mental cultivation and high principles in a self-instructed working man'.[48]

Mary Anne Plummer wrote to Taylor explaining that:

> It is a matter of regret to me that I have not been able to obtain more [signatures], but Mr Plummer has been lately so much taken up with the business of Victoria Park that I have been unable to get out as much as usual. It will always afford me much pleasure to help you in any such matters and I am sure that the same may be said of my husband.[49]

Plummer was occupied with a campaign to prevent the construction of a gas storage station in East London's Victoria Park, the lungs of the East End, which also involved John Stuart Mill. Despite her diffidence, the cluster of signatures in Hackney Wick strongly suggests that Mary Anne canvassed her neighbours Mrs C. A. Dawson, Mrs A. Young and Mrs Emma Dornbusch at 11 Grove Villas.

Emma Dornbusch was the second wife and former housekeeper of an exiled German Communist, George Dornbusch. Emma's stepdaughter, Ada, also signed the petition. The Dornbusch family was engaged in a range of radical causes. The Dornbusch family home was called 'Vegetarian Cottage' in a public show of their commitment to vegetarianism, which they shared with many Chartists including Elizabeth and Charles Neesom.[50] Dornbusch was a member of the anti-slavery Emancipation Society, along with John Stuart Mill, Peter Alfred Taylor MP and Dr Richard Pankhurst. In 1868, George and Emma Dornbusch were both members of the National Society for Women's Suffrage.[51] Support for the 1866 suffrage petition was embedded within circles connected with the National Charter Association and represented a continuity, rather than a rupture, with the outlook of the Moral Force Chartists.

Clusters, canvassers and communities

The 1866 petition originated in London, which provided 424 out of the 1,499 signatures. A proportion of these signatories came from a radical counterculture, which flourished among London's radical booksellers who were clustered around the Strand. Many booksellers were active in the campaign for a free press and provided support for free-thinking radicalism and for Chartism. James Watson, Henry Hetherington and William Lovett had all run radical bookshops in the capital.[52] Mrs and Harriet Truelove signed the petition from 240 the Strand. They were the wife and daughter of Edward Truelove, Owenite, Chartist, bookseller and publisher.[53] Just down the Strand at number 282 was a bookshop run by Edward and Louisa Farrah, which had sold Chartist publications, and this was the address from which Louisa signed the 1866 petition. Miss K. Ackland, Sarah Colmar, Mrs Alfred Comfort, Miss Davies, Mrs Lane and Miss R. Lane all gave their address as 226 the Strand. This may have been a multi-occupancy house or the address of a sympathetic book-shop owner which the women could use to protect their privacy.

Travelling east along the Strand, a campaigner seeking signatures would have arrived at number 150, a working men's club, which was the address given by signatory Jane Horsburgh. Positioned a little further east, 41 Fore Street, Moorgate, was the home of signatories Esther and Elizabeth Vialls. The Vialls ran a coffee house, established in the 1830s by their father William Vialls and the radical and Chartist Francis Place as a 'free space' for working-class people to gather without the temptation of alcohol.[54] In his autobiography, William Lovett remembered frequenting coffee houses in Holborn and Clerkenwell, where he was initiated into the art of political debate by listening to influential radicals including Richard Carlile and George Thompson.[55] From the 1820s onwards, booksellers and coffee-shop proprietors were engaged in political campaigns for working-class access to knowledge and public spaces. The radical attitudes associated with such trades and the London streets in which they clustered proved to be very resilient, and they continued to support radical causes into the 1860s.

Some 106 women from Leeds signed the petition. Their addresses suggest that the names were collected during a house-to-house canvas in the working-class Woodhouse area now home to the University of Leeds. Signatories from along Woodhouse Lane included Sarah and B. Loftus, who ran a baby linen shop at number 88, and Mary Newton, who owned a stationery shop at number 99. Signatories from the nearby Woodhouse Street included Martha Fenton, laundress, and Emma Tingle, charwoman. Signatories from surrounding streets included lodging housekeeper Sarah Fisher and Ellen Heaton, daughter of a wealthy bookseller. Heaton campaigned for female suffrage, education for girls, environmental protections and against vivisection on animals. She was a member of the Pre-Raphaelite Brotherhood and an art collector.[56] The signatories from Leeds demonstrate that more middle-class, educated women did not always constitute the most signatories in a city, and shared political sympathies could transcend social divisions and penetrate deeply into the class structure.

Some 173 signatories lived in Manchester, the city at the heart of the Industrial Revolution and a major site of reform agitation throughout the nineteenth century. Elizabeth Crawford has identified Elizabeth Wolstenholme-Elmy as the likely organiser of support for the female suffrage petition in the city. Wolstenholme was the granddaughter of a Lancashire cotton-spinner;

she had a long association with the Langham Place circle and joined the Kensington Society when it was first established in 1865.[57] Whoever organised the petitioning in Manchester, the signatories included women from across different classes. Several signatories were prosperous women living in the healthier suburbs of the city, such as Mary Anne Gaskell, daughter of the novelist and Unitarian Elizabeth Gaskell. Many other Manchester signatories were working women and small traders.

A closer look at one signatory in the Lancashire mill town of Salford offers a glimpse of how political interactions played out in the lived experience of working-class women. Elizabeth Dracup was the daughter-in-law of John Dracup, a linen draper.[58] Dracup was a prominent figure in Manchester's radical circles. In 1819, he provided bail money for John Wroe, a radical journalist with the *Manchester Guardian,* and his wife, when they were arrested at Peterloo. By 1844, John Dracup was sufficiently established to be elected to Salford's new borough council. In the same year, Dracup's son, William, married Elizabeth Askew.[59] William died eighteen months later and in 1847, the widowed Elizabeth, who must have had some education, opened a school with her sister-in-law, Frances. Elizabeth then disappeared from the historical record until January 1861, when she began to run another school at Seawood House, Newton-in-Cartmel, Lancashire, the address she gave when she signed the 1866 petition.

Salford had a history of supporting radical causes, of sending delegations to Peterloo, agitating against the New Poor Laws and providing support for Chartism.[60] This tradition was crucial for generating support for the female suffrage petition in Lancashire. Elizabeth's connections with the Dracups survived her bereavement, and her political and familial relationships reinforced each other. The petition gives us the chance to look beyond the well-known families who left written records of their lives and consider the role played by women such as Elizabeth Dracup in creating the women's suffrage movement.

Suffrage and sexuality

In the 1830s and 1840s, radical political organisations created spaces in which women could explore ways of living beyond the confines of the conventional family. American actor Charlotte Cushman first appeared in this book as the lover of Eliza Cook. When Cushman settled in London in 1845, her home became such a space. Regular visitors included her future partner Matilda Hays, Robert Owen, William Linton, lovers Ellen Braysher and Amelia Edwards, and Eliza Lynn before her marriage to Linton.[61] As this space narrowed in the 1850s, the possibility of expressing heterodox sexuality became more limited. Some historians of female Chartism identified 'respectability' as a cultural and political concept which united working-class and middle-class radicals at the expense of women's freedom.[62] Some women, however, could pursue a degree of sexual freedom which went far beyond the constraints imposed by the monogamous family and heterosexuality.

Among the signatories to the 1866 petition were women whose lives demonstrated that ideas of respectability did not extinguish the possibility of sexual relationships outside marriage. Susanna Inge, who we met in Chapter 1, gave birth to a son in 1847 and assumed the identity of a widow, although there is no record of her getting married. Mother and child emigrated to America in 1858. Barbara Bodichon's father did not marry her mother, a milliner who bore him several children. Harriet Taylor had an open sexual relationship with John Stuart Mill before they could marry. Elizabeth Wolstenholme lived with Benjamin Elmy for years before they married when she became pregnant in 1874. The petition shows that working-class women could also live outside the narrow prescriptions of appropriate relationships. Elizabeth Bucknall, a Manchester cotton winder, was an unmarried mother of one when she signed the 1866 petition.

Women involved in same-sex relationships formed another group among the signatories to the 1866 petition. These were women who formed sexual relationships with other women which took the form of 'female marriages', which were acknowledged by their friends and acquaintances. Signatory Matilda

Hays was an author, translator and activist who was involved in a female marriage with Charlotte Cushman. Hays was often known as Max or Mathew.[63] Hays and Cushman lived together, exchanging rings and referring openly to their 'marriage'. When Hays published a translation of a George Sand novel in 1851, she dedicated it to Cushman. The following year, poet Elizabeth Barrett Browning wrote to her cousin Arabella with her impressions of meeting Cushman: 'I understand that she & Miss Hayes [sic] have made vows of celibacy & and of eternal attachment to each other – they live together, dress alike ... it is a female marriage.'[64]

These informal marriages may have helped to reconcile others to the lesbianism of those involved. Cushman's biographer suggests that her successive marriages to Eliza Cook, Matilda Hays and the sculptor Emma Stebbins helped to incorporate the actress into many networks by giving her an aura of respectability.[65] Another female marriage was established between Amelia Edwards, novelist and Egyptologist, and Ellen Drew Braysher. The couple lived together for thirty years and signed the petition from the home they shared in Westbury-on-Trym, near Bristol. These relationships both radically subverted conventional ideas of marriage and reinvented it to express monogamous, lesbian relationships.

Signatory Frances Power Cobbe was famous among radical circles for her journalistic exposés of the horrors of slavery and domestic violence and her philosophical writings on women's rights. Cobbe lived in an artistic, lesbian community, which coalesced around Cushman and her circle in Italy in the early 1860s. In her autobiography, Cobbe describes meeting the mathematician Mary Somerville, another signatory, and how she could 'hardly keep herself from caressing her' as the two sat on a bed.[66] Cobbe formed a lasting relationship with the sculptor Mary Lloyd and the couple lived together from 1864 until Lloyd's death in 1896.[67] Both signed the petition from their home in 26 Hereford Square, London. Cobbe was circumspect regarding their relationship in her autobiography, comparing Lloyd's love to a mother's affection and concluding that she could not be expected to write more. In her private correspondence, Cobbe was free to be more candid and she referred to Lloyd as 'my wife' in a letter to Somerville.[68]

Emily Faithfull, a member of the Langham Place Group and campaigner for women's employment, signed the 1866 petition. Six years earlier, she had set up the successful Victoria Press, which employed women as compositors in the face of opposition from the printers' union. Census records for 1861 show that Faithfull was living at the home of Matilda Hays in Langham Place. Faithfull was propelled into the public eye during the Codrington Divorce Case in 1864. In the spring of 1856 Admiral Codrington went to fight in the Crimea. His wife, Helen Jane, chose Emily Faithfull to be her companion while the Admiral was away. He returned in the autumn of 1856. Within months Mrs Codrington was refusing to sleep with him and insisted that she needed to share her bed with Faithfull, which she said helped her asthma. Faithfull alleged that one night, the Admiral got into the marital bed and tried to rape her. The Admiral claimed in court that he was looking for a poker. He retaliated against her accusations of attempted rape by accusing Helen Jane of adultery with a man and beginning divorce proceedings in what became the scandalous *Codrington v Codrington*. Faithfull was named in court as having 'alienated' Helen Jane's affections from her husband.[69] Faithfull was not permanently damaged by the scandal. She continued to campaign, publish and lecture, completing three successful speaking tours of America in the 1870s and 1880s, and was awarded a pension by Queen Victoria in 1895. She ended her life living with another woman, Charlotte Robinson, who was described as 'home art decorator' to Queen Victoria and to whom Faithfull left all her worldly goods.[70]

These signatories to the 1866 petition pursued heterodox sexual relationships which modified ideas of respectability to incorporate same-sex marriages. Gender conformity was strongly promoted by the religious, political and cultural institutions of the mid-nineteenth century and reinforced through the criminal law, but there were social spaces within radical political networks in which lesbian relationships were accepted and celebrated.

Some prominent female radicals lived with their lovers, and some gave birth outside marriage. The pressure to conform imposed itself on them and many eventually married or, like Susanna Inge, assumed the identity of a widow. Women in same-sex relationships, however, could not transition into conformity, so they created a parallel institution of female marriage. Radical women had to face accusations of immorality when they appeared in public. Some responded by emphasising their purity and virtue, but others were prepared to explore different ways to live and to love. A small but discernible current which advocated sexual freedom for women flowed from the early socialists of the 1820s and 1830s, through the writings of radicals such as Frances Wright and Eliza Cook, and women's friendship networks into the later women's suffrage movement.

Female suffrage in the era of civil war

The American Civil War broke out on 12 April 1861. Radicals might have expected Britain's once-powerful anti-slavery movement to revive, but they would have been disappointed. On 27 November 1862, Harriet Beecher Stowe issued an 'Appeal to the Women of England' in the first of several attempts to resurrect the anti-slavery cause. It was Mentia Taylor, the initiator of the 1866 petition, who answered Beecher Stowe's appeal. Mentia had been fighting her own battles with the established anti-slavery movement. She had applied to join the London Anti-Slavery Society but was refused because women were not accepted as members. Taylor's response to this rebuff was to establish the Ladies' London Emancipation Society.[71] Taylor provided the organisational means for women to engage with this later campaign against slavery, just as she provided a catalyst for the female suffrage campaign and there was significant cross-fertilisation between the two campaigns. In the 1860s, the veteran campaigner Frederick Douglass shared platforms with another black American abolitionist and reformer, Sarah Parker Remond, who was probably the only black woman to sign the

1866 women's suffrage petition, although Matilda Hays was sometimes referred to as 'Creole'.[72]

Abolitionist friendships and political networks proved to be of vital importance in the 1860s when the movement against slavery confronted a changed political landscape. Britain had become heavily dependent on importing cotton produced by enslaved people in the Southern states of the US. The Cotton Kingdom of the South was the twin of Cottonopolis, as Manchester was known. Three decades after the abolition of slavery, and fifty years since the abolition of the slave trade, Britain was up to its neck in slavery. The blockade of the South during the American Civil War created severe shortages and unemployment, which became known as the Cotton Famine. By 1862, some 312,200 men and women, about 70 percent of the Lancashire cotton workforce, were out of work.[73] As David Olusoga has argued, patterns of support for the North did not fall along simple class lines with employers supporting the South and workers siding with the North. In towns which had been strongholds of Chartism, such as Ashton-under-Lyne and Oldham, there were large meetings of textile workers who opposed the blockade of the South, motivated by a desperation for their predicament to be alleviated and by underlying racism. Neighbouring Rochdale, however, remained resolutely hostile to the South.[74]

The families which provided support for the 1866 petition also provided a bedrock of support for the North and enjoyed sufficient influence to activate wider political networks in opposition to American slavery. Rochdale was one of the most consistently anti-slavery towns in Lancashire. John Bright had been the MP for the town and owned mills in Rochdale which closed during the Cotton Famine but continued to pay their workers.[75] Bright was a friend of black American abolitionist Frederick Douglass and a committed opponent of slavery. John's daughter, Helen Bright Clark, invited Douglass to visit her home in Street, Somerset where he met Catherine Impey, a Quaker living with her mother in the town. Both Catherine and her mother, Mary Hannah, signed the 1866 petition. Shortly after meeting Douglass, Catherine and Mary Hannah Impey began to write, edit and publish a periodical, *Anti-Caste,* one of the first anti-racist publications in Britain.[76]

Between 1888 and 1895, *Anti-Caste* exposed atrocities committed by British colonialists, campaigned against lynching in the American South and gave black writers a platform. Catherine hosted black American activist Ida B. Wells, and the two women set up an organisation, the Society for the Recognition of the Universal Brotherhood of Man, and went on a national lecture tour together. The well-to-do Bright family and families of more modest means such as the Impeys created national and international networks of solidarity which transcended geographic distance and distinctions of race and class. The 1866 petition reveals the multilayered webs of abolitionism and solidarity between black and white which was deeply embedded among radical families such as the Brights, Ashursts and Sturges, who with black activists – such as Frederick Douglass and Sarah and Charles Remond – created reciprocal relationships between anti-slavery and pro-suffrage networks which strengthened both movements.

These connections were obscured by historians of Chartism who were concerned to present the movement as a legitimate ancestor of the later nineteenth-century labour movement. The presence of independent women who had broad and inclusive aspirations disrupted the retrospective creation of a moderate and respectable working-class movement. In reacting against the failures of labour historians to recognise women's contribution to radical movements, later feminist historians sought and found an antagonism between the aspirations of women and the demands of the organised working class. They did not look beyond Chartism's failure to articulate specifically feminist demands to explore the insurgent nature of female Chartism.

The female suffrage campaign drew strength from the political experience of female Chartists and their family and community networks. The mid-nineteenth-century women's movement did not have to invent its own rhetoric, strategies and organisations. Rather, mid-century feminists could engage with, modify and re-energise pre-existing traditions and networks in support of a renewed campaign to improve women's lives by expanding the franchise. Their movement would not have had the capacity to engage with so many working women had it not found fertile ground in the pre-existing working-class histories of supporting women's right to vote and engaging with political activism.

The Many Faces of Eliza Lynn Linton

Eliza Lynn was born in Keswick in the Lake District in 1822, the youngest of twelve children. Her father was an Anglican vicar. When she was twenty-one, she moved to London to make an independent living by writing. She became one of the first female professional journalists when she took up a post with the *Morning Chronicle* in 1845.[1] In London, Lynn mixed with a circle of political and sexual radicals, which included her future husband, William Linton, and several lesbian couples. Lynn called them her 'insurgents'.[2]

After spending a year working in Paris, Lynn returned to the Lake District where she again met William Linton, a founding member of the LWMA, a close friend of James Watson and a leading figure within London Chartism. In October 1837, William Linton had married Laura Wade, a member of William Fox's radical Unitarian congregation. When she died just six months later, Linton began a relationship with Laura's sister, Emily, another radical Unitarian.[3] The law prohibited a marriage between a widower and his sister-in-law, so they lived in a common-law marriage. Emily gave birth to seven children before she too died.[4] Linton left London in 1852 and moved to Coniston, where he met Eliza Lynn again. They married in 1858.

There is no evidence that Lynn Linton joined any political organisation but in the early 1850s, contemporaries observed that she supported the Rebecca Riots and defended the French Revolution of 1848. Lynn Linton befriended Felice Orsini, an Italian revolutionary living in exile in England. Orsini was executed in 1858 for attempting to assassinate Napoleon III.[5] By 1866, Lynn Linton's political allegiances were shifting in contradictory directions.[6] She signed the 1866 female suffrage petition and also signed a similar petition the following year. Just a few months later, however, Lynn Linton became a celebrity for her vitriolic attacks on women's habits and political aspirations. In her most famous article, 'The Girl of the Period' published in 1868, she mocked women who thought only of shallow pursuits, the woman, 'who dyes her hair and paints her face, as the first articles of her personal religion'.[7] At this point, Lynn Linton could reconcile her satirical critiques of vacuous women with support for electoral and legal reforms which could benefit independent women. As her reputation grew, however, she focused her attacks more explicitly on women seeking political rights.

In 1889, Lynn Linton signed an 'Appeal against Female Suffrage', organised by Mrs Humphrey Ward, a prominent opponent of votes for women. Lynn Linton's 1891 article, 'Wild Women as Politicians', was a vitriolic attack on women with political ambitions, who she called 'the Shrieking Sisterhood'. Lynn Linton was frequently accused of hypocrisy because she had separated from her own husband and earned her own living while demanding that other women exhibit wifely submission and limit themselves to domestic concerns. Lynn Linton's own access to financial independence came to depend on her opposition to female independence in general. Lynn Linton articulated support for 'manliness and manly virtues', which were closely bound up with her growing support for British colonialism as a civilising force. She advocated 'the manly doctrine of readiness for war, should war be necessary, and the steady expansion of the empire'.[8] Eliza Lynn Linton was not the first prominent writer to make the journey from political radical to conservative and to benefit financially from their apostasy. What is perhaps more interesting in Lynn Linton's case was how complex and contradictory that process was.

Lynn Linton's 1851 novel, *Realities*, attracted such hostility from the critics that she abandoned novel writing for two decades and concentrated exclusively on her journalism. In the 1870s, when she returned to fiction, she also seemed to return to her earlier feminism and radicalism. She often referred to herself as a Communist, espousing a vision of cooperation steeped in Christian ethics. Her most controversial novel, *The True History of Joshua Davidson* (1872) was subversive because Lynn Linton imagined Christ as a poor, persecuted man, and pure Christianity as communistic and egalitarian. *The Rebel of the Family* (1880) contained a sympathetic portrayal of women's rights activists and the first literary portrait of London's lesbian community.[9] In the novel, *Bell Blount*, 'The Lady President of the West Hill Society for Women's Rights', is a lesbian. Her 'good little wife' Connie, 'was everything that one woman could be to another'. Lynn Linton's extraordinary novel, *The Autobiography of Christopher Kirkland* (1885) switched the gender of all the main characters, which allowed Lynn Linton to explore her own sexual attraction for women. In the novel, she protests the 'hideous injustices' women had had to endure but suggests their demands have gone too far and would result in women becoming masculine and men becoming feminine.[10]

One character in the novel is clearly based on Mentia Taylor and the Aubrey House set. Lynn Linton's depiction of Mentia's companion, the black American abolitionist campaigner Sarah Parker Remond, was deeply racist. But Lynn Linton was never consistently reactionary. She explores her contradictory attitudes to her 'unlovely' heroines, both repulsed and fascinated by her 'boy-women'.[11] In her Chartist days, Eliza Lynn Linton could reconcile her belief in a distinct female nature with support for women's right to vote. As radicalism and working-class activism declined, a fissure between these two beliefs deepened. Lynn Linton evolved from radical and female suffrage campaigner into an anti-feminist and imperialist, but her evolution was not smooth or predictable. Her sympathy with the condition of the poor, and her interest in exploring unconventional sexuality and female rebellion continued to find expression in her writings.

8

Chartist Afterlives: 'Thanks to My Mother'

The links between Chartism and the 1866 female suffrage petition are one dimension of Chartism's contested legacy which have been overlooked. A small number of historians have identified Chartism's lasting impact in terms of constitutional reform and working-class aspiration to education.[1] Many historians see Chartism as a short-lived movement, a huge and powerful wave which crashed over British politics and swiftly receded, leaving little trace. The legacy of Chartism was eradicated by the incorporation of more skilled workers into consensual Liberal politics. David Goodway has observed that, while Chartism had an indissoluble bond with its predecessors, a

> profound hiatus exists around mid-century and although Chartism and former Chartists could not fail to influence developments in trade unionism and the renewed movement for parliamentary reform, the connections appear amazingly slight given the psychological hold, combined with the mass penetration of Chartism in its hey-day.[2]

Where Chartism did leave a legacy, it was considered to be one which was detrimental to working-class women's engagement with radical politics.[3]

Exploring Chartist legacies through the lens of female activism provides a challenge to this interpretation of the movement. Chartism left a vibrant legacy, which encouraged rather than undermined women's activism. Evidence of Chartist support for the later female franchise campaign does not rest exclusively on the 1866 petition. Chartist leader Ernest Jones, and Chartist and historian of Chartism Robert Gammage were both listed as supporters of the Manchester Women's Suffrage Society in 1868.[4] George Howell was a bricklayer who joined the Chartist movement in 1848 and went on to become secretary to the Reform League and the Trade Union Congress and Lib–Lab MP for Bethnal Green. His archive contains memorabilia from the women's suffrage movement, including several adverts for pro-suffrage meetings and pamphlets, including a speech, 'Women's Suffrage', delivered by William Fox in Oldham in February 1853, and published as a pamphlet in 1868. He also kept records of the London National Society for Women's Suffrage, the Manchester Society for Women's Suffrage and the National Society for Women's Suffrage, established in 1878. The executive committee of the National Society for Women's Suffrage included many familiar names: the Garretts, the Ashursts, the Taylors, the Sturges and Helen Taylor. Among the members of the General Committee were former Chartists Benjamin Lucraft and Alfred Mundella, and radicals associated with Chartism including William and Mary Howitt, Edward Miall, Elizabeth Pease Nichol, William Shaen, Mentia Taylor and Eliza Wigham. These suffrage campaigners shared the broad, reforming aspirations of their Chartist fathers and mothers, and grandfathers and grandmothers. They blended concern for women's political rights with organising to redress the economic inequalities which shaped working-class women's lives.

Political sympathies were passed down from mothers to daughters, through extended families and female friendship networks, and sustained by women who were influential within their families and communities. These networks have been cast into shade by the presence of articulate, well-connected middle-class suffragettes whose dramatic family sagas have overshadowed the contributions made by working-class women. There was a stable intergenerational network of radicals and Chartists who consistently supported the women's suffrage campaign from the 1840s to the 1870s and beyond. Amie Hicks was the daughter of a Chartist who lived in London. In 1884, she joined the Social

Democratic Federation and was also a member of the Women Ropemakers' Union, the National Union of Women Workers and the National Society for Women's Suffrage.[5] Bradford-born Julia Varley was the great-granddaughter of a radical who protested at Peterloo and the granddaughter of a Chartist. Varley began work in a textile mill at the age of twelve and later became a prominent trade union organiser and suffragette in Bradford and Birmingham.[6] She was awarded an OBE for her public service in 1931. Derbyshire-born Hannah Mitchell was also the granddaughter of a Chartist. She worked as a servant and a dressmaker before joining the Independent Labour Party and becoming a full-time activist for the Women's Social and Political Union.[7]

Annie Kenney was born in Oldham and became a trade unionist and a leading figure in the Women's Social and Political Union. In her autobiography, Kenney recalled how her mother had encouraged her to read the writings of Tom Paine and Robert Blatchford's socialist paper *The Clarion*:

> Thanks to my mother, who allowed us great freedom of expression on all subjects, whether it was dancing, the Athanasian Creed, Spiritualism, Haeckel,[8] Walt Whitman, Blatchford or Paine, I grew up with a smattering of knowledge on many questions.[9]

The biographies of prominent male figures in the late nineteenth and early twentieth-century labour movement also provide evidence that Chartist women kept radical traditions alive. Philip Snowden, the first Labour chancellor of the exchequer, was born in Cowling, West Yorkshire, to a Chartist father.[10] Fred Jowett, a power-loom operative elected as Labour MP for Bradford West in 1900, recalled that his mother's descriptions of the Chartist meetings she attended as a young girl made a deep impression on him.[11]

The nineteenth-century female suffrage campaign was never exclusively middle class in either its personnel or its ideology. The movement did not have to invent its own rhetoric, strategies and organisational structures. Rather, women's rights campaigners could engage with, modify and re-energise existing

Chartist traditions and networks in support of a renewed campaign to improve women's lives by expanding the franchise. Their movement would not have had the capacity to engage with so many working women had it not found fertile ground in working-class communities with a history of support for women's right to vote. Over the decades, the story of female suffrage campaigning became the story of prominent families such as the Garretts and the Pankhursts. This narrow perspective has distorted our understanding of this history.[12] The socialist and suffrage campaigners of the later nineteenth and early twentieth centuries were following in the footsteps of their mothers and grandmothers when they campaigned so tirelessly for their right to vote, and they repeatedly asserted their right to interfere in politics.

The Political Journeys of Sarah Parker Remond

Sarah Parker Remond was an African American woman who was born into a free family of committed abolitionists in Salem, Massachusetts, on 6 June 1826. She pursued a dream of education which took her from her hometown, across the Atlantic to Britain, and finally to Italy where she settled and became a qualified midwife. She established herself as a pivotal figure in international movements against slavery and racism in the US, for women's rights in the US and Britain and for the liberation of Italy from colonial domination. Sarah defied the restrictive 'race-gender expectations that constructed African American women as powerless when she became one of the first and few antebellum women to take the lecture pulpit'.[1] She sustained her tireless political campaigning through a series of strong friendships with other women, including members of an expat lesbian community in Italy and a radical female milieu in London.

Sarah's first experience of dynamic female relationships was with the women in her family. Remond's mother, Nancy Lenox, established the first black women's anti-slavery society in Salem. Her sisters were successful businesswomen and entrepreneurs who valued their life outside the family home. They were respected within the wider community and developed formal campaigns against slavery and racism. Free black people such as Sarah and her family were subjected to systematic racist discrimination. They were repeatedly refused entry to public buildings, trains, museums and theatres because they were black. On one occasion, Sarah and her sister were forcibly ejected from their box at the opera. Sarah, who was injured in the process, took the case to court and won compensation of $500, which makes her one of the first black women to win a legal case against segregation.[2]

Sarah's older brother, Charles Lenox Remond, was a noted abolitionist lecturer who had toured the US and visited Britain in 1840, where he attended the anti-slavery conference in London. Sarah began her own career as an abolitionist lecturer in 1856 when she gave talks for the American Anti-Slavery Society, a non-segregated organisation that reached a membership of 250,000.[3] At this time, anti-slavery gatherings which involved black and white, and men and women regularly attracted violence including arson attacks, smashed windows and the beating of participants. Free black people could never be free from the fear of violence, and after the Fugitive Slave Act of 1851, from the threat of being kidnapped and forced back into slavery. In the late 1850s, Sarah was growing in power as a speaker, and she went from addressing local meetings to speaking to national conventions. A contemporary described how her speeches 'waked up dormant aspirations which would vibrate through the ages'.[4]

International travel was out of the reach of all but a tiny number of black women in the mid-nineteenth century. For that small number, which included Sarah, travelling abroad offered new possibilities of freedom and autonomy and the possibility of social and cultural advancement and reinvention.[5] However independent they were, and Sarah travelled alone, black women knew they had to be prepared to face racism as well as sexism wherever they travelled. In November 1858, the *Anti-Slavery Advocate* published a letter from Remond in which she described her feelings as she was about to embark on a ship to Britain: 'I still hope to reach London before winter, but I dread starting for many reasons. I do not fear the wind nor the waves, but I know that no matter how I go, the spirit of prejudice will meet me.'[6] Her experiences in America would have filled Sarah with anxieties about what lay ahead, but she arrived in Liverpool in January 1859 without incident. Her sister Caroline and her family were not so lucky. They crossed the Atlantic a year after Sarah and were denied access to the dining tables because American passengers objected to being seated with black people. Sarah mobilised her friends and supporters to create a mighty stink about the Cunard Line's racist treatment of her sister.[7]

The warmth and friendship Sarah was offered by the British abolitionists surprised and cheered her. In March 1859, Sarah gave a speech in Warrington. At the end of the meeting, the abolitionist women of Warrington presented Sarah with an inscribed watch. She responded, 'I have been received here as a sister by white women for the first time in my life, I have been removed from the degradation which overhangs all persons of my complexion.'[8] Sadly, such supportive experiences were not universal and Sarah was excluded from the platforms of the mainstream abolitionist movement. Among the more radical abolitionists, however, Sarah was a valued comrade. She shared a platform with Frederick Douglass in Wakefield's Corn Exchange Building, which was 'crowded to excess' by an audience of more than 1,500.[9] A report in the local paper described Sarah as a 'lady of colour', who spoke for an hour and a half in a very fluent style and 'gave a dissertation on the abomination of slavery'.[10] Through 1859 and 1860, Sarah spoke to packed audiences in Liverpool, Warrington, Manchester, Leeds, Bristol, London, Scotland and Ireland.

Sarah settled in London, where she engaged as an equal in radical circles and 'reinvented herself as a new, distinct model of blackness, one of empowerment and elaborate identity'.[11] In London, she met Giuseppi Mazzini and embraced the cause of Italian unification and freedom from the Austrian Empire. Remond owned a copy of Elizabeth Barrett Browning's poem, 'Casa Guidi Windows' (1851), a celebration of Italian resistance, and Margaret Fuller's *Woman in the Nineteenth Century* (1843).[12] Fuller was an American author, journalist and activist who participated in the Roman Republic of 1848. Remond met Frances Power Cobbe and stayed with her in Bristol, in Florence and in Dublin. In Florence, Cobbe was part of a lesbian community which included Charlotte Cushman and Matilda Hays. From December 1861 to October 1864, Remond lived with Mentia and Peter Taylor at Aubrey House in London, which was the centre of abolitionist, female suffrage and Italian nationalist agitation. Sarah must have become very close to Mentia Taylor. According to one contemporary, Sarah, 'had for some years been adopted as Mrs Taylor's companion'.[13]

Remond was an executive member of the London Emancipation Committee and the Ladies' London Emancipation Society, both based at Aubrey House. Sarah studied at Bedford Ladies College, which had opened in 1849 to provide higher education for women. The college was set up by two signatories of the 1866 petition, Elizabeth Jesser Reid, who had been a delegate to the 1840 World Anti-Slavery Convention and Sophia De Morgan, the daughter of London radical William Frend who worked as a tutor to Ada Lovelace, the daughter of Lord Byron and Annabella Milbanke, who was herself an active abolitionist.

In 1866, Remond left London to pursue her studies in Florence which was known as a cosmopolitan and politically liberal city. In January 1869, Sarah qualified as a midwife, an achievement which was widely reported by British newspapers, which circulated the following notice: 'Sarah Parker Remond after a regular course of study at Hospital S. Maria Nuovo Florence received a diploma in midwifery.'[14] Sarah practised midwifery for twenty years. She never returned to the US but her sisters, Caroline and Maritcha, joined her in Italy. In April 1877, Sarah married Lazzaro Pintor, an Italian office worker from an educated, middle-class family. Sarah was nearly fifty-one and he was forty-four years old.

Sarah was an audacious campaigner against prejudice and lived a life of adventure. Her challenge to convention depended on her relationships with other women, with her mother and sisters, and women in the radical circles of London and Italy. She died in Rome in 1894 just over a century after the birth of Frances Wright, the subject of the first portrait in this book. Wright was an heiress; Remond was a professional woman. Wright envisaged eradicating slavery from above, according to her own schemes. Remond understood slavery from the perspective of a black American woman. Her fight to end slavery was allied to her own struggle for self-emancipation from racism and sexism. But both women shared a breadth of ambition, a willingness to engage with multiple, interlocking campaigns for independence, equality and social change.

The hundred years that lies between Frances's birth and Sarah's death witnessed repeated outbursts of working-class female activism. The women of the labouring classes were Jacobins, they were reformers, they campaigned against the New Poor Law and slavery, they were Chartists, they were trade unionists and they were suffrage campaigners. Many women were active in more than one radical campaign or organisation and developed multiple, overlapping identities. Between these visible eruptions of resistance, women continued to disseminate oppositional ideas and contest the gender conventions imposed upon them. Considering their tenacity, it is possible to see resistance, rather than acquiescence, as the normal state for working women. Historians have done them a disservice by marginalising their voices and erasing their contribution. Women were not side players in the making of the English working class. They were central to constructing its radical traditions, and their activism should be celebrated as a source of strength and confidence for our continuing struggle for equality and liberation.

Every generation thinks it has invented radical protest and experiments in free love. And, of course, they all do. Yet, we also have an inheritance of ideas and strategies passed down through grandmothers, mothers, sisters, aunts and friends, transferred through the subterranean channels of ideas, stories and poems that flows through communities, workplaces and families. The women of the 1840s participated in the creation of a radical counterculture which prefigured that of the 1960s. They debated, drank and danced together. They stopped eating meat and found ways to explore living harmoniously with the natural world. Some found spaces in which they could explore their sexuality. Many not only rejected the emerging capitalist society but also envisaged alternatives in which solidarity replaced competition and a degree of sexual freedom was the norm.

The Chartist women did not seek individual advancement. Their vision was always a collective one, in which all fought for reform, and all expected to reap the benefits of that reform. Our lives are so different from the those of the Chartist women but in so many fundamental ways, they are the same. We are still struggling to reconcile work and childcare and assert our rights to interfere in politics without abuse and derision. If the Chartist women had known that nearly two centuries later, we would still be fighting for the radical change they believed to be imminent, I am confident they would have found the right words to encourage us to keep the flame alive.

Further Reading: The Changing Faces of Female Chartism

In the two centuries since the Chartist movement, only one book devoted to female Chartism has been released: *Women in the Chartist Movement*, published by Jutta Schwarzkopf in 1991. The first historical accounts of Chartism were written by men who had participated in the movement. These early histories focused on elected leaders and official procedures, conventions and resolutions. Women, who tended to engage with the movement in less official and less easily recorded ways, were marginalised or entirely absent from these accounts. A subsequent generation of Marxist historians set themselves the task of rescuing plebian and artisan reformers from the condescension of history, in Edward Thompson's famous phrase. They tended to treat women, however, as an undifferentiated part of the crowd without their own interests and concerns.

Dorothy Thompson, Edward's wife and comrade, began the long process of unearthing working women's contribution to radical politics with her 1976 essay 'Women in Radical Politics: A Lost Dimension' in the *Rights and Wrongs of Women*, edited by Anne Oakley and Juliet Mitchell. More widespread interest in female Chartism did not develop until feminist historians of the 1980s contested the ways in which women's experiences and activism needed to be written back into historical accounts of the nineteenth-century reform movement. Jutta Schwarzkopf's *Women and Chartism* (1991) and Anna Clark's *The Struggle for the Breeches* (1997) both made a huge contribution to establishing female Chartism as a significant force. They inserted gender into E. P. Thompson's seminal account of the making of the English working class and explored how some working-class radicals failed to challenge female exclusion and amplified popular misogyny. Schwarzkopf and Clark tended to judge female Chartism according to the standards of the 1970s feminist movement. The framework of patriarchy cast women as the victims of men and failed to give sufficient weight to the voices of Chartist women themselves. Schwarzkopf's and Clark's research has been developed and refined by scholars including Michelle de Larrabeiti, Eileen Janes Yeo, Helen Rogers and Matthew Roberts. Chartist women fashioned themselves as 'glorious auxiliaries' to deflect criticism of their political activism, but these auxiliaries were conscious of their authority and influence over the movement.

In its early days, Chartism offered women the opportunity to create their own organisations and to write and speak in public. Historians have cast doubt on whether such opportunities were sustained throughout the 1840s. Dorothy Thompson suggested that women may have been alienated from increasingly formal political structures, which they found it hard to access, and that growing pressure to conform to standards of respectability encouraged women to withdraw from radical politics.

Schwarzkopf and Clark amplified the idea of female withdrawal, which they attributed to the actions of male Chartists who excluded women from the movement in order to restore their patriarchal authority. This interpretation has been widely accepted by historians of Chartism, and Chartism has been represented as a historical moment in which the organised working class could have embraced gender solidarity but instead chose to reinforce male supremacy and female subordination. I hope this book will contribute to a revision of that consensus and demonstrate how energetically and creatively women continued to challenge inequality. The Chartist commitment to women's rights was a minority current within the wider movement, but it was neither transitory nor ephemeral. Working-class women never submitted to being marginalised, silenced or intimidated out of fighting for their rights.

Acknowledgements

This book is based on research undertaken for a PhD at Leeds University. My first supervisor, the incomparably knowledgeable, generous and supportive Malcolm Chase, died on 29 February 2020, but I hope he would have approved of the finished result. All historians of Chartism owe Malcolm an enormous debt of gratitude.

I would like to thank my supervisors, Professor Laura King and Professor Peter Maw, who steered me through this loss and the COVID lockdown, and gave both their expertise and unfailing encouragement. I have benefitted greatly from presenting my research at Chartism Day events and socialist history seminars, as well as local history events organised by Halifax Trades Council. Thank you to all the labour and women's history enthusiasts who have kept the radical flame alive.

My thanks are also due to Tom Hazeldine, my editor at Verso, for his invaluable help and guidance.

My partner and comrade, Robert Hoveman, my mother, Elisa Cox, and my son, Frederick Cox, also deserve my thanks for their support, and for living with Chartism over many holidays and family events.

My father, Peter Cox, did not live to see me finish the project, but I know that he would be enormously proud and fascinated by the rebellious women whose stories I have told in this book.

Notes

Preface

1 The idea of women as 'glorious auxiliaries' of the men's struggle first appears in an address by the female Chartists of Ashton-under-Lyne. It has been widely used by historians of Chartism to express women's position as active, but subsidiary, supporters of the male cause. See, for example, Emmanuelle Morne, '"Glorious Auxiliaries?" Gender, Participation, and Subordination in the Chartist Movement', *Labour History Review*, April 2020, Liverpool University Press.
2 Malcolm Chase, *A New History of Chartism* (Manchester: Manchester University Press, 2007), p. 10.
3 The nadir of this trend must surely be *The Book of Gutsy Women: Favorite Stories of Courage and Resilience* (New York: Simon & Schuster, 2019) co-authored by Hillary and Chelsea Clinton.
4 Sheila Rowbotham, *Dreamers of a New Day: Women Who Invented the Twentieth Century* (London: Verso, 2010), p. 1.

1. The 'Hen Chartists' Take Flight

1 'Female Chartists', *Bell's New Weekly Magazine*, 23 October 1842, p. 2.
2 'Meeting of the Female Chartists', *London Evening Standard*, 19 October 1842.
3 'Female Chartists', *Bell's New Weekly Magazine*, 23 October 1842, p. 2.
4 'Domestic Intelligence', *Bradford Observer*, 3 November 1842, p. 2.
5 'The Pollywalkerites', *Bell's New Weekly Messenger*, 30 October 1842, p. 4.
6 'Miscellaneous Selections' *Newcastle Journal*, October 1842, p. 4.
7 'Political Proceedings of the Week', *Bristol Times*, 5 November 1842, p. 3.
8 'The Chartist Meeting – Miss Mary Ann Walker Again', *The Times*, 25 October 1842.

9 'The Hen Chartist, Miss Walker', *Monmouthshire Beacon*, 24 December 1842, p. 3.
10 *Hereford Journal*, 9 November 1842, p. 3.
11 'Metropolitan News', *Illustrated London News*, 29 October 1842, p. 7.
12 'Mary Ann Walker', *West Kent Guardian*, 5 November 1842, p. 4.
13 *John Bull*, 29 October 1842, p. 6. and 31 October 1842, pp. 7–8.
14 'Miss Mary Ann Walker on the People's Charter', *The Northern Star*, 10 December 1842, p. 7.
15 Anna Clark, *The Struggle for the Breeches: Gender and the Making of the British Working Class* (California: University of California Press, 1997), p. 228.
16 'Sketches of Female Politicians. No. 1-Miss Walker', *Punch, or the London Charivari*, 1842, p. 192.
17 Rogers, 'Any Questions?', p. 4.
18 *John Bull*, 31 October 1842, pp. 7–8.
19 'Miss Mary Ann Walker Presented Herself on the Platform', *Ballyshannon Herald*, 4 November, p. 1.
20 'The Female Chartists', *Morning Advertiser*, 3 November 1842, p. 3.
21 'The She-Chartists', *Morning Herald*, 23 November 1842, p. 6.
22 This may have been at William Lovett's National Association Hall, established in January 1842.
23 'Miss Mary Ann Walker on the People's Charter', *The Northern Star*, 10 December 1842, p. 15.
24 Ibid.
25 'Miss Mary Ann Walker', *Bristol Times and Mirror*, 14 January 1843, p. 4.
26 'Miss Mary Ann Walker on the People's Charter', *The Northern Star*, 10 December 1842, p. 7.
27 'Notes of the Week', *Atlas*, 18 February 1843, p. 7.
28 'Miss Mary Ann Walker', *Bristol Times and Mirror*, 14 January 1843, p. 4.
29 'Miss Mary Ann Walker', *Bristol Times and Mirror*, 14 January 1843, p. 4.
30 'Miss Mary Ann Walker Presented Herself on the Platform', *Ballyshannon Herald*, 4 November 1843, p. 1.
31 'To the Women of England', *The Northern Star*, 2 July 1842, p. 7.
32 Jutta Schwarzkopf, *Women in the Chartist Movement* (New York: St Martin's Press, 1993), p. 218.
33 'Unlicensed Theatricals', *Bells' New Weekly Messenger*, 20 August 1843, p. 5.
34 Dr Philip Salmon, 1832 Reform Act, 2022, historyofparliament.com.
35 Men had been granted the vote if they married a freeman's

daughter, but this was abolished by the Act. There were many bureaucratic and financial obstacles to overcome before a man who fulfilled the £10 property qualification could vote.

36 'The People's Charter on being an outline of an Act to provide for the just representation of the people of Great Britain and Ireland, 1838', quoted in Schwarzkopf, p. 59.

37 Chase, *A New History*, p. 19.

38 Clark, *The Struggle for the Breeches*, p. 38.

39 'Address of the Ashton Female Political Union to the Women of Great Britain and Ireland', *The Northern Star*, 2 February 1839, p. 4.

40 Chase, *A New History*, p. 28.

41 Tom Scriven, 'The National Charter Association and its Legacy, 180 years on', *History Workshop*, 30 July 2020.

42 Schwarzkopf, *Women and the Chartist Movement*, p. 61.

43 Chase, *A New History*, p. 186.

44 'Chartist Intelligence', *The Northern Star*, 1 May 1841, p. 17.

45 Michelle de Larrabeiti, 'Conspicuous Before the World: The Political Rhetoric of Chartist Women', in *Radical Femininity: Women's Self-Representation in the Public Sphere*, ed. Eileen Janes Yeo (Manchester: Manchester University Press, 1998), pp. 106–26.

46 'The London Female Democratic Association to the Women of England, Particularly the Women of the Metropolis', *The Charter*, 11 May 1839, p. 2.

47 'Female Radicals', *The Charter*, 10 November 1839, p. 13.

48 Ibid.

49 Matthew Roberts, *Democratic Passions: The Politics of Feeling in British Popular Radicalism, 1809–1848* (Manchester: Manchester University Press, 2023), p. 13.

50 'Address of the Female Political Union of Newcastle Upon Tyne to the Fellow-Country Women', *The Northern Star*, 9 February 1839, p. 6.

51 Helen Rogers, *Women and the People: Authority, Authorship, and the Radical Tradition in Nineteenth-Century England* (Abingdon: Routledge, 2000), p. 90.

52 Ibid., p. 91.

53 Ibid.

54 Ibid., p. 92.

55 Clark, *The Struggle for the Breeches*, pp. 67–84.

56 Dorothy Thompson, *The Early Chartists* (London: Macmillan Press, 1971), p. 115.

57 *The Operative*, 28 April 1839, p. 12.

58 Neville Kirk, 'In Defence of Class: A Critique of Recent Revisionist Writing Upon the Nineteenth-Century English Working Class', *International Review of Social History*, 17 (1987), 2–47.

'The Apostle of Progress' Frances Wright

1 Tithi Bhattacharya, 'How Not to Skip Class: Social Reproduction of Labour and the Global Working Class,' in *Social Reproduction Theory: Remapping Class, Recentering Oppression*, ed. Tithi Bhattacharya (London: Pluto, 2018), pp. 68–93 (pp. 70–1).
2 'Address from the National Female Chartist Association', *The Northern Star*, 8 July 1848, p. 2.
3 'Great metropolitan meeting in honour of the memory and writing of Thomas Paine', *The Northern Star*, 12 February 1848, p. 11.
4 'Madame D'Arusmont', *The Northern Star*, Saturday 29 June 1844, p. 4; 'Madame D'Arusmont', *The Northern Star*, 6 July 1844, p. 3; 'Madame D'Arusmont', *The Northern Star,* 13 July 1844, p. 3; 'Madame D'Arusmont', *The Northern Star,* 27 July 1844, p. 3; 'Madame D'Arusmont', *The Northern Star,* 3 August 1844, p. 3; 'Madame D'Arusmont', *The Northern Star,* 17 August 1844, p. 3.
5 *Saint James Chronicle*, 1 May 1827; *Sussex Advertiser* and the *Belfast Commercial Chronicle*, 7 May 1827; *Liverpool Mercury,* 11 May 1827; *Birmingham Journal*, 12 May 1827.
6 Carol A. Kolmerten, *Women in Utopia: The Ideology of Gender in the American Owenite Communities* (Bloomington: Indiana University Press, 1990), p. 119.
7 Gail Bederman, 'Revisiting Nashoba: Slavery, Utopia and Frances Wright in America, 1818–1826', *American Literary History*, Volume 17, Issue 3, Fall 2005, pp. 438–59.
8 Margaret Lane, *Frances Wright and the 'Great Experiment'* (London: Rowman & Littlefield, 1972).
9 Bederman, 'Revisiting Nashoba', pp. 438–59.
10 'Sketches About Town', *Dundee Courier*, 3 October 1849, p. 2.
11 'Anti-Corn Law Movement', *Derry Journal*, 12 February 1839, p. 4, 'A Meeting of the Unsympathisers', *Derry Journal*, 11 December 1838, p. 1.
12 Mike Sanders, ed., *Women and Radicalism in the Nineteenth Century: Frances Wright* (Abingdon: Routledge, 2001), p. 12.
13 Ibid., p. 255.
14 Kolmerten, *Women in Utopia*, p. 127.
15 Alice Perkins and Theresa Wolfson, *Frances Wright: Free Inquirer: The Study of a Temperament* (London: Harper & Brothers, 1939), pp. 291–2.
16 'Reviews', *The Northern Star*, 26 August 1848, p. 3.
17 See, for example, 'Advertisements & Notices', *The Northern Star*, 24 November 1849, 10 November 1849 and 5 January 1850; 'Advertisements & Notices', *The Odd Fellow*, 27 June 1840, 8 August 1840 and 18 September 1841.

18 Perkins and Wolfson, *Frances Wright*, p. 253.
19 Frances Wright, *Course of Popular Lectures, with Three Addresses and a Reply to the Charges against the French Reformers of 1789* (New York: Office of the Free Inquirer, 1829), p. 157.
20 'Reviews', *The Northern Star*, 7 September 1844, p. 3.
21 Ibid.
22 'Frances Wright', *The Northern Star*, 15 May 1847, p. 8.
23 'Reviews', *The Northern Star*, 21 August 1847, p. 12.
24 'Thomas Paine', *Sheffield Independent*, 12 February 1848, p. 8.
25 'Madame D'Arusmont's Lecture', *Sheffield Independent*, 26 February 1848, p. 6.
26 'Women's Rights', *Sheffield Independent*, 26 April 1851, p. 8.

2. Radical Foremothers

1 Matthew Roberts, 'The Cult of the Radical Hero', *Labour History Review*, 78, Number 1 (2013), 3–32 (p. xi).
2 'Mary Ann Walker', *West Kent Guardian,* 5 November 1842, p. 4.
3 'The Female Reformers', *Liverpool Mercury*, 28 September 1838, p. 3.
4 Samuel Bamford, *Passages in the Life of a Radical and Early Days, Volume II* (London: T. Fisher Unwin, 1893), p. 141.
5 Richard Poole, *Peterloo: An English Uprising* (Oxford: Oxford University Press, 2019), p. 25.
6 'Knowledge is Power' was the motto on the front page of the *Poor Man's Guardian.*
7 Chase, *A New History*, p. 185.
8 Frow and Frow, 'Women in the Early Radical Movement', *Marxism Today*, April 1968.
9 Malcolm Chase, 'Mann [nee Burnett] Alice (1791–1865) Radical and Publisher', *Oxford Dictionary of National Biography*, September 2019.
10 *The Poor Man's Guardian*, 26 May 1832.
11 Mary Wollstonecraft, *Vindication of the Rights of Women* (London: Penguin Books, 2004), p. 99.
12 Richard Pankhurst, 'Anna Wheeler: A Pioneer Socialist and Feminist', *The Political Quarterly*, 25 (1954), 132–43.
13 Abbie L. Kory, 'William and Thompson's Appeal: A Radical Revisioning of Gender', *New Hibernia Review / Iris Éireannach Nua*, Vol. 8, No. 2 (Summer 2004), pp. 106–20.
14 '*The Times* versus Mary Smith', *The Spectator*, 11 August 1832, p. 13, archive.spectator.co.uk, accessed August 2019.
15 Michael Taylor, *The Interest: How the British Establishment Resisted the Abolition of Slavery* (London: Vintage, 2021), p. xv.

16 Ibid.
17 David Olusoga *Black and British: A Forgotten History* (London: Pan, 2017), p. 208.
18 Clare Midgley, *Women and Slavery: The British Campaigns, 1780–1870* (London: Routledge, 1992), p. 61.
19 Ibid., p. 69.
20 Ibid., p. 36.
21 Ibid., pp. 117–18. This was part of a sustained tradition of female activism in Sheffield, which would later include the Women's Rights Association.
22 Ibid., p. 13; Adam Hochschild, *Bury the Chains: The British Struggle to Abolish Slavery* (London: Pan, 2012), p. 326.
23 Taylor, *The Interest*, p. 24.
24 Betty Fladeland, *Abolitionist and Working-Class Problems in the Age of Industrialization* (New York: Macmillan, 1984), p. 87.
25 Seymour Dresher, 'Women's Mobilisations in the Era of Slave Emancipation: Some Anglo-French Comparisons', in ed. Seymour Dresher, *Pathways from Slavery: British and Colonial Mobilisations in Global Perspective* (Abingdon: Routledge, 2018), p. 115.
26 Midgley, 'Anti-Slavery and Feminism', p. 346.
27 Ibid., p. 347.
28 Ryan Hanley, 'Slavery and the Birth of Working-Class Racism in England, 1814–1833', *Royal Historical Society* (2016), pp. 107–8; Robbie Shilliam, *Race and the Undeserving Poor: From Abolition to Brexit* (Newcastle: Agenda Publishing, 2018), p. 20.
29 Betty Fladeland focuses on co-operation in *Abolitionist and Working-Class Problems* while Tom Scriven identifies the 'racist republican' current within Chartism, 'Slavery and Abolitionism in Chartist Thought, 1838–1850', *The Historical Journal*, Number 65 (2022), 1,262–84 (p. 1,264).
30 Hanley, 'Slavery', p. 121.
31 Ibid., p. 122.
32 'Chartism at a Discount', *The Taunton Courier*, 19 June 1839, p. 8.
33 Fladeland, *Abolitionist and Working-Class Problems*, p. 79.
34 'Address of the Bristol Female Patriotic Association', *The Northern Star*, 3 August 1839, p. 6.
35 Fladeland, *Abolitionist and Working-Class Problems*, p. xii.
36 Hanley, 'Slavery', pp. 103–23.
37 Satnam Virdee, *Class, Nation and the Racialized Outsider* (London: Palgrave Macmillan, 2014), p. 256.
38 Scriven, 'Slavery and Abolition', p. 1,270.
39 Ibid.
40 Ibid., p. 1,275.
41 Universal suffrage usually meant universal male suffrage.

42 Malcolm I. Thomis and Jennifer Grimmett, *Women in Protest 1800–1850* (London: Routledge, 1982), p. 63.
43 John Gurney, *Wanting and Having: Popular Politics and Liberal Consumerism in England 1830–70* (Manchester: Manchester University Press, 2015), pp. 81–90.
44 Pat Thane, 'Women and the Poor Law in Victorian and Edwardian England', *History Workshop*, No. 6 (Autumn 1978), pp. 29–51.
45 Thomas Malthus, *An Essay on the Principle of Population, as it Affects the Future Improvement of Society with Remarks on the Speculations of Mr Godwin, M. Condorcet, and Other Writers* (St Paul's Church Yard: J. Johnson, 1798), p. 204.
46 Kathryn Gleadle and Sarah Richardson, 'The Petticoat in Politics: Women and Authority', in *Women in British Politics, 1760–1860: The Power of the Petticoat*, eds Kathryn Gleadle and Sarah Richardson (London: Macmillan, 2000), pp. 1–18 (pp. 7–8).
47 Thomis and Grimmett, *Women in Protest*, p. 60.
48 Ibid., p. 61.
49 'Leeds and West Riding News', *The Northern Star*, 5 October 1839, p. 4.
50 Lynn Hollen Lees, *The Solidarities of Strangers: The English Poor Laws and the People, 1700–1948* (Cambridge: Cambridge University Press, 2008), p. 114.
51 Ibid., p. 135–6.
52 Ibid p. 137.
53 Clark, *The Struggle*, p. 191.
54 Nicolas C. Edsall, *The Anti-Poor Law Movement, 1834–44* (Manchester: Manchester University Press, 1971), p. 182.
55 Ibid., p. 167.
56 Thomis and Grimmett, *Women in Protest*, p. 59.
57 Ibid., p. 58.
58 'Horrible Treatment of the Poor in the Sevenoaks Union Workhouse', *The Northern Star*, 11 December 1841, p. 7.
59 'The Andover Workhouse Abominations', *The Northern Star*, 20 September 1845, p. 8.
60 Ibid.
61 Thomis and Grimmett, *Women in Protest*, p. 60.
62 'Elland', *The Northern Star*, 17 February 1838, p. 8.
63 'Public Meeting of Women against the New Poor Law', *Morning Herald*, 20 February 1838, p. 6.
64 'Elland', *The Northern Star*, 17 February 1838, p. 8.
65 Grogram is a term derived from grosgrain, heavy woven cloth often stiffened with gum.
66 *The Globe*, 20 February 1838, p. 2.
67 'A curious report from the Times', *Bombay Gazette*, 30 April 1838, pp. 3–4.

68 *The Globe*, 20 February 1838, p. 2.
69 Ibid.
70 'Original Correspondence', *The Northern Star*, 21 April 1838, p. 7.
71 *The Globe*, 27 March 1838, p. 4.
72 *The Globe*, 22 March 1838, p. 3.
73 'Imperial Parliament', *The Northern Star*, 14 April 1838, p. 8.
74 Chase, *A New History*, pp. 22–9.
75 Ibid.
76 'Solemn Appeal to the People', *Southern Star*, 2 February 1840, p. 12.
77 'Births, Deaths and Marriages and Obituaries', *Hull Packet*, 20 May 1870, p. 8.
78 Robert Owen, *Lectures on the Marriages of the Priesthood of the Old Immoral World: Delivered in the Year 1835, Before the Passing of the New Marriage Act* (Leeds: J. Hobson, 1840).
79 Richard Pankhurst, *William Thompson (1775–1833): Pioneer Socialist* (London: Pluto Press, 1991), p. 120.
80 Barbara Taylor, *Eve and the New Jerusalem: Socialism and Feminism in the Nineteenth Century* (London: Virago Press, 1983), p. 16.
81 Taylor, *Eve*, p. 52.
82 Schwarzkopf, *Women in the Chartist Movement*, p. 102.
83 David Jones, 'Women and Chartism', David V. Jones, 'Women and Chartism', *History*, 68 (1983), 1–21 (p. 12).
84 Yeo, 'Mary Lovett', p. 97.
85 Taylor, *Eve*, p. 247–50.
86 Sophie Lewis, *Abolish the Family: A Manifesto for Care and Liberation* (London: Verso, 2022); M. E. O'Brien, *Family Abolition: Capitalism and the Communizing of Care* (London: Pluto Press, 2023).
87 Schwarzkopf, *Women in the Chartist Movement*, pp. 151–78.
88 Sylvia Mason, *Mary Frost: Wife, Mother, Chartist* (Monmouthshire: Saron Publishing, 2022), p. 98.
89 Angela Y. Davis, Gina Dent, Erica R. Meiners and Beth E. Richie, *Abolition. Feminism. Now.* (London: Penguin, 2022), pp. 14–15.

'White Slavery' and the Radical Poetics of Mary Hutton

1 Meagan Timney, 'Mary Hutton and the Development of a Working-Class Women's Political Poetics', *Victorian Poetry*, 49 (Spring 2011), 127–46 (p. 139).
2 Ibid., p. 128.
3 Ibid., p. 130.
4 Hutton, *Cottage Tales and Poems*, pp. 20, 25.

5 Timney, 'Mary Hutton', p. 128; Haywood, *Chartist Fiction*, p. 20.
6 Mary Hutton, '"The Wrongs of Man"', in Ian Haywood ed., *Chartist Fiction*, p. 189.
7 Hutton, *Cottage Tales and Poems*, p. 25.
8 Timney, 'Mary Hutton', p. 140.
9 Haywood, *Chartist Fiction*, p. 189.
10 Ibid., p. 20.
11 Timney, 'Mary Hutton', p. 140.
12 Ibid., p. vi.
13 Matthew Roberts, 'Women and Late Chartism: Women's Rights in Mid-Victorian England', *The English Historical Review*, 136 (581), pp. 918–49 (p. 23).
14 Ibid., p. 21.

3. Insurrection, 1839: 'The Time of War'

1 Kelly J. Mays, '"Slaves in Heaven, Labourers is Hell": Chartist Poets' Ambivalent Identification with the (Black) Slave', *Victorian Poetry*, 39 (2001), 137–63 (p. 147).
2 Chase, *A New History*, p. 4.
3 'Twelve Thousand Women', *The Northern Star*, 5 May 1838, p. 4.
4 'Radical Demonstration in Sheffield', *Birmingham Journal*, 29 September 1838, p. 3.
5 'Radical Meeting on Kersal Moor', *Liverpool Mercury*, 28 September 1838, p. 8.
6 'To the unrepresented people of Great Briton and Ireland', *The Northern Star*, 8 September 1838, p. 4.
7 'Meeting of Females', *The Northern Star*, 1 September 1838, p. 8.
8 'Address of the Female Radical Association of Carlisle', *The Northern Star*, 22 December 1838, p. 2.
9 Ibid.
10 'Carlisle Female Radical Association', chartistancestors.co.uk.
11 'Address of the Ashton Female Political Union', *The Northern Star*, 2 February 1839, p. 4; 'Address of the Female Political Union of Newcastle-Upon-Tyne', *The Northern Star*, 9 February 1839, p. 6.
12 'Great Meeting of the Women of Darlington', *The Northern Star*, 13 July 1839, p. 3.
13 'New Durham: Hurrah for the Women', *The Northern Star*, 30 March 1839, p. 7.
14 'Durham County Charter Meetings', *The Northern Star*, 30 March 1839, p. 7.
15 'Address of the Ashton Female Political Union to the Women of Great Britain and Ireland', *The Northern Star*, 2 February 1839, p. 4.

16 *The Operative*, 28 April 1839, p. 12.
17 Gurney, *Wanting and Having*, pp. 159–60.
18 'The Mercury', *Leeds Mercury*, 6 May 1837, p. 6.
19 Schwarzkopf, *Women in the Chartist Movement*, p. 176.
20 Ibid., p. 178.
21 Gurney, *Wanting and Having*, p. 155.
22 'A Voice from Prison', *The Northern Star*, 9 April 1842, p. 23.
23 Gurney, *Wanting and Having*, p. 146.
24 James Epstein, 'Some Organisational and Cultural Aspects of the Chartist Movement in Nottingham', in *The Chartist Experience: Studies in Working-Class Radicalism and Culture, 1830–1860*, eds James Epstein and Dorothy Thompson (London: Macmillan, 1982), pp. 221–68 (p. 37). Women's role in such commemorations was largely overlooked by historians until Matthew Roberts' article, 'Chartism, Commemoration and the Cult of the Radical Hero, 1770–1840' (2013), in which he explored how the gender dimensions of Chartist commemoration cast new light on the movement's political culture: Roberts, 'The Radical Hero', p. xvi.
25 James Epstein, 'Understanding the Cap of Liberty: Symbolic Practice and Social Conflict in Early Nineteenth-Century England', *Past & Present*, 122 (February 1989), 57–118 (p. 79).
26 Epstein, 'Understanding the Cap of Liberty', p. 79.
27 Clark, *The Struggle*, p. 161.
28 Epstein, 'Understanding the Cap of Liberty', p. 105.
29 Ibid.
30 'Full Text of the Petition for the Charter, 1839', chartistancestors.co.uk.
31 'Harlem, A Dream Deferred', 'Hope deferred makes the heart sick, but a desire fulfilled is a tree of life.'
32 'The National Petition', *London Courier and Evening Gazette*, 13 July 1839, p. 3.
33 Chase, *A New History*, p. 42.
34 Ibid., p. 42.
35 'The National Petition', *Weekly Chronicle*, 16 June 1839, p. 20.
36 Richard Huzzey and Henry Miller, 'Petitions, Parliament and Political Culture: Petitioning the House of Commons, 1780–1918', *Past & Present*, Volume 248, Issue 1, (2020), 123–64.
37 Malcolm Chase, 'What did the Chartists Petition For?', *Social Science History Association*, White Rose Research, 2019, p. 9.
38 Ibid., p. 1.
39 Ibid., p. 11.
40 'Death', *The Northern Star*, 1 September 1849, p. 9.
41 Chase, 'What did the Chartists Petition For?', p. 2.
42 Chase, *A New History*, p. 59.

43 Ibid., p. 62.

44 Kathryn, Gleadle, *The Early Feminists: Radical Unitarians and the Emergence of the Women's Rights Movement* 1831–51 (London: Palgrave Macmillan, 1998), p. 78.

45 Chase, *A New History*, p. 10.

46 Jennifer Bennett, 'The London Democratic Association 1837–41: A Study in London Radicalism', in *The Chartist Experience: Studies in Radicalism and Culture, 1830–1982* (London: Palgrave Macmillan, 1982), pp. 87–119 (p. 87).

47 Schwarzkopf, *Women in the Chartist Movement*, p. 234.

48 'The London Female Democratic Association', *The Operative*, 14 April 1839, p. 9.

49 'Apprehension of Thirteen Chartists in London', *Leeds Intelligencer*, 18 May 1839, p. 7. 'The London Female Democratic Association', *The Operative*, 14 April 1839, p. 9. *Bolton Chronicle*, 18 May 1839, p. 4. 'Examination of the Thirteen Chartists Arrested in the City', *Weekly Chronicle*, 19 May 1839, p. 22.

50 'Examination of the Thirteen Chartists Arrested in the City', *Weekly Chronicle*, 19 May 1839, p. 22.

51 'Final Examination at Bow Street of the Twelve Chartists who were taken into Custody on Thursday Last, *The Northern Star*, 25 January 1840, p. 1; 'Central Criminal Court', *The Northern Star*, 15 February 1840, p. 7.

52 'Bow Street', *Morning Herald*, 22 January 1840, p. 7.

53 Malcolm Chase found evidence that there were 100 women present. 'The Chartists in London', *Morning Post,* 22 January 1840, p. 4; 'Meeting of the Chartists in London', *Northern Liberator*, 25 January 1840, p. 3; Chase, *A New History*, p. 187.

54 'Final Examination at Bow Street', *The Northern Star*, 25 January 1840, p. 1.

55 'Meeting of the Women's Political Union', *Birmingham Journal*, 10 November 1838, p. 6.

56 Ibid.

57 'Women's Union', *Birmingham Journal*, 26 January 1839, p. 3.

58 'Women's Union', *Birmingham Journal*, 9 March 1839, p. 3.

59 Ibid.

60 Helen Rogers, 'What Right have Women to Interfere with Politics? The Address of the Female Political Union of Birmingham to the Women of England 1838', in *Explorations in Cultural History*, eds T. Ashplant and G. Smythe (London: Pluto Press, 2001), pp. 65–100 (p. 98).

61 'Women's Union', *Birmingham Journal*, 9 March 1839, p. 3.

62 'Meeting of the Women's Union', *Birmingham Journal*, 9 March 1839, p. 7.

63 *The Northern Star*, 18 May 1839, p. 6.

64 'Birmingham Female Political Union', *Manchester and Salford Advertiser*, 25 May 1839, p. 4.
65 Ibid.
66 Rogers, 'What Right have Women' in *Explorations in Cultural History*, eds T. Ashplant and G. Smythe (London: Pluto Press, 2001), pp. 65–100 (p. 97).
67 Ibid., p. 98.
68 'Nottingham Female Political Union', *The Northern Star*, 8 December 1838, p. 6.
69 Rogers, *Women and the People*, p. 105.
70 Matthew Roberts, 'Women and Late Chartism: Women's Rights in Mid-Victorian England', *The English Historical Review*, 136 (581), (2021), 918–49 (p. 9).
71 Chase, *A New History*, p. 79.
72 Ibid., p. 65.
73 Ibid., p. 65.
74 Ibid., p. 79.
75 Ibid., p. 80.
76 Ibid., p. 81.
77 Ibid., p. 61.
78 Ibid., p. 84.
79 'Doings of the Chartists', *Derbyshire Courier*, 11 May 1839, p. 4. 'Awful result of the Arming of Female Chartists at Cockermouth', *Manchester Courier*, 27 July 1839, p. 6.
80 Mason, *Mary Frost*, p. 55.
81 Ibid., p. 58.
82 Ibid., p. 71.
83 Edward Hamer, *The Chartist Outbreak in Llanidloes* (Llanidloes: John Ellis Caxton Printing Works, 1939), p. 31.
84 'Evening Riots at Newport', *Sun*, 13 November 1839, p. 3.
85 'The Case of Frost, Williams and Jones', *The Patriot*, 27 February 1840, p. 5.
86 'More Young Patriots', *The Northern Star*, 3 October 1840, p. 8, and the same column for 12 December 1840.
87 'The Females of Holbrook to the Chartists of Great Britain on behalf of Mrs Frost, Mrs Williams and Mrs Jones', *The Northern Star*, 5 February 1849, p. 16.
88 Mason, *Mary Frost*, p. 76.
89 'Mrs Frost', *The Northern Star*, 26 February 1842, p. 14.
90 Mason, *Mary Frost*, p. 134.
91 George Rude, 'John Frost (1784–1877)', *Australian Dictionary of Biography*, Volume I, 1966.
92 John Baxter, *Samuel Holberry 1814–1842: Sheffield's Revolutionary Democrat* (Sheffield: Holberry Society Publications, 1978), p. 10.

93 Ibid., p. 16.
94 Ibid., p. 18.
95 Ibid., p. 23.
96 'To the Editor of *The Northern Star*', *The Northern Star*, 31 July 1841, p. 5.
97 '*York*', *The Northern Star*, 4 September 1841, pp. 6–8.
98 'Public Meeting of Women at Bradford', *The Northern Star*, 30 March 1839, p. 3.
99 'Address from the London Delegate Meeting', *The Northern Star*, 11 September 1841, p. 26.
100 'To the Editor of *The Northern Star*', *The Northern Star*, 31 July 1841, p. 5.
101 'Advertisements and Notices', *The Northern Star*, 10 July 1841, p. 10.
102 *The Northern Star*, 13 March 1841.
103 David Goodway, *London Chartism: 1838–48* (Cambridge: Cambridge University Press, 2010), p. 36; Chase, *A New History*, p. 177; Schwarzkopf, *Women in the Chartist Movement*, p. 83.
104 Gleadle, *Early Feminists*, p. 78.
105 David Stack, 'William Lovett and the National Association for the Political and Social Improvement of the People,' *The Historical Journal*, 42 (December 1999), 1027–50 (p. 1,029).
106 Ibid., p. 1,028.
107 Ibid., p. 1,003.
108 Scriven, *Popular Virtue*, p. 7.
109 Gleadle, *Early Feminists*, p. 151.
110 Stack, 'William Lovett', p. 1044.
111 John Collins and William Lovett, *The Rules and Objects of the National Association for Promoting the Political and Social Improvement of the People* (London: William Ostell, 1841), p. 4.
112 'National Association', in William Lovett Archive, reference M.S. 753.
113 Schwarzkopf, *Women in the Chartist Movement*, p. 61.
114 Stack, 'William Lovett', p. 1,043.
115 *National Association Gazette*, 8 January 1842.
116 Margaret Josephine Shaen, *William Shaen: A Brief Sketch* (London: Kessinger Legacy Reprints, 1912), p. 22.
117 Gleadle, *Early Feminists*, p. 79.
118 Judith Walkowitz, *Prostitution and Victorian Society: Women, Class and the State* (Cambridge: Cambridge University Press, 1980), p. 121.
119 Elizabeth Crawford, *The Women's Suffrage Movement in Britain and Ireland: A Regional Survey* (Abingdon: Routledge, 2006), p. 172.
120 'The General Convention', *The Charter*, 14 July 1838, p. 13.

121 'Copies of any Memorials or Correspondence relating to the Treatment of William Lovett and John Collins', 4 February 1840, William Lovett Archive, MS.
122 George Vargo, *An Underground History of Early Victorian Fiction: Chartism, Radical Print Culture and the Social Problem Novel* (New York: New York University, 2018), p. 120.
123 Ibid., p. 120.
124 Gleadle, *Origins*, p. 4.
125 Gleadle, *Early Feminists*, p. 77.
126 'Reviews', *The Northern Star*, 26 September 1846, p. 12. 'Reviews', *The Northern Star*, 6 February 1847, p. 12. 'Reviews', *The Northern Star*, 9 January 1847, p. 11.
127 Gleadle, *Early Feminists*, pp. 33–62.
128 *Manchester Examiner and Times*, 9 February 1853.
129 Gleadle, *Early Feminists*, p. 149.
130 Ibid., p. 141.
131 Ibid., p. 161.
132 Dorothy Thompson, *The Dignity of Chartism* (London: Verso Books, 2015), p. 43.
133 James Mill, *Essays on Government, Jurisprudence, Liberty of the Press and Law of Nations* (London: J. Innes, 1924), p. 21.
134 Ben Griffin, *The Politics of Gender in Victorian Britain: Masculinity, Political Culture and the Struggle for Women's Rights* (Cambridge: Cambridge University Press, 2012), p. 38.
135 Ibid., p. 39.
136 Ibid., p. 43.
137 Rogers, *Women and the People*, p. 92.
138 Schwarzkopf, *Women in the Chartist Movement*, p. 72.
139 Vargo, *An Underground History*, p. 17.
140 'An Appeal to the Women of Great Britain', *The Northern Star*, 20 May 1843, p. 4.
141 Ibid., p. 4.
142 Schwarzkopf, *Women in the Chartist Movement*, p. 97.
143 Rogers, *Women and the People*, p. 91.
144 Ibid., p. 88.
145 Schwarzkopf, *Women in the Chartist Movement*, p. 97.

'Bid the Outraged World, Be Free!': Making Common Cause with Elizabeth Pease and Anne Knight

1 Midgley, *Women Against Slavery*, p. 1.
2 Anna Stoddart, *Elizabeth Pease Nichol* (Michigan: E. P. Dutton & Co., 1899), p. 120.
3 Ibid., p. 136.

4 Ibid., p. 141.
5 Ibid.
6 Elizabeth Pease to Anne Warren, 24 June 1841, quoted in Bonnie Anderson, *Joyous Greetings: The First International Women's Movement 1830–1860* (Oxford: Oxford University Press, 2000), p. 13.
7 Stoddart, *Elizabeth Pease*, pp. 76–7.
8 Ibid., pp. 77–9.
9 Ibid., p. 229.
10 Malmgreen, 'Anne Knight', p. 104.
11 Anderson, *Joyous Greetings*, p. 13.
12 Malmgreen, 'Anne Knight', p. 106.
13 Marion Reid, *A Plea for Woman* (London: Polygon, 1988), p. 15.
14 Ibid., p. 12.
15 Ibid., p. 10.
16 Anderson, *Joyous Greetings*, p. 138; Suzanna Ferguson, 'Foreword', in Reid, *A Plea for Woman*, p. 1.
16 Anne Knight archive, Friends Library, MS Box 2.
17 Knight inserted Linton's appendix after p. 94 of Reid's *A Plea*.
18 Malmgreen, 'Anne Knight', p. 100.
19 Ibid., pp. 109–10.
20 Ibid., pp. 105, 109.
21 Ibid., p. 107.
22 'The Rights of Women', *The Northern Star,* 29 March 1851, p. 8.
23 Malmgreen, 'Anne Knight', p. 113.

4. General Strike, 1842: 'Every Woman Ought to be a Politician'

1 Hansard, 3 May 1842, volume 63, cc12-25.
2 Ibid.
3 'The Women of the Insurrection', *The Leeds Times*, 20 August 1842, p. 4.
4 Ibid.
5 Clark, *The Struggle*, p. 84
6 Mick Jenkins, *The General Strike of 1842* (London: Lawrence & Wishart, 1981), p. 214.
7 Ibid.
8 'Riots in Lancashire', *York Herald*, 20 August 1842.
9 Jenkins, *The General Strike*, p. 21
10 'State of the Country', *The Northern Star*, 20 August 1842, p. 20.
11 'The women of the Insurrection', *Leeds Times,* 27 August 1842.
12 Jenkins, *The General Strike,* p. 215.
13 'State of the Country', *The Northern Star*, 20 August 1842, p. 20.

14 Jenkins, *The General Stike*, p. 215.
15 Ibid.
16 Ibid.
17 Ibid., p. 217.
18 Ibid., p. 215.
19 'State of the Country', *The Northern Star*, 17 September 1842.
20 Jenkins, *The General Stike*, p. 216.
21 'Before Mr Baron Rolfe', *The Northern Star*, 15 October 1842.
22 'To the Females of the Metropolis and its Vicinity', *The Northern Star*, 10 September 1842, p. 13.
23 Ibid.
24 Matthew Roberts, 'Women, Late Chartism and the Land Plan in Nottinghamshire', *The Midland Review*, Volume 48, No. 2 (2023), 196–216 (p. 1).
25 Margaret Hewitt, *Wives & Mothers in Victorian Industry* (London: Loxley Press, 1958).
26 Clark, *The Struggle*, p. 239.
27 Schwarzkopf, *Women in the Chartist Movement*, p. 92.
28 Schwarzkopf argues that the extent of baby farming was exaggerated, *Women in the Chartist Movement*, p. 21, while Clark refers to childcare as a trope of Chartist rhetoric rather than an urgent practical problem which shaped women's lives, *The Struggle*, pp. 229, 238, 240.
29 Hewitt, *Wives and Mothers*, p. 21.
30 Ibid., p. 103.
31 'Address of the Female Political Union of Newcastle-Upon-Time to their Fellow-Country Women', *The Northern Star*, 9 February 1839, p. 6.
32 John A. Leatherland, *Essays and Poems, with a Brief Autobiographical Memoir* (London: W. Tweedie, 1862), p. 8.
33 Scriven, *Popular Virtue*, p. 144.
34 Schwarzkopf, *Women in the Chartist Movement*, p. 189.
35 Chase, *A New History*, p. 247–8.
36 Ibid., p. 248.
37 Ibid., p. 254.
38 Roberts, 'Women, Late Chartism and the Land Plan', p. 1.
39 Scriven, *Popular Virtue*, p. 120.
40 'To the Women of England', *The Northern Star*, 4 December 1847, p. 11.
41 Schwarzkopf, *Women in the Chartist Movement*, p. 187.
42 Chase, *A New History* p. 269.
43 Scriven, *Popular Virtue*, p. 147.
44 'Chartist Intelligence', *The Northern Star*, 4 September 1847, p. 9.
45 Ibid.

46 Ibid.
47 Scriven, *Popular Virtue*, p. 7.
48 Roberts, 'Land Plan', p. 5.
49 'Chartist Intelligence', *The Northern Star*, 6 May 1843, p. 2.
50 Roberts, 'Land Plan', p. 7.
51 Ibid., p. 20.
52 Ibid., p 15.
53 Ibid., p. 16.
54 Ibid., p. 13.
55 Schwarzkopf, *Women in the Chartist Movement,* p. 285.

The 'Red-Hot Radical' Eliza Cook

1 John Dix, *Lions: Living and Dead, or Personal Recollections of the 'Great and Gifted'* (London: Tweedie, 1852), p. 52.
2 Alexis Easley, *Victorian Iconoclast: Eliza Cook (1812–1889), Celebrity, Authorship and Afterlives in English and American Literature* (Basingstoke: Palgrave Macmillan, 2016), p. 68.
3 Susan Rutherford, '"Loud and Open Speak the People's Mighty Name": Eliza Cook, Music and Politics', *Journal of British Studies*, 60 (April 2021), 416–29 (pp. 416–17).
4 Gleadle, *Early Feminists,* p. 144.
5 'Public Meetings', *The Northern Star*, 2 June 1849, p. 13.
6 Solveig C. Robinson, 'Of "Haymakers" and "City Artisans": The Chartist Poetics of Eliza Cook's "Songs of Labor"', *Victorian Poetry,* 39 (Summer 2001), 229–54 (p. 229).
7 See, for example, 'Poetry', *The Northern Star*, 8 June 1839, p. 7; 'Poetry', *The Northern Star*, 4 November 1843, p. 3; 'Sunshine and Shadows', *The Northern Star,* 26 May 1849, p. 3.
8 'Poetry', *The Northern Star*, 6 April 1844, p. 3.
9 Robinson, 'Haymakers', p. 234.
10 'The Nottingham Election', *The Northern Star*, 14 August 1847, p. 1.
11 Easley, 'Eliza Cook', p. 68.
12 Lisa Merrill, *When Romeo Was a Woman: Charlotte Cushman and Her Circle of Female Spectators* (Ann Arbor: University of Michigan, 1999), p. 138.
13 Easley, 'Eliza Cook', p. 67.
14 Dix, *Lions*, p. 43.
15 Robinson, 'Haymakers', p. 230

5. Revolution, 1848: 'Breaking the Chains of Women'

1 Carol Diethe, *Towards Emancipation: German Women Writers of the Nineteenth Century* (Berghan Books, 1998), p. 101.
2 Ophélie Siméon, '"Goddess of Reason": Anna Doyle Wheeler, Owenism and the Rights of Women', *History of European Ideas*, 47, 2 (2021), 285–98 (p. 295).
3 Dolores Dooley, *Equality in Community* (Dublin: Cork University Press, 1996), pp. 96–9.
4 'Free Correspondence', *The Northern Star*, 17 January 1852, p. 9.
5 Sabine Freitag, 'Jeanne Deroin: Feminist, Socialist, Exile', in *Exiles from European Revolutions: Refugees in Mid-Victorian England*, and Pamela Pilbeam, *French Socialists before Marx: Workers, Women and the Social Question in France* (Teddington: Acumen Publishing, 2000), pp. 41–56.
6 A. J. P. Taylor quoted in Mike Rapport, *1848: Year of Revolution* (London: Abacus, 2009), p. 401.
7 Eric Hobsbawm, *Age of Capital* (London: Phoenix Press, 2000), p. 14.
8 Christopher Clark, 'Why Should We Think about the Revolutions of 1848 Now?', *London Review of Books*, 7 March 2019.
9 Rapport, *1848: Year of Revolution*, p. 176.
10 Dorothy Thompson, 'Women and Nineteenth-Century Radical Politics', in *The Rights and Wrongs of Women*, eds Juliet Mitchell and Anne Oakley (London: Penguin, 1976), p. 137.
11 Jones, 'Women and Chartism', pp. 13–14.
12 *The Banner of Ulster*, 16 June 1848, p. 3.
13 Roberts, 'Women's Rights', p. 925–6.
14 'Brutal Atrocities by the "Special" Ruffians at Leicester', *The Northern Star*, 3 June 1848, p. 22.
15 'The Midland Counties', *The Northern Star*, 3 June 1848, p. 22.
16 Roberts, 'Women's Rights', p. 926.
17 'An Address from the Male and Female Chartists of Birmingham to Feargus O'Connor, Esq', *The Northern Star*, 21 May 1842, p. 12.
18 Sabine Freitag, ed., *Exiles from European Revolutions: Refugees in Mid-Victorian England* (New York: Berghahn Books, 2003), p. 2.
19 Ibid., p. 211.
20 Diana M. Garno, '"Gendered Utopia": Women in the Icarian Experience 1840–1898', unpublished dissertation 1190 (Wayne State University, 1998).
21 Freitag, *Exiles*, p. 225.
22 'To the Female Chartists', *The Northern Star*, 24 June 1848, p. 23.

23 'To the Men and Women of France', *The Northern Star*, 11 March 1851, p. 14.
24 'Female Political Rights Association', *The Northern Star*, 14 June 1851, p. 9.
25 Bennett, 'The London Democratic Association', p. 88.
26 Emma Harris, '"Health and Fraternity": The Schell Viettinghoffs in Mid-19th-Century London', in *From Queen Anne to Queen Victoria: Readings in 18th- and 19th-Century British Literature and Culture*, eds Grazyna Bystydzienska and Emma Harris (Warsaza: Uniwersytet Warszawski, 2012), p. 197.
27 Ibid., p. 195.
28 Ibid.
29 Ibid., p. 199.
30 Thierry Drapeau, 'Marx and the Chartist', 5 May 2019, tribune .co.uk [accessed September 2020].
31 'Belgium', *The Northern Star*, 25 March 1848, p. 3.
32 'The Fraternal Democrats', *The Northern Star*, 9 October 1847, p. 12.
33 Weerth was nominated by the English Chartists to be their representative at an international gathering to celebrate the seventeenth anniversary of the 1830 revolution in Poland, 'Poland: The Fraternity of Nations', *The Northern Star*, 4 December 1847, p. 5. In March 1848, Weerth was described as 'our Chartist friend' when he appeared on a platform with Ernest Jones and Karl Marx at an international gathering of radicals, 'Report of the Delegation to Paris', *The Northern Star*, 11 March 1848, p. 5.
34 Jenny Marx, 'Short Sketch of an Eventful Life', in *Marx and Engels Through the Eyes of the Contemporaries* (Moscow: Progress, 1972), p. 254.
35 Mary Gabriel, *Love and Capital: Karl and Jenny Marx and the Birth of a Revolution* (New York: Little, Brown and Company, 2011), p. 180.
36 Freitag, *Exiles*, pp. 25–55.
37 Chase, *A New History*, p. 295.
38 'To the Men and Women of France', *The Northern Star*, 11 March 1848, p. 14.
39 Thomas C. Jones and Robert Tombs, 'The French Left in Exile: Quarante-huitards and Communards in London, 1848–80' in *A History of the French in London: Liberty, Equality and Opportunity*, eds Debra Kelly and Martyn Cornick (London: University of London Press, 2013), 165–91 (p. 166).
40 Johanna Da Costa, 'Revolution in France: "The Women of 1848", How the Revolution of 1848 Finally Gave Women a Voice', *The Collector*, 18 March 2021.

41 Pamela Pilbeam, 'Jeanne Deroin (1805–1894)', *Oxford Dictionary of National Biography* (26 May 2005).
42 'Foreign Intelligence', *John Bull*, 14 April 1849, p. 3; Freitag, *Exiles*, p. 285.
43 'Rights of Women', *Reynolds's Weekly*, 22 June 1851, p. 7.
44 'Female Political Rights Association', *The Northern Star*, 14 June 1851, p. 1.
45 *Illustrated London News*, 14 April 1849, p. 2; *Dublin Evening Post*, 14 April 1849, p. 1; *John Bull*, 14 April 1849, p. 3; *Evening Mail*, 11 April 1849, pp. 4–5; *Shipping and Mercantile Gazette*, 11 April 1849, p. 3; *London Evening Standard*, 11 April 1849, p. 3; *Express (London)*, 11 April 1849, p. 1; *Bell's Life in London*, 15 April 1849.
46 'France', *Monmouthshire Merlin*, 25 November 1848, p. 2.
47 *Illustrated London News*, 14 April 1849, p. 2; *Dublin Evening Post*, 14 April 1849, p. 1; *John Bull*, 14 April 1849, p. 3; *Evening Mail*, 11 April, pp. 4–5; *Shipping and Mercantile Gazette*, 11 April, p. 3; *London Evening Standard*, 11 April, p. 3; *Express (London)*, 11 April, p. 1; *Bell's Life in London*, 15 April.
48 'Female Political Rights Association', *The Northern Star*, 14 June 1851, p. 1; 'Woman's Rights' Convention', *The Northern Star*, 9 November 1851, p. 4.
49 Françoise Kunka, 'The French Teacher at Kelmscott House: Cécile Desroches, Jeanne Deroin and the Utopian Socialist Connection', morrissociety.org, accessed June 2019.
50 Martin Hoyles, *William Cuffay: The Life and Times of a Chartist Leader* (London: Hansib Publication, 2012), p. 130.
51 Ibid., p. 187.
52 'Literature', *Morning Post*, 22 March 1853, p. 3.
53 *Staffordshire Advertiser*, 15 April 1848, pp. 8–9; *Stonehaven Journal*, 25 April 1848; *Bradford Observer*, 20 April 1848.
54 *Birmingham Journal*, 15 April 1848, p. 8.
55 'Metropolitan Gossip', *Southern Reporter and Cork Commercial Courier*, 25 May 1848, p. 4.
56 'Nooks and Corners of Character – the Charwoman', *Punch*, January 1850, victorianlondon.org.
57 'Advertisements & Notices', *The Northern Star*, 6 January 1849, p. 5.
58 'Meetings and Democratic Intelligence', *Reynolds's Weekly*, 7 November 1852, p. 16.
59 See, for example, *Taunton Courier and Western Advertiser*, 21 June 1848; *Bedfordshire Mercury*, 24 June 1948; *Cork Examiner*, 5 July 1848; *Leicester Journal*, 7 July 1848; *Arbroath Guide*, 8 July 1848; *John O' Groat Journal*, 21 July 1848.

60 'The Political Rights of Women', *Reynolds's Weekly*, 23 March 1851, p. 7.

61 Keith Flett, *Chartism After 1848: The Working Class and the Politics of Radical Education* (London: Merlin, 2006), chapter 7, pp. 174–94.

Irish Nationalism, Chartism and the 'Lady Insurrectionist' Sarah Theobald

1 Thompson, *Dignity of Chartism*, p. 123.

2 Chase, *A New History*, p. 317.

3 'Mary Ann Walker', *West Kent Guardian*, 5 November 1842, p. 4.

4 'Miss Mary Ann Walker Again', *London Evening Standard*, 25 October 1842, p. 1.

5 Clifford O'Connor, *Arthur O'Connor: The Most Important Irish Revolutionary You May Never Have Heard of* ... (London: Universe, 2009), p. 29.

6 Nini Rodgers, 'The Irish in the Caribbean 1641–1837: An Overview', *Irish Migration Studies in Latin America* 5 (November 2007), 145–55 (p. 111).

7 She features on only one page of Schwarzkopf's *Women in the Chartist Movement*.

8 *Kilkenny Journal and Leinster Commercial and Literary Advertiser*, 21 June 1848, p. 1; *Roscommon Messenger*, 14 June, p. 2; *The Pilot (Dublin)*, 12 June 1848.

9 'Chartist Meeting at Manchester', *The Northern Star*, 9 July 1848, p. 7.

10 *London Evening Standard*, 3 August 1848, p. 1.

11 *Norfolk News*, 12 August 1848, p. 1; *Fife Herald*, 24 August 1848, p. 4; *Westmeath Independent*, 30 September 1848, p. 2–3.

12 'Chartist Outbreak in Lancashire', *Halifax Guardian*, 19 August 1848, p. 4.

13 Ibid.

14 *Kilkenny Journal and Leinster Commercial and Literary Advertiser*, 21 June 1848, p. 1; *Roscommon Messenger*, 14 June 1848, p. 2; *The Pilot (Dublin)*, 12 June 1848.

15 Ibid.

16 'Chartist Intelligence', *The Northern Star*, 27 January 1849, p. 5.

17 'Mr Kydd's Tour', *The Northern Star*, 30 December 1848, p. 4.

18 'Chartist Intelligence', *The Northern Star*, 26 May 1849, p. 16.

19 *Kilkenny Journal and Leinster Commercial and Literary Advertiser*, 21 June 1848, p. 1; *Roscommon Messenger*, 14 June, p. 2; *The Pilot (Dublin)*, 12 June 1848.

20 *Bradford Observer*, 24 August 1848, p. 7.
21 *Christian News*, 27 October 1855, p. 6–7.
22 'Local News', *Newcastle Guardian and Tyne Mercury*, 6 October 1855, p. 5.

6. Resistance, 1850s: 'The Strong-Minded Women of the Party'

1 'Demonstration to meet John Frost, The Pardoned Chartist Leader', *Morning Post*, 16 September 1856, p. 3; 'Chartist Demonstration', *Westmoreland Gazette*, 20 September 1856, p. 8; 'Chartist Demonstration', *The Era*, 21 September 1856, p. 5.
2 'Chartist Demonstration', *Western Times*, 20 September 1856, p. 2.
3 Roberts, 'Women and Late Chartism', p. 6.
4 Trygve Tholfsen, *Working-Class Radicalism in Mid-Victorian England* (London: Croom Helm, 1976), p. 128.
5 Griffin, *The Politics of Gender,* p. 230.
6 Tholfsen, *Working-Class Radicalism,* p. 157.
7 Sometimes known as the Sheffield Women's Political Association, see Schwarzkopf, *Women in the Chartist Movement*, p. 251.
8 Schwarzkopf, *Women in the Chartist Movement*, p. 249.
9 'Meeting at Sheffield – the Rights of Women', *The Northern Star*, 8 February 1851, p. 13.
10 Schwarzkopf, *Women in the Chartist Movement*, p. 249.
11 Roberts, 'Women's Rights', p. 933–4.
12 Roberts, 'Women's Rights', p. 934.
13 Schwarzkopf, *Women in the Chartist Movement*, p. 252.
14 Margot Finn, *After Chartism: Class and Nation in English Radical Politics 1848–1874* (Cambridge: Cambridge University Press, 1993), p. 69.
15 'Women's Rights', *Sheffield Independent*, 26 April 1851, p. 8.
16 'The Rights of Women', *Reynolds's Weekly*, 4 May 1851, p. 6.
17 Schwarzkopf, *Women in the Chartist Movement,* pp. 254–5.
18 Roberts, 'Women's Rights', p. 945.
19 'To the Women of England', *Reynolds's Weekly*, 4 May 1851, p. 6.
20 'The Rights of Women', *The Northern Star*, 22 February 1851.
21 'Female Political Rights Association', *The Northern Star*, 14 June 1851, p. 9.
22 'The Chartist Programme', *The Northern Star*, 9 August 1851, p. 1.
23 'Female Political Rights Association', *The Northern Star*, 14 June, p. 1; Roberts, 'Women's Rights', p. 939.
24 'Female Political Rights Association', *The Northern Star*, 6 March 1852, p. 1.

25 'Chartist Intelligence', *The Northern Star*, 15 November 1851, p. 10.
26 Ibid.
27 Helen Taylor, 'The Enfranchisement of Women', *Westminster Review*, July 1851.
28 'Democratic Movements', *The Northern Star*, 8 May 1852, p. 13.
29 Schwarzkopf, *Women in the Chartist Movement*, p. 254.
30 'Chartist Intelligence', *The Northern Star*, 13 January 1849, p. 14.
31 A Mrs Holmes is listed as a member of the league's board, and a Mr Holmes was active in Sheffield Chartism, *The Northern Star* 25 May 1850 and 16 November 1850, but I have been unable to establish a more definite connection.
32 'Democratic Movement', *The Northern Star*, 5 June 1852, p. 5.
33 'The Metropolis', *The Northern Star*, 4 October 1851, p. 6.
34 Scriven, *Popular Virtue*, p. 83.
35 Ibid., p. 86.
36 'Co-operative Intelligence', *The Northern Star*, 27 December 1851, p. 13.
37 'Bloomerism', *The Northern Star*, 13 September 1851, p. 5.
38 'Lecture on Bloomerism', *The Northern Star*, 20 September 1851, p. 16.
39 Ibid.
40 'Democratic Movement', *The Northern Star*, 1 May 1852, p. 6.
41 'Women's Emancipation', *Punch*, 1851, quoted in Ana Stevenson, '"Bloomers" and the British World: Dress Reform in Transatlantic and Antipodean Print Culture, 1851–1950', *Culture and Society*, 14:5 (2017), 621–46 (p. 33).
42 'Contemporary Press', *Reynolds's Weekly*, 11 January 1852.
43 Clark, *The Struggle*, p. 267.
44 Scriven, *Popular Virtue*, p. 133.
45 'The Midland Counties', *The Northern Star*, 3 June 1848, p. 22.
46 Ibid.
47 Jane Humphries, *Childhood and Child Labour in the British Industrial Revolution* (Cambridge: Cambridge University Press, 2010), pp. 27–9, 40–2.
48 Lindsey German, *Sex, Class and Socialism* (London: Bookmarks, 1989), p. 40.
49 H. I. Dutton and J. E. King, *Ten Percent and No Surrender: The Preston Strike, 1853–1854* (Cambridge: Cambridge University Press, 1981), p. 94.
50 'The Wages Movement', *Preston Chronicle*, 8 October 1853, p. 8.
51 'The Labour Movement, *The People's Paper*, 24 September 1853, p. 8.
52 Dutton and King, *Ten Percent*, p. 2
53 'Meeting on Behalf of the Chartist Exiles', *The Northern Star*, 17

January 1846, p. 23; 'Chartist Meeting at Preston', *The Northern Star*, 25 May 1839, p. 5; 'To Feargus O'Connor M.P.', *The Northern Star*, 30 March, p. 25.

54 Dutton and King, *Ten Percent*, p. 52.
55 'Manchester Millocrats', *The People's Paper*, 26 November 1853, p. 3.
56 Janet Greenlees, 'Women and the Preston Lock-Out: Not Just 'ten per cent', *Transactions of the Historic Society of Lancashire and Cheshire*, 2024, p. 35.
57 'The Preston Strike', *Preston Chronicle*, 7 October 1854, p. 3.
58 'The Wages Movement', *Preston Chronicle*, 12 November 1853, p. 3.
59 Ibid.
60 *Manchester Courier*, 10 December 1853, p. 8.
61 *Huddersfield and Holmfirth Examiner*, 12 November 1853, pp. 6–7.
62 *Morning Post*, 9 November 1853, p. 2.
63 'The Wages Movement', *Preston Chronicle*, 12 November 1853, p. 3.
64 'Burnley', *Preston Chronicle*, 31 December 1853, p. 5.
65 Clark, *The Struggle*, p. 197.
66 *Morning Post*, 11 November 1853, p. 4.
67 'Strike of Women', *Huddersfield and Holmfirth Examiner*, 12 November 1853, pp. 6–7.
68 Ibid.
69 Rogers, *Women and the People*, p. 83.
70 Dutton and King, *Ten Percent*, p. 178.
71 Brian Harrison, 'The Sunday Trading Riots of 1855', *The Historical Journal*, VIII, 2 (1965), pp. 219–45.
72 Harrison, 'Sunday Trading Riots', p. 221.
73 *The People's Paper*, 15 March 1856, p. 1.
74 Harrison, 'The Sunday Trading Riots', p. 223.
75 Ibid.
76 Ibid.
77 'Sunday Riots in Hyde Park', *Illustrated Times*, 7 July 1855, p. 7.
78 'The Hyde Park Riot', *The Express*, 21 July 1855, p. 4.
79 Harrison, 'The Sunday Trading Riots', p. 224.
80 Ibid., p. 225.

Chartism and Communism in the Life of Helen Macfarlane

1 Historian David Black has done historians of female Chartism a huge service by researching Helen Macfarlane's personal and political history.

2 David Black, *The Red Antigone: The Life and World of Helen Macfarlane 1818–1860* (London: BPC Publishers, 2024), p. 41.
3 Ibid., p. 42.
4 Ibid., p. 68.
5 Ibid., p. 47
6 Ibid., p. 65.
7 Ibid., p. 67.
8 David Black ed., *Helen Macfarlane: Red Republican, Her Essays, Articles and Her Translation of the Communist Manifesto* (London: Unkant Publishers, 2014), p. 49.
9 Black, *Red Antigone*, p. 45.
10 Black, *Helen Macfarlane*, p. 99.
11 Ibid., pp. 48–9.
12 Ibid., p. 69.
13 Ibid., p. 81.
14 David Black suggests that Macfarlane was caught in the middle of a political row in which Mary Harney opposed Marx and Engels' influence (ibid., pp. 117–19).
15 Ibid., p. 111.

7. Suffrage, 1866: 'Dangerous, Go-ahead, Revolutionary' Women

1 Mary Smith, *The Autobiography of Mary Smith, Schoolmistress and Nonconformist: A Fragment of a Life* (London: Bemrose & Sons, 1892), pp. 147–8.
2 Ibid., p. 258.
3 Schwarzkopf, *Women in the Chartist Movement*, p. 286.
4 'Social Science', *English Woman's Journal*, cited by Kathleen E. McCrone in 'The National Association for the Promotion of Social Science and the Advancement of Victorian Women', *Atlantis*, 8 (1982), 44–66 (p. 47).
5 Crawford, *Reference Guide*, p. 48.
6 Chase, *A New History*, p. 42.
7 Letters to Mentia Taylor from Emily Davis, Taylor Mill Archive, Women's History Library, Archive Mill/Taylor paper/13 ff 242.
8 Jane W. Grant, *In the Steps of Exceptional Women: The Story of the Fawcett Society 1866–2016* (London: Francis Boutle Publishers, 2016), p. 3.
9 Ibid.
10 Elizabeth Crawford, 'Suffrage Stories: the 1866 Petition: The Aldeburgh Connection', womanandhersphere.com
11 Jenifer Glynn, *The Pioneering Garretts: Breaking the Barriers for Women* (London: Hambledon Continuum, 2008), pp. 10–11.

12 Elizabeth Crawford, *Woman and Her Sphere: 1866 Women's Suffrage Petition: The Aldeburgh Connection,* 12 May 2015, available at womanandhersphere.com.
13 Crawford, *The Women's Suffrage*, p. 85.
14 Crawford, *Woman and Her Sphere.*
15 Schwarzkopf, *Women in the Chartist Movement*, p. 61.
16 Roger Fulford, *Votes for Women* (London: TBS Book Service, 1976), p. 48.
17 Janet Smith, 'The Feminism and Political Radicalism of Helen Taylor in Victorian Britain and Ireland', unpublished PhD thesis, repository.londonmet.ac.uk, p. 32.
18 Millicent Garrett Fawcett, *Women's Suffrage: The History of a Great Movement* (London: T.C. & E.C. Jack, 1912), p. 20.
19 Two historians of the women's movement, Christine Bolt and Barbara Caine, mention the petition only in passing, although they discuss its organisers and the societies they established: Christine Bolt, *The Women's Movements in the United States and Britain from the 1790s to the 1920s* (Amherst: University of Massachusetts Press, 1993), p. 121. Barbara Caine, *Victorian Feminism* (Oxford: Oxford University Press, 1992), p. 35. Exceptions to the relative lack of interest in the petition are the researcher Ann Dingsdale who has identified 600 of the signatories, and suffrage historian Elizabeth Crawford who has excavated the biographies of many signatories and placed them in the context of later suffrage activity in their geographical locations: Elizabeth Crawford, *Women's Suffrage Movement: A Reference Guide*, 1866–1828 (London: University College London Press, 1999) and Ann Dingsdale, 'Generous and Lofty Sympathies: the Kensington Society, the 1866 Women's Suffrage Petition and the Development of Mid-Victorian Feminism' unpublished PhD, University of Greenwich, 1995.
20 Sandra Holton Stanley, *Suffrage Days: Stories from the Women's Suffrage Movement* (Abingdon: Routledge, 1996), p. 7.
21 Olive Banks, Barbara Caine and Helen Rogers make no mention of either woman in their studies of nineteenth-century feminism. Jane Rendell mentions Mentia Taylor only as the treasurer of the London Suffrage Society, *Origins*, p. 319.
22 'The 1866 Women's Suffrage Petition: The First Mass Votes for Women Petition', parliament.uk.
23 Harriet Grote, *The Philosophical Radicals of 1832, Some Incidents Connected with the Reform Movement from 1832 to 1842* (London: Saville & Edwards, 1866).
24 'Receipts and Expenditure of the National Association', 22 February 1842 to 24 June 1843, William Lovett Archive, reference M.S. 753.

25 Elizabeth Crawford, *Women's Suffrage Movement: A Reference Guide, 1866–1928* (London: University College London Press, 1999), p. 47.
26 Elizabeth Cady Stanton, Susan B. Anthony and Matilda Joslyn Gage, *History of Woman Suffrage, Volume III* (New York: Charles Mann, 1887), p. 840.
27 Holton Stanley, *Suffrage Days*, p. 24.
28 Crawford, *Women's Suffrage Movement*, p. 139.
29 Elizabeth Crawford, 'Ostler, nee Taylor, Catherine Courtauld', *Oxford Dictionary of National Biography* (2013).
30 Crawford, *Women's Suffrage Movement*, p. 118.
31 Jane Rendell, 'The English Woman's Journal', *Equal or Different: Women's Politics 1800–1914* (London: Blackwells, 1987), pp. 114–15.
32 Glynn, *The Pioneering Garretts*, p. 36.
33 Caine, *English Feminism*, p. 95.
34 Daisy Plant, *A History of Women's Lives on the Isle of Wight* (Pen and Sword History, 2019), p. 82.
35 Ibid., p. 114.
36 Joel Wiener, *William Lovett* (Manchester: Manchester University Press, 1989), p. 119.
37 Schwarzkopf, *Women in Chartism*, p. 78; Yeo, 'Mary Lovett', p. 174.
38 Yeo, 'Mary Lovett', pp. 176, 77.
39 C. P. Lucas, 'George Tansley', *The Working Men's College 1854–1904* (London: Macmillan and Co, 1904), pp. 129–80.
40 William J. Linton, *James Watson: A Memoire of the Days of the Fight for a Free Press in England and of the Agitation for the People's Charter* (New York: Augustus M. Kelly, 1880), p. 17.
41 Ibid., p. 83.
42 Bouthaina Shaaban, 'Shelley and the Barmbys', *Keats-Shelley Journal*, 1992, Vol. 41 (1992), 122–38 (p. 124).
43 A. L. Morton, *The English Utopia*, Part V, Chapter II (London: Lawrence & Wishart, 1952), p. 268.
44 Taylor, *Eve*, p. 282.
45 Crawford, 'Woman and Her Sphere', 7 June 2016.
46 Letter from Mary Ann Plummer to Helen Taylor, 5 June 1866, The Women's Library, Archive Mill/Taylor paper/13 ff 242.
47 John Plummer, *Songs of Labour, Northamptonshire Rambles and Other Poems* (London: W. Tweedie, 1860), p. xxi.
48 John Stuart Mill, *Principles of Political Economy*, ed. Jonathon Riley (Oxford: Oxford University Press, 1994), p. 151. Mill and Plummer corresponded and met regularly throughout the 1860s and 1870s. H. David, 'John Plummer's Northamptonshire "Lace Songs"', 2 March 2017, available at laceincontext.com.

49 'Mary Anne Plummer', available at suffrageresources.org.uk (accessed January 2020).
50 James Gregory, *Of Victorians and Vegetarians: The Vegetarian Movement in Nineteenth-Century Britain* (London: I.B. Tauris, 2007), p. 28.
51 Anne Knight archive, Friends Library, MS Box W2 2/6.
52 G. D. H. Cole, *Chartist Portraits* (London: Macmillan & Co., 1965), p. 53.
53 Edward Truelove compiled a 'Reformer's Library' in 1850 and later published the proceedings of the First Working Men's International, see Finn, *After Chartism*, p. 116.
54 Esther E. Vialls, Women's Suffrage Database, available at suffrage resources.org.uk (accessed May 2026).
55 Lovett, *My Struggle*, p. 37.
56 Crawford, *Reference Guide*, p. 40–1.
57 Sandra Stanley Holton, *Suffrage Days*, pp. 9, 14.
58 Tim Dracup, 'The Life and Times of John Dracup, Salford Radical – Eponymous' (November 2017), available at timdracup .wordpress.com (accessed May 2022).
59 *Manchester Guardian*, 3 July 1847, p. 3.
60 Chase, *A New History*, pp. 38–9, 62, 195.
61 Merrill, *When Romeo Was a Woman*, pp. 154–5.
62 Clark, *The Struggle*, pp. 246–7; Schwarzkopf, *Women in the Chartist Movement*, p. 270.
63 David McKie, *Bright Particular Stars: A Gallery of Glorious British Eccentrics* (London: Atlantic Books, 2013), p. 168.
64 Sharon Marcus, *Between Women: Friendship, Desire and Marriage in Victorian England* (Princeton: Princeton University Press, 2007), p. 201.
65 Marcus, *Between Women*, p. 202.
66 Bonnie Zimmerman, ed., *Lesbian Histories and Cultures: An Encyclopaedia* (Abingdon: Routledge, 2013), p. 678.
67 Ibid., p. 782.
68 Sally Mitchell, *Frances Power Cobbe: Victorian Feminist, Journalist, Reformer* (Virginia: University of Virginia Press, 2004), p. 157.
69 Martha Vicinus, 'Lesbian Perversity and the Victorian Marriage: The 1864 Codrington Divorce Trial', *Journal of British Studies*, 36 (January 1997), 70–98 (pp. 71–2).
70 McKie, *Bright Particular Stars*, p. 170.
71 Midgley, *Women Against Slavery*, p. 116.
72 McKie, *Bright Particular Stars*, p. 168.
73 Olusoga, *Black and British*, p. 351.
74 Ibid., p. 362.
75 Ibid., pp. 362–3.

76 Vron Ware, *Beyond the Pale: White Women, Racism, and History* (London: Verso, 2015), pp. 184–5.

The Many Faces of Eliza Lynn Linton

1 George Somes Layard, *Mrs Lynn Linton: Her Life, Letters and Opinions* (London: Methuen, 1901), pp. 57–8.
2 Merrill, *When Romeo Was a Woman,* pp. 154–5.
3 F. B. Smith, *Radical Artisan: William James Linton 1812–1897* (Manchester University Press, 1973), pp. 15–16.
4 Smith, *Radical Artisan*, p. 43.
5 Layard, *Mrs Lynn Linton*, p. 86.
6 Nancy Fix Anderson, *Woman against Women in Victorian England: A Life of Eliza Lynn Linton* (Indianapolis: Indiana University Press, 1987), pp. 57–9.
7 Eliza Lynn Linton, *Modern Women and What Is Said about Them: A Reprint of a Series of Articles in* the Saturday Review (New York: J. S. Redfield, 1868), p. 26.
8 Anderson, *Woman against Women*, p. 192–3.
9 Deborah T. Meem, 'Introduction', *The Rebel of the Family* (Canada: Broadview Literary Texts, 2002), p. 4.
10 Eliza Lynn Linton, *The Autobiography of Christopher Kirkland* (London: Richard Bentley and Son, 1885), p. 9.
11 Deborah T. Meem, 'Eliza Lynn Linton and the Rise of Lesbian Consciousness', *Journal of the History of Sexuality*, Volume 7, April 1997 (537–60), p. 547.

8. Chartist Afterlives: 'Thanks to My Mother'

1 Keith Flett, *Chartism After 1848,* pp. 146–74.
2 Goodway, *London Chartism*, p. 13.
3 Schwarzkopf, *Women in Chartism*, p. 288.
4 Anne Knight Archive, MS W2 2/6.
5 Crawford, *Women's Suffrage Movement*, pp. 815–16.
6 Martin Greenwood, 'Mill Girl Julia Varley Devoted Life to Trade Union Movement', *Telegraph & Argus*, 18 December 2022, thetelegraphandargus.co.uk.
7 Crawford, *Women's Suffrage Movement*, pp. 1,178–80.
8 Ernst Haeckel was a German zoologist and ecologist.
9 Annie Kenney, *Memories of a Militant* (London: Edward Arnold & Co, 1924), p. 1.
10 Philip Viscount Snowden, *My Autobiography: Volume One 1864–1919* (Edinburgh: The Edinburgh Press, 1934), p. 19.

11 Fred William Jowett, *What Made Me a Socialist* (Glasgow: Strickland Press, 1925), p. 4.

12 As Jill Liddington and Jill Norris have demonstrated for Lancashire and Yorkshire: Jill Liddington and Jill Norris, *One Hand Tied Behind Us: The Rise of the Women's Suffrage Movement* (London: Virago, 1978); Jill Liddington, *Rebel Girls: How Votes for Women Changed Edwardian England* (London: Virago, 2006).

The Political Journeys of Sarah Parker Remond

1 Sirpa Salenius, *An Abolitionist Abroad: Sarah Parker Remond in Cosmopolitan Europe* (Boston: University of Massachusetts Press, 2016), p. 2.

2 Ibid., p. 45.

3 Ibid., p. 54.

4 Ibid., p. 69.

5 Ibid., p. 8.

6 'A Letter from Sarah Parker Remond', *Anti-Slavery Advocate*, 1 November 1858, p. 4.

7 Salenius, *An Abolitionist Abroad*, pp. 76–8.

8 'The Lecture at the Lion Hotel', *Warrington Times*, 11 March 1859.

9 'Anti-Slavery Meeting', *Bradford Observer*, 19 January 1860, p. 6.

10 *Wakefield and West Riding Herald*, 13 January 1860, p. 5.

11 Salenius, *An Abolitionist Abroad*, p. 72.

12 Ibid., p. 41.

13 Conway Moncure, *Autobiography, Memories and Experiences* (London: Cassell & Company, 1904), p. 422.

14 *Morning Herald*, 2 January 1869, p. 3; *Western Daily News*, 4 January 1869, p. 3; *Bath Chronicle*, 7 January 1869, p. 6; *Illustrated London News*, 9 January 1869, p. 23.

Index